Design After Modernism

Design
After Modernism

BEYOND THE OBJECT

•

Edited by
JOHN THACKARA

THAMES AND HUDSON

Acknowledgments and copyright notices for the individual
contributions can be found on p.229.

First published in the United States in 1988 by
Thames and Hudson Inc., 500 Fifth Avenue,
New York, New York 10110

Library of Congress Catalog Card Number 87-51020

Typeset in Great Britain by Q-Set, Gloucester
Printed and bound in the German Democratic Republic

Contents

•

Contents

Preface

•

Although design has been the subject of increased interest and investment during the 1980s, theoretical discussion of the subject has only swirled in eddies around its edges. Debates concerning postmodern architecture, aesthetics and popular culture, or philosophical and literary postmodernism, have tended to make but glancing contact with the world of product development and new technology, software and systems design.

The explanation for this lies partly in the structure of design education, and of the design professions. The number of graduate and postgraduate architecture schools vastly outnumbers those for industrial, graphic or interior design, to name just three high-profile examples; and it is not generally necessary to possess a higher degree in order to practise as a non-architectural designer. Where theoretical work does take place, it is usually based in history departments – often in disguise.

Neither have the governments of industrialized countries felt it important to fund or promote theoretical design research – the realization that design is an important ingredient of innovation strategy is a recent phenomenon. Even now, where governments do intervene in design education, it is usually to make it more vocational, rather than to strengthen its analytical content. There is a parallel here with philosophy; even though its study is important to the development of fifth-generation information technology, it too is being cut back in many universities.

This leaves design research stuck in a ghetto, confined for the most part to the consideration of discrete products, ranging from cars to buildings – or to the compilation of designer biographies. This anthology is an attempt to help redress the balance. It contains much diversity of opinion, and should not be looked to for a unified world view of design in the postmodern age. The contributions are united not by a consistent strategy, but by their critical approach to a subject which has for too long been considered either neutral or 'technical'.

That said, the collection is not arbitrary; it is organized into sections which represent the three arenas in which debate is beginning to develop. After two introductory chapters which reconsider the present situation of design, and the meaning of modernity and modernism itself, Part One considers the city, building and street – not just as architectonic phenomena, but as the geographical and cultural context for technology and design. Part Two examines the so-called crisis of functionalism, product design and decoration, and the craft aesthetic; it considers arguments that we are entering a post-industrial age in which *things* will be less valuable than ideas and cultural production. Part Three analyses the changing nature of the design process itself, looking at parallels between the design of intangibles, such as software, and the continous re-design of tangible products made possible by information technology, automation and flexible manufacturing.

The reader may be forgiven for asking whether all of this is strictly the province of design at all; some design theorists, notably in Japan, have asked whether an entirely new word is needed for such a wide range of issues. Many contributors have come from outside the world of design – from art criticism, from philosophy or from technology. But if this book has a point, this is it: traditional notions of 'design' are, both practically and theoretically, defunct. Reality has seen to that. If our new understanding of 'design' is too broad to be subsumed into a single word, then that is a separate problem.

London, October 1987

INTRODUCTION

•

—1—

Beyond the object in design
•
JOHN THACKARA

Revolts against modern design have been a recurrent feature of recent cultural history. Every campaign against the architecture of a new public building, or controversy surrounding an exhibition of new art or sculpture, is evidence that people no longer accept that 'progress' in the arts is either inevitable or, for that matter, a good thing. There are two popular prejudices about modernist practice: first, that it treats all places and all people in the same way, an approach perceived to be a threat to individual identity and local tradition; and second, that it elevates expert judgment over everyday experience and learned, tacit knowledge. Reinforcing these objections is an insecurity caused by the constantly renewed modernization of industry and of society itself, with all that implies – unemployment, the deskilling of work, the feeling that technology is out of control, fear of impending nuclear catastrophe or war.

Design occupies an important place in the history of modernism. In contrast to the fine arts, or to political theory, design has expressed in material form the ideas that modernism has thrown up: the progressive nature of technology, celebration of the machine, an awareness that the present is radically different from the past. Designed objects express ideas clearly. The century provides us with a stage play of objects charting modernism's trajectory – triumphs of the early years, exciting new products and buildings embodying the vision of a future made abundant and ordered by machines – giving way gradually to disillusion as tower blocks and concrete motorways came to symbolize our loss of control over events, and the overweening power of corporations and the state.

Today, design is promoted not as a force for good, but as a neutral tool to be used by technicians in the planning of complex urban environments, the harnessing to profitable use of new technology, and the communication of information by visual or other means. Because it has been disarticulated in the public mind from progress, design has managed somehow to evade blame for the negative consequences of its role in our thoroughly modern lives: the automation of production in industry, resulting in unemployment and the hollowing out of the manufacturing economy; the de-aestheticization of environments and products in the name of marketing and economic manufacture;

John Thackara

the formation of a system of perpetual innovation which creates a superabundance of products, and mass user dissatisfaction with them, at the same time as production is unable to meet the most basic of human needs in non-industrial countries.

Design is not a neutral tool; it is a planning activity whose aims and procedures are dictated by commercial and political interests. Design is about decisions and priorities, not equations and logic. Its appropriation by marketing as a sales prefix (e.g. 'designer' furniture), and its recent transformation in media-speak from a process into a commodity, are attempts to depoliticize design – just when its political role has become acutely important. As the century expires, we are entering a new 'modern' age, an upheaval in world politics and economy fuelled by new technologies, demographic changes and other historical forces. Only this time, the new, the 'modern', in design as in everything else, is by no means so attractive as it was early in the century. The 'modern' needs rehabilitating, and design is being called upon to help.

There is now broad consensus that we live in a new era, and that the period since World War Two is qualitatively different from previous periods. As the American critic Fredric Jameson describes it, it is 'a new kind of society, variously described as postindustrial society, multinational capitalism, consumer society, media society ... new types of consumption, planned obsolescence; an ever more rapid rhythm of fashion and styling changes, the penetration of advertising, television and media generally to a hitherto unparalelled degree throughout society; the replacement of the old tension between city and country, centre and province, by the suburb and by universal standardization; the growth of superhighways; these are some of the features which would seem to mark a radical break with that old prewar society in which high modernism was still an underground force.'[1] Jameson argues that postmodernism has one central theme, the disappearance of a sense of history, the way in which our entire contemporary social system has little by little begun to lose its capacity to retain its own past; as he puts it, we have 'begun to live in a perpetual present and in a perpetual change that obliterates traditions'.[2]

It is a condition that the French critic Jean Baudrillard calls an 'ecstasy of communication', an explosion of information and ideas dating back to the 1940s and 1950s when the birth of mass electronic media created the communications industry. The proponents of postmodernism as a distinctly new era argue that our culture has become so saturated by short-lived electronic imagery that artists and designers can no longer claim that their work expresses or reflects timeless, universal theories. Baudrillard, putting the extreme case, believes the spread of mass communications has destroyed any possibility for art or design to play a socially progressive or even meaningful role. In a world of simulated reality and pseudo-events, art and design retreat into themselves.[3]

As well as being classed as a new feature of the so-called information age, postmodernism has been described in negative terms as a kind of vacuum

—12—

created by the loss of modernism's hold on the popular imagination. Jameson talks about the loss of the emotional ground tone we associate with the modernist period, modernism's self-confidence, 'the loss of significant connection with others, the anxiety deriving from this radical solitude; there has been a detemporalization of the culture . . . a loss of any vital imaginative sense of the past . . . a virtual incapacity to imagine historical difference'.[4]

One corollary of this failure of historical sensibility is a misrepresentation of modernism itself: postmodernism, in proclaiming the end of 'progress' as an ideal, sets itself in opposition to an idealized, ahistorical version of modernism itself. Postmodernists and historians have conspired to separate modernism as an art movement from the changes in science and technology, and the social, political and economic conditions, that were the context for its evolution. Modernism is too often treated as a series of discrete art movements – Futurism, Cubism, Constructivism, Dada, Surrealism – in isolation from world wars, revolutions and changing technology. This one-dimensional analysis enables some postmodernists to claim cultural pluralism and diversity, openness to change, and enthusiasm for the new, as their own – even though these ideas were central to modernism too at various moments.

Postmodernism as a kind of cultural *laisser faire* looks even more problematic when it is compared to the political and social realities of, to name one example, Mrs Thatcher's policies. The British prime minister is positively anti-modern in her talk of a 'return to Victorian values' – but she has proved to be the most ruthless modernizer of industry, technology and finance the century has seen. No tears are shed by this traditionalist for those, such as the miners, whom she considers to be anachronistic remnants of an industrial past. Or take the Agnelli family in Italy, pouring millions of dollars into an exhibition on Futurism, that once most radical of modernist movements. Futurism seems to have been given a new lease of life as late 1980s capitalism preaches the message that technology in general, and high technology in particular, is a good thing. Conveniently, the political allegiances of the Futurist movement (fascism), and the social consequences of the new gospel of technology such as unemployment, do not need to be mentioned. After all, this is a 'cultural' event.

The mainstream of postmodernism divorces debate about cultural modernization from that of social modernization – and therefore confines its attention to surface phenomena (the ecstasy of communication . . .) at the expense of the social and political developments these express. As Jürgen Habermas puts it, 'the neoconservatives sever the cultural from the social, then blame the practices of the one (modernism) for the ills of the other (modernization). With cause and effect thus confounded, "adversary" culture is denounced, even as the economic and political status quo is affirmed – indeed, a new "affirmative" culture is proposed.'[5]

In the last few years, however, particularly in the United States, a refined version of postmodernism has been articulated, a 'postmodernism of resistance', which, while critical of the 'official' modernism adopted by capitalism in support of its restructuring programme, promotes a less quiescent form of postmodernism in response. In the words of Hal Foster, an American critic who edited an influential anthology of essays on this subject, this radical postmodernism supports 'a desire to think in terms sensitive to difference, a scepticism regarding autonomous "spheres" of culture, or separate "fields" of experts . . . it signals a practice, cross-disciplinary in nature, that is rooted in a vernacular or sensitive to forms that deny the idea of a privileged realm.'[6]

It is on this idea, that art and design cannot be allowed to lurk in a 'privileged realm', that this book is based. While governments and multinational corporations appear to have decided that design is a wonder weapon in the fight for world markets (in Britain, a non-interventionist government has poured millions into design support, while allowing all kinds of core manufacturing industries to disappear), most critics have contented themselves with diatribes against the one design movement, modernism, which actually attempted to harness technology and industrial modernization to the general good. The theme of this book is that if progress and modernization have ceased automatically to be benign, it does not follow that modernism's strategic drive to make them so has failed.

Contributions have been grouped according to four themes: first, the nature of our century's previous 'modernization programmes', their relationship to the cultural modernisms which have accompanied them, and the transformation of modernism from adversarial, opposition culture into a corporate one; second, re-defining the city – the largest man-made object, and site of the revolutions in politics, ideas and technologies with which design must now grapple; third, product aesthetics in the age of global production which is in conflict with the potential of flexible manufacturing to support postmodernism's demand for differentiation; and finally, the implications of software for design strategy, the nature of open-ended systems and continuous redesign . . . design 'beyond the object'.

All our modernisms

MARSHALL BERMAN's book *All That Is Solid Melts Into Air*[7] has been a notable catalyst in changing the parameters of debates about modernism; he argues here that the problem for design is not modernism itself, but the way that it has absorbed uncritically the futurist ideology of capitalism. The problem with all modernisms in the futurist tradition, he explains, is that with brilliant machines and mechanical systems playing all the leading roles, 'there is precious little for man to do' – the early twentieth-century modernists combine a celebration of the idea of the modern world with an almost total lack of feeling for the people in it. Twentieth-century modernists, suggests Berman, have argued almost exclusively about style, whereas their nineteenth-century predecessors found in modernity a framework for the major questions of life in the modern world – such as the purpose of modern cities, how people can live together, and what they want from their environment. Berman argues that we should try to 'bring some of the dynamic and dialectical modernisms of the past back to life'. In his rediscovery of the prophetic vision and traditions of early modernism, Berman resembles a latter-day Ruskin. A singularly postmodern pan-culturalism, an interest in popular culture, and the attention paid to the role of producers in the modern world make up Berman's idiosyncratic world view; they also make a uniquely rich contribution to our search for a handle on our own modernity. Despite his determination to locate the various manifestations of modernism in their historical context, to 'periodicize' modernism, Berman has been criticized for ignoring, in his attempt to rescue modernism from the dustbin of history to which neoconservatives and/or postmodernists would consign it, the specific *political* conjunctures under which enthusiasm for modernity as a cultural style was first encouraged. According to Perry Anderson, the present improbability of an alternative to consumer capitalism, 'blocks the likelihood of any profound cultural renovation comparable to the great Age of Aesthetic Discoveries in the first third of this century. Gramsci's words still hold true: "the crisis consists precisely in the fact that the old is dying, and the new cannot be born; in this interregnum a great variety of morbid symptoms appears".'[8] But Berman is unwilling to be complacent in the face of such morbid symptoms; against a postmodernism of simultaneity, placelessness and the disappearing context, he attempts to assemble an alternative programme for (among other things) design, recalling for us what was popular, hopeful, communal and egalitarian about the early period of modernism.

City, building, street

It is worth stressing that postmodernists have discovered nothing new in the dynamic, perpetual change that they perceive to be a key feature of contemporary life and culture; Berman recalls that Baudelaire, who invented the idea of the city as a subject of modern history, 'used fluidity ("floating existences") and gaseousness ("envelops and soaks us like an atmosphere") as symbols for the distinctive quality of modern life'.[9] Indeed, the 'moving chaos' of nineteenth-century urban life, that century's own brand of postmodernism, was seen as a one of the principal challenges facing early modernist architects; as Sanford Kwinter reminds us, not only did the modern city compound technical innovations which have had profound effects on mental and physical life, but 'the culture of cities also belongs to much more fundamental moments in our history – the rise of the first "artificial" civilizations as they break more and more fully from the "organic" earth-based world with its single lived time and legible naturalistic space'.[10] The result was early modernism's historic campaign to bring order and rational planning to the great metropolises.

The intractability of that problem led many to develop a hatred for the traditional city: Siegfried Giedion claimed that the modern highway 'demonstrates that there is no longer any place for the city street, with heavy traffic running between rows of houses; it cannot possibly be permitted to persist';[11] more commonly recalled is Le Corbusier's 1929 slogan, 'We must kill the street!' Berman, in his discussion of architectural modernism's propensity to an elite, urban pastoralism, argues that the inner logic of the new urban environment, 'from Atlanta's Peachtree Plaza to Detroit's Renaissance Center' has been the functional segmentation and the class segregation of the 'old modern street, with its volatile mixture of people and traffic, businesses and homes, rich and poor'. The writer Mike Davis, in discussing the postmodern city, adds to this 'the decisive role of urban counterinsurgency in defining the essential terms of the contemporary built environment. Since the ghetto rebellions of the 1960s, a racial, as well as class, separation has been paramount. No wonder then that the contemporary American inner city resembles the classic colonial city, with the towers of the colons and white rulers militarily set off from the casbah or indigenous city.'[12]

It is in opposition to this corporatist architecture, which is oblivious to context, and in favour of the rediscovery of place and time, that KENNETH FRAMPTON addresses the problems facing architecture. Frampton agrees that there is a new conservative tendency in American architecture, one that has become more dominant during the eighties: 'populist collage giving way to cannibalized forms of eclectic historicism, used by an architectural profession whose task is to provide a marketable image, once an optimal rental return has been assured by the general arrangement of the plan'. Seeking an alternative theoretical framework within which to continue the critical practice of architecture, Frampton is inspired less by the great industrial conurbations than by the periphery of the so-called developed world, 'peripheral nodes able to sustain a more multilayered complexity of architectural culture'. Frampton's approach, which he calls 'critical regionalism', is an attempt to develop a critical resistance to the abstraction, atonality and atemporality of modernism as a style taken over by big capital and enshrined as a principle in corporate architecture and over-planned cities.

There is a tension in this debate between those such as Frampton who look to the edges, and critics who are less pessimistic about prospects for the traditional city. For example Michael Piore, a professor of economics at MIT, argues that, with the disintegration of the institutional structures of mass production in favour of what he calls 'flexible specialization', a new mode of production is emerging 'that flourishes in the traditional urban economy where many small producers operate in close proximity to one another, each dependent on a dense industrial community'.[13] Piore's analysis replicates on a metropolitan scale the argument that while new technology *can*, theoretically, lead to the dispersal of work, to the 'home office' for example, geographical proximity has a greater claim to operational efficiency for business.

For the European critic, too, less enervated by the formless sprawl of American urbanism, the city remains the focus for most strategies to rescue design from the grip of corporatism. The Italian professor of architecture

Manfredo Tafuri has fulminated against utopian objections to the 'inhuman metropolis'; in Europe, he says, such sentiments are 'only nostalgia, the rejection of the highest levels of capitalist organization, the desire to regress to the infancy of humanity'.[14] In solidarity with this view, NIGEL COATES positively immerses himself in the city; he welcomes and seeks out what Walter Benjamin called 'the countless places in the big cities where one stands on the edge of the void'.[15] Coates takes the 'improbability, multifunctionality, multiplicity and lack of organic structure – in short all the contradictory aspects assumed by the modern metropolis' as his base line for a critique of modernist design strategy for the city.

Coates is critical of the constrictive tendency of recent modernisms to treat the history of architecture as a history of styles. As the architect Bernard Tschumi puts it, 'There is no space without event, no architecture without programme; the meaning of architecture, its social relevance and its formal invention, cannot be dissociated from the events that "happen" in it.'[16] The emphasis on styles, Tschumi contends, 'also corresponds to a wider pheno-menon: on the one hand, the increasing role of the developer, encouraging architects to become mere decorators; on the other, to the tendency of many critics to concentrate on surface readings, signs, metaphors, and other modes of presentation, often to the exclusion of spatial or programmatic concerns. These are two faces of a single coin, the increasing desertion by the architectural profession of its responsibilities vis-à-vis the events and activities taking place in the spaces it designs.'[17]

The American architectural critic Sanford Kwinter considers that the single most important contribution of Futurist theory to our modern conception of the world is that 'the physics of space-time given rise to a fundamental new entity, the event, as well as the geometry through which it could be ex-pressed.'[18] It is in solidarity with this discovery, and against an architecture moulded by profit, and for that matter a criticism obsessed with signs, that Coates promotes *narrative* architecture. It lies, he says, 'somewhere between the body and the city . . . it therefore has to consider fleeting meanings as well as solid architectural forms, movement as well as the volumes that contained them, the subjective as well as the rational.' Narrative architecture is not the first articulation of architecture-in-use: after all, Le Corbusier considered himself to be an organizer of collective life rather than just a designer of objects. Tafuri reminds us that early modernist architecture 'summoned the public to participate in its work of design . . . the single building was no longer an "object", it is only the place in which the elementary assemblage of single cells assumes physical form.'[19]

There is nothing 'postmodern', then, about the notion of 'architecture-as-use'. On the contrary, in its concentration on the style and appearance of buildings, mainstream postmodernism is closer to the concerns of today's developer who needs to market his buildings, and designs them accordingly. But postmodernism does acquire a critical cutting edge when it addresses the way buildings are *produced*; it opposes the rigidity of plan and sterility of affect produced when attempts are made to 'mass produce' buildings, and in its espousal of craft and the re-introduction of hand-made building components postmodernist architecture contributes to a 'softening' of the built environment.

But the importance of narrative architecture lies in its method, rather than in particular building forms or details that it may advocate. As the English critic Brian Hatton has put it, 'only by metamorphosing the madness of life into the magic of architecture are we going to get real cities, and not the monofunctionally-zoned, zombie and gnomescapes that an unholy alliance of the market and misunderstood modernism has produced in our midst.'[20] Where the early modernist planners and architects concentrated on laws of organization, some of today's designers are interested in subverting and opening up the rigid structures and patterns of behaviour the modern city attempts to impose on its inhabitants.

There is nothing inherently radical in the 'new flexibility'; the change from static to flexible models has a purely functional rationale: it corresponds to the new demands placed on the city by information technology and the imperatives of continuous innovation in business. In 1986, for example, the buildings and infrastructure of London's financial district were subject to immense pressures by the 'Big Bang', when markets and procedures were de-regulated. Everything from the pedestrian traffic to the wiring of 'smart buildings' was affected. But as RICHARD BOLTON observes, capitalism's motive in improving the programming of the modern city is improved productivity, not a concern with natural and humane lifestyles. One other 'anti-narrative' example: the dramatic rise in out-of-town shopping centre developments, increasing by 50 per cent annually in Britain, is a logical consequence of the decentralization of information and distribution networks in retailing – but their impact on city centre life is disastrous.

Marshall Berman recalls a quotation from Thomas Berger's 'Crazy in Berlin', in which an ex-GI wanders around the war-torn city asking, 'Why, when things are broken, do they seem like more than when they're together?' Berger's implicit answer is that, for the survivors, urbicide reduces everything to its bare essentials and so, ironically, makes all that is left look and feel larger than life. In narrative architecture, 'salvage design' and other strands within the avant-gardes of the eighties, and for that matter on the streets of the South Bronx and countless other development 'problem areas', the lesson, as Berman puts it, is that 'there are plenty of people in the fire zones who have the will and energy to rebuild . . . there's cultural creativity in those ruins.'[21]

The sites of this creativity move around, emerging and dying like exotic moths – the East Village in New York, the mansion houses of Tokyo, the scruffy suburbs of Milan – areas which do not look like designer precincts or immaculate middle-class suburbs, but which generate more ideas, and sustain more life, than more controlled urban environments. As the combined effect of what the French economist Marc Guillaume calls the 'invasive functionality' of industry, and street-level creativity of dispossessed ruin dwellers, the post-modern city, like the earliest modern city, is subject to continuous destruction and rearrangement. 'No longer having an equivalent for what Jean-François Lyotard calls "grand narratives", the cities try to compensate for this loss . . . [hence] the obsession with patrimony, the conservation of a few scattered centres, monuments and remains. But what remain are merely stereotypical signs of the city: these efforts do not make a memory – merely a global sign system consumed by tourists.'[22] To quote Rem Koolhaas, 'More important than the design of cities is the design of their decay.'[23]

Technology and innovation

Design in the city remains in a state of permanent crisis, subject to the competing claims of corporatist modernism, with its search for productive order, and 'narrative', postmodern claims for the virtues and romance of creative disorder.

In industry, parallel but distinct pressures are evident. The advent of mass communications since the war, which postmodernists say has changed our very culture, has also changed the nature of business. The prospect of 'world markets', brought about by a combination of mass production in its highest form and mass marketing through the new communication channels, has excited the bigger corporations. For them, incredible economies of scale and super-efficient sales and distribution mean bigger profits and the elimination of smaller, less efficient, competitors.

But there is a reverse side to this globalist coin – namely, the reaction by consumers against the homogenization of products and advertising, and a rediscovery of national and cultural differences as virtues in all things consumable. This 'market pull' is matched by the development of sophisticated new production systems, incorporating innovations such as flexible manufacturing, which make possible the economic manufacture of a more or less infinite variety of products. This tendency in marketing and technology is a problem for the global multinationals for whom selling high-quality, high value-added products to affluent consumers is no substitute for the mass production upon which they were reared.

Whichever strategy is preferred, niche or global marketing, a remarkable feature of recent years has been the importance given to design by companies of both persuasions. In fact, design has emerged in the past five years as a principal element in innovation strategy. In the words of one of Britain's biggest design groups, it is 'the means by which each company can humanize technology in its own way, and go on to diffuse it to the masses more quickly and more widely. Increasingly, companies compete with one another to express their commitments and identity through design. Once more, design mediates on the consumer's behalf. It is a force for progress.'[24] Attention has switched to design in the context of a worldwide recession and intensified competition not only between companies, but between industrial centres of the world – North v. South, Europe v. America, East Coast America v. Pacific Rim, and so on. A common feature of competition in all these markets is that the cost of translating technology into commercial products is as great as, or greater than, the cost of developing the technology itself; design, which is used to make products out of inventions, is thus one key determinant of costs and profitability.

Design has started to be regarded by some companies as a magic ingredient that can resolve the contradictions thrown up in this worldwide struggle for markets. Apart from its use in the application of technology, design can be employed in the analysis and implementation of consumer needs, in the automation of production, in the improvement of product quality at a time of rising consumer expectations, and in the modelling and development of software (the fastest growing sector). The trouble is that in the 'triad' economies of Japan, the USA and Europe, where pressure from new competitors has been felt most keenly, industrial design practice remains at an infantile stage of development. Until recently, design has been used in most manufacturing merely to improve surface styling, or to cut costs. Its use to create products of quality and originality that consumers want, or even need, has been rare. Hartmut Esslinger, founder of frogdesign, a world leader in product development, reckons only five per cent of European industry – principally automobiles, electronics, high-tech consumer goods and appliances – invest in deep-rooted design throughout their operation.[25] In America a similarly small proportion of industry operates a widely applied and integrated design policy. The huge size of domestic markets has protected manufacturing from world competition, and the military has hogged a huge proportion of scientific research. The result is that the economy is now 'hollowing out' as high valued-added technology is imported by Europe and America from the developing Pacific economies. Ironically, industrial design actually promotes this process – by cladding the foreign-made working parts in 'home designed' casings.

Design strategy is technically, if not politically, much more advanced in Japan. Companies such as Sharp, which produce a staggering 5000 new models and products every year, have developed elaborate theoretical and organizational models to control the innovation process. Sharp's design chief Kiyoshi Sakashita talks of 'humanware' design, the consideration of products in terms of the total environment in which they will be used.[26] Sharp employs sociologists to study how people live and behave, and then plans products to fill the gaps they discover. As a design strategy this marks a dramatic change: most Western design has been 'production-led': it attempts to fit product specifications to the capabilities of existing factories and laboratories. The Japanese approach, based on their investment over decades in 'smart' production systems, is the opposite: new technology is used to create what consumers are discovered to 'want'.

Hiroshi Shinohara, who runs Canon's research division, says of this new process that in most of his company's products, 'software and hardware comprise a single unit. As a result our design strategy has had to be restructured in order to shift attention from what we call static symbolization [of hardware] to "dynamic images" '[27] – a change the Italian design theorist Augusto Morello refers to as the 'tertiarization' of products.[28]

With the subordination of hardware's importance in product planning, new influences come into play: for example, changing patterns of housework, or new kinds of social organization such as single parent families, gay households, and so on . As CLAUDIA DONÀ recounts, some designers have suggested that these new social patterns add up to a 'new domestic landscape', and have attempted to develop new design forms to match. But feminist writers argue that modernist design has always operated with specific notions of femininity in mind – assumptions which influence women by shaping patterns of work (and thus access to skills), or by architectural planning which controls their use of space. The effect of innovations such as microwave ovens and other food technology, or of washing machines, has been to increase the woman's 'duties' (by creating a market/demand for more meals than she had to provide before, and by shifting the burden of labour from the laundry into the home).[29] The adaptability in product design afforded by software has not, in other words, been matched by a fundamental change in their social impact.

'Soft' products, then, are not unique to the postmodern period: industrial design has always been influenced by social factors to express values, even if these have changed. What is new is the development of *continuous* software-led innovation, an ideological feedback system which destabilizes the attempt, started by early modernism, to create a stable global product language.

While the production and communications apparatus for world products may finally be in place, the nature of product innovation itself has changed. Until recently European and American companies have operated an evolutionary strategy, whereby continuous feedback from markets and production is used to modify products bit by bit; increasingly, as we have seen, the Japanese work backwards from the market, or from raw technological breakthroughs, creating product 'concepts' which it is the job of designers and engineers to develop. Globalist ambition is foundering in a super-heated world market in which timing and sensitivity to fashion trends are as important as large-scale production.

The frenetic innovation and increasing pressure on costs and profitability in world markets has forced many Western manufacturers to opt for a strategy of increasing the quality and value of their products, and to aim at smaller, more specialized markets. But this quality 'niche marketing' strategy has serious drawbacks. There is disagreement, for a start, about what 'quality' means. Few companies share the commonplace notion of quality as products which people actually need, which are made well, and which offer good value for money. Some see technical performance as an index of quality, and proceed to add-on functions whose worth is questionable, and which in any case are mimicked in a matter of months by quick-footed competitors. Others define quality in terms of durability and reliability, a fairly unprofitable approach now that electronics are so widespread; (modularity in components has made the servicing and repair of products such a simple matter). Although rationalized as a positive response to rising consumer expectations, the quality strategy can also be seen as an aspect of de-industrialization, a retreat from mass markets won by more efficient competitors.

Product aesthetics

Today's crisis of product design thus involves many of the problems modernism attempted to tackle during the early part of the century. The pressure from engineering and production for global designs seeking maximum economies of scale has not changed. The stress caused by the need to translate technical innovation into saleable products, while still making a profit, is the same today as it was when, for example, electricity was first introduced. For all the important implications of software-based products, and the advent of 'black box' styling as a challenge to designers, the problem is not actually with 'functionalism', and, by association, with modernist design, at all. Rather as JEAN BAUDRILLARD argues, the crisis lies in the diminishing satisfaction afforded by *all* the products of a system which literally consumes its own children in the rush to gain competitive advantage by innovation. Because product design is thoroughly integrated in capitalist production, it is bereft of an independent critical tradition on which to base an alternative.

The results are there for all to see. In addition to the flood of new products, design in recent years has been responsible for the widespread updating of shops, and the transformation of a whole range of services from travel to finance. The trouble is that the quality of our experience in highly designed hypermarkets, high-tech interiors, 'theme pubs' and starter homes is not demonstrably superior to life in less designed locations. On the contrary, the prefix 'designer' has become in some cases a byword for unsympathetic, artificial and over-controlled environments, or a marketing device used to sell poorly conceived, over-priced goods. The design of today's consumer, leisure and service enterprises and products *is* technically proficient, but it is also manipulative, and aesthetically bankrupt. And people are rebelling against it.

The decline in quality offered to the masses, as Jean Baudrillard explains, can be seen not only in the commodities themselves but also in the way they are presented. The style of presentation, thanks to the perfection of techniques which exploit new materials and technologies to the limit, is pushed to extreme refinement of mere surface. As Wilhelm Alff, a German writer, has argued 'the commodities offer, as in the style of Louis XV, an ever more shiny and shallow skin, which promises more and more while giving less.'[30] And his colleague

W.F. Haug, writing in the same book on 'commodity aesthetics', has observed that, 'It's not that the commodities have no use-value at all; [rather] they really provide almost nothing of what they promise aesthetically. In so far as commodity aesthetics scores a "hit" with buyers, and determines their behaviour and, not least, their spending, the buyers are in a position similar to Tantalus, finding himself surrounded by the most beautiful delusions of his needs; when he reaches for them, he clutches empty space. Tantalus is the addicted buyer.'[31]

The reasons why design promises so much, and delivers so little, are developed by PETER FULLER. He argues, against Adolf Loos, that the destruction of ornament within the modernist movement was 'one of the cultural crimes of our age', and makes the parallel criticism that modernism is fatally compromised by its espousal of the idea that 'progress' is synonymous with an increase in the quantity of manufactured goods. One needs to remember, in reading Fuller's contribution, that the functionalist aesthetic which led to the destruction of ornament in design was a relatively late phenomenon in modernism; in fact, much of high modernism's anti-ornament polemic was directed against what its reformers considered the eclectic excesses of the nineteenth century. The 'machine syle' as such came later, and has been lifted out of its historical context and quoted by some post-modernists as evidence that modernism was by its nature against decoration; postmodernism is enabled by this distortion to put itself forward as an alternative, when it is not.

This particular debate, in which modernism and functionalism are conflated, has tended to divert attention from the aesthetic to the tactical; there is nothing inherently 'modern' about 'function' – design has always had a functional element. The important issue, as FRANÇOIS BURKHARDT comments, is the *values* a design expresses. The advent of the microchip did not, in other words, pose a qualitatively new problem for design: 'black box' aesthetics were simply a new version of an old problem: what values should any product express? In his chapter, Peter Fuller does not propose a fully worked-out programme for a new product aesthetics, but he does suggest that one possible source for a postmodern design programme could be the higher reaches of modern mathematics, where scientists are discovering new geometries and patterns in nature more complex and varied than the Euclidean forms that obsess so many contemporary designers.

Nature is of key importance in the search for a design aesthetic in the postmodern period that is not dominated by the 'imperatives' of production. John Berger has made a fascinating attempt to put flesh on this proposition in talking about the hand-made white birds that are found in many parts of central Europe. He lists some of the qualities which make them pleasing and mysterious to everyone who sees them, which 'provoke an aesthetic emotion': 'First, there is a figurative representation. One is looking at a bird, thus there is a reference to the surrounding world of nature. Secondly, the choice of subject (flying bird), and the context in which it is placed (indoors, where live birds are unlikely), render the object symbolic. Thirdly, there is respect for the material used; the wood has been fashioned according to its own qualities of lightness, pliability and texture. Looking at it, one is surprised how well wood becomes bird. Fourthly, there is formal unity and economy. Despite the object's apparent complexity, the grammar of its making is simple, even austere. Its richness is the result of repetitions which are also variations. Fifthly, this man-made object provokes a kind of astonishment: how on earth was it made? . . . one is looking at something that has been worked with a mysterious skill and a kind of love.'[32]

Of course, urban life has always tended to produce a sentimental view of nature; one of the valuable legacies of early modernism is its determined opposition to ruralist kitsch. But early modernism's attempt to find a positive link between the natural order and the man-made world provides us with a number of useful pointers for an appropriate design aesthetic today – an alternative to more recent design in which, as Claudia Donà observes, the aesthetics of the machine and the marketplace, and the desire for 'mastery' and exploitation, have distracted our attention from the unity in diversity of nature, and our place within it.

Viennese modernism, for example, saw as its essential quest salvation through sensuous experience, not through super-rationality, or the aesthetics of production. Edward Timms recalls an exhibition on the subject: 'Every dimension of sensuous experience was explored to its limit: through music and through colour, through the tactile value of materials and the geometrical lines of design, the sensuous appeal of the body and the subliminal realm of the unconscious, the austere delights of language and the pleasures of the palate . . . rarely have the delights of the senses been so insistently explored.'[33]

Again, Eugène Vallin, an influential architect of the Nancy school, thought that Nature could be explored as inspiration for formal design purposes; there was a quality to be found in natural forms, 'rather than a final form, a formal principle; rather than an excuse for embellishment, a basic element of construction'.[34] Naturalistic ornament offered seemingly endless variations of shape and form that could be drawn on to prevent, as Emile Galle wrote, 'the ornamentalist . . . from servile insipid copying from objects devoid of meaning, reality and charm'.[35] The Art Nouveau designers are obvious examples: they accentuated the delicate but vigorous twists found in nature and turned them into formally elaborated design effects.

As PETER DORMER observes, a re-examination of craft aesthetics and methods is one way that diversity and originality may be institutionalized in design. Dormer shares Fuller's view that while there is much that is reactionary in the history and ideology of craft, this is not an *a priori* characteristic of craft, either as an idea or as a practice. Many late modernist designers, obsessed with the high-tech idiom, cite the poor quality of the 'craft' knick-knacks sold in church precincts and village bazaars, from California via the Cotswolds to Sydney (most of which *is* junk) to prove that product quality means, by definition, machine quality – amd appearance – achieved only through the scientific organization of industrial production. The fact that consumers persist in their enthusiasm for the hand-made, or anything that looks like it, leads to several contradictions. General Motors, for example, have taken to including horny-handed upholsterers in their car advertising at the very same time as they invest billions to create the worker-free factory of the future in which to manufacture these 'craft' products. Audi, too, have recently extolled the virtues of robots and craftsmen working together on the Audi 80.

While General Motors have flirted with the craft aesthetic, other attempts have been made, albeit on a modest scale, to subvert the monolithic character of recent product design but it has to be admitted that many such stylistic experiments have been cosmetic, leaving untouched the relationships – between design, production and the consumer – that determine the nature of the products most people buy.

Movements such as Memphis and Alchymia, the international designers active in Milan during the early eighties, were 'ideological' phenomena, as the Italians put it, an extension of that country's avant-garde tradition that dates back to the fifties. Although Memphis was the occasion for much discussion about the crisis facing traditional design methods, it could only take physical form thanks to Italy's unique production infrastructure, a network of small production units nourished by a surviving craft tradition which made the development of short-run prototypes feasible. Ettore Sottsass, one of the founders of Memphis, likes to compare the group's catalytic impact to that of early Cubism, but it must be questioned whether Memphis, given the moment at which it flourished, was actually more than a new product of the 'culture industry' – a system which deals in vicarious experience and changes according to fashion, but remains fundamentally the same. It would certainly be hard to argue that Memphis offered the kind of 'informational aesthetic for a simulacral world'[36] that critics have been looking for.

Memphis and the craft revival apart, the hardiest surviving minority tendency in product design during the seventies and eighties has been a rarefied form of high modernism – the production in small quantities of early twentieth-century artefacts such as chairs and lights that pay homage to the golden age of modernism as a style. This plethora of chrome and black denotes the designer as connoisseur, with two curious consequences: first, preserving the machine aesthetic in the form of rare and expensive reproductions, the designer's self-image as a cultured and expert professional is reinforced by the *rarity* of the products he (and occasionally she) is surrounded by. Second, the designer, as fashionable connoisseur caught in his or her own paradox, watches these timeless, universally 'right' trappings quickly relegated by obsolescence, as the designer-modern style is consumed by a voracious style system which must always turn its attention to pastures new (at the time of writing, a kind of baroque English romanticism had come into favour).

In Europe, a second stream of criticism of traditional modernist design has emerged in recent years. Called, variously, *design primario* or 'soft', this developing theory (based in Milan where the designer Clino Castelli has used the ideas for clients such as Fiat and Herman Miller) attacks the systematic exclusion of aesthetic and sensual delight from so many industrial products and buildings, and has developed a new critical interest in the links between mechanism and organism, between artificial mechanical order and natural variety, that so intrigued early modernists. Because architecture and product design is still executed through the medium of two-dimensional drawing (or its electronic equivalent), the 'objective' properties of the product or place tend to be stressed at the expense of subjective aspects, including sensual qualities, such as light, heat, sound, humidity and so on which cannot easily be quantified or specified. The writer Julian Gibb has explained that '*design primario* aims to exploit high technology's protean potential to shape sensorial space flexibly and economically; technology can control levels of light, sound temperature and humidity, and reduce the burden on hard structures to create favourable environments sympathetic to human use.'[37]

One of the ironies of the development of *design primario* is that big business, not avant-garde design, has been keenest on the idea so far. While designers invoke what they see as the finest traditions of modernism as they create sterile, impersonal, machine-made objects and interiors, it is left to organizations like NASA and Fiat to mount research into ways by which sensual pleasure may be reintroduced into high-tech contexts; NASA is attempting to make its Space Lab cabin habitable for long periods by designing high-tech 'r&r modules' which contain holograms portraying landscape vistas, recorded messages from loved ones back home and other ersatz stimuli. Their assumption is that 'pleasure' is more social and psychological than physical – that the smallest sensory input can be made pleasurable when applied in the right way.[38] This theme is developed by PETER YORK, when he observes that what the world wants of British 'design' is not actually products at all, but our history, and images thereof, which is the one thing other countries cannot reproduce.[39] It would be stretching things to describe York's analysis as a 'postmodernism of resistance', but his introduction of the concept 'undesign' does have critical implications for the organization of design practice.

Design and work

In the design of products, then, much that is described by postmodernism as a break with modernist orthodoxy – a rediscovery of ornament, a return to craft and a renewed priority given to sensuality in places and things – turns out to have been a concern of early modernism, too. The same applies when we turn to the key question of production.

THIERRY CHAPUT and other contributors such as PHILIPPE LEMOINE talk here about fundamental shifts in the structure of industrial production. Novel features of the 'postmodern' scene include the 'tertiarization' of products, in which hardware becomes functionally, and economically, less important than software; the development of continuous innovation systems, in which design, production and market research feed on themselves at an ever more frantic rate; and finally the radical division of labour ushered in by large-scale automation and artificial intelligence, leading to the prospect of the final displacement of human beings from design altogether.

But is the break from the past as sharp as it seems? MIKE COOLEY notes that it is possible in the history of conflicts between man and machine – a central concern from Ruskin through to high modernism – to draw an unbroken line from Brunelleschi, through the development of industrial production, to automation and, in the future, to digital information systems and 'artificial intelligence'. Cooley explains that the qualitative difference between the roles of architect and stone mason in a cathedral building programme is slight; and it compares to the division of purely 'intellectual' tasks into modules in software development. Separating theory and practice precludes the exploitation of intuition, subjective judgment and tacit knowledge. The result is the displacement of live, let alone collective, human labour, physical *or* mental, from production.

Most discussions of design take place in sublime ignorance of the scope of automation planned by the multinational corporations. The so-called Advanced Manufacturing Technologies offer staggering opportunities to the makers of nearly all engineered products to cut costs and improve flexibility and control in production. (To take a well-known, albeit not very high-tech example: the Benetton knitwear chain operates a system which links its point-of-sale terminals in different countries to a central automated plant which can initiate production automatically.) By 1990, the AMT industry is expected to have annual sales of more than \$30 billion.[40] As the *Financial Times* has explained 'The main issues are not so much technological, as conceptual and managerial; for the suppliers, system programming is largely uncharted territory; for the users, automation is a human problem because it can affect the organization of an entire company. Automation obviously eliminates manual and skilled jobs. But it also plays havoc with the traditional roles of supervisors and even directors.'[41] This is because totally automated production systems such as Benetton's, which are already coming on stream, make direct links between the market and production – machining, handling, assembly; such systems can even initiate orders for new materials and tools, to replace those used.

The objective is 'total control', and people are seen as obstacles in the way. Although high modernism claimed to have found, in its principles for the rational organization of production, a way to reconcile the conflict between man and machine, the human element in industry today is typically seen as an unreliable factor of production compared with the dependability and subservience of machines. Some high priests of the automation crusade in the US even recommend hiring a workforce with a low IQ in semi-automated plants – on the basis that they are less likely, by thinking too much, to mess up the system.

But what happens economically at the instant in which living labour ceases to be involved in the productive process, when, according to the labour theory of value, this fragment of the process ceases to generate surplus value? Envisaging this event repeated throughout industry, Ernest Mandel has concluded that 'we have arrived here at the absolute inner limit of the capitalist mode of production.'[42] The problem with this vision of automation as the end of capitalism is that it views the changes as a linear process in which machines grow larger and larger, and workers fewer and fewer, until all that remains is the single megamachine presiding over an economy devoid of human workers. In fact, as the Australia-based researcher Tessa Morris Suzuki has argued 'the phase of automation which gathered pace during the 70s and 80s was not simply the direct continuation of mechanization, but marked a radical departure from earlier forms of the development of machinery. The separation of hardware from software may be seen as constituting a revolutionary fission of the labour process itself.'[43]

As TOM MITCHELL explains in his contribution, the use of software in production changes the relationship between knowledge, labour and machinery, and forces capitalist enterprises and economies to become *perpetual innovators*. The focus of activity shifts from the way in which the enterprise produces *products* to the way in which it introduces *new* products. In Suzuki's words, 'its whole structure is centred on the development, alteration and refinement of productive processes.'[44] One indication of the shift in resources is the declining share of Japan's corporate capital expended on material inputs, such as machinery and raw materials, and the growing share expended on non-material inputs such as software, data services, planning and research – the so-called 'softening' of the economy mentioned earlier.

The notion that all design and planning in an information society, because it does not involve manual work, is necessarily intellectual and creative, is one eagerly propagated by the ideologues of the information society. But the reality is quite different. The commodity production of knowledge has become central to corporate profit making, and the urge to increase efficiency in this process has led to the growing fragmentation of tasks. The complex information networks and database systems play a role similar to the conveyor belt in the factory; they are connected together by wires and modems, rather than by belts and pulleys, but they make possible the breaking down of previously complex integrated tasks into a series of small isolated components which can be performed by less skilled workers – just like a production line in a factory, only it is a production line with no beginning and no end.

In offices, for example, the serried ranks of typists and filing clerks so beloved of the proponents of 'scientific management', Taylorism and so on, are disappearing – but the actual tasks performed by the vast majority of people operating computer terminals continue to be data capture and manipulation, not decision making. The same people – a small minority at the top – continue to make all the important decisions; new technology merely makes sure they are better informed.

For so-called creative activities, too, the separation of tasks imposes a crucial isolation on those involved: more and more, engineers and programmers are genuinely ignorant of the precise application of the products they design. As *Processed World* (a radical monthly magazine for workers in offices and information processing) reports from Silicon Valley, USA: 'A new "structured" approach to programming formalizes the task-by-task division of design; programmers write "slave" modules of code that perform relatively simple tasks; project leaders can assign an entire computer program design without mentioning that, for example, the Pentagon will use the software to refine an experimental missile. Management benefits directly: many people may not enjoy creating office automation technology and weapons systems that destroy life, but if the work seems as harmless as a game of chess, so much the better.'[45]

Beyond the object

So although some aspects of our experience in the postmodern world are novel, the relationship of design to production has not changed fundamentally. The objects of design have evolved, but the nature of the design system has not – so far. Design's crisis lies in the broader political and cultural context, the 'postmodern condition' of a society, full of proliferating images, which has lost confidence in the idea of progress, and in which 'technoscience' seems to have taken on a life of its own.

Two features of this new state of mind preoccupy postmodern philosophers greatly: first, our inability to comprehend the sheer complexity of a world full not just of products and buildings, but also of 'systems'; and second, the 'informational isolation' and insecurity we feel in the face of the *intangible* technologies which surround us. JOHN CHRIS JONES calls these features of the non-objective world 'softecnica . . . the coming of live objects, a new presence in the world'. Jones, who in the sixties pioneered the study of 'design methods', before abandoning the subject as a blind alley, has a particular interest in the continuous re-design of computer software; he opposes the radical separation of reason, intuition and experience within the design system we have outlined, and calls for the re-introduction of personal judgment, imagination and what may be called 'artistic sensibility' into design. His programme flies in the face of modernism's historic faith in rationalism and science; it also challenges the inexorable advance of technology towards automated, autonomous design systems.

For its part, the artificial intelligence community which is creating such autonomous systems tends to be unimpressed by our postmodern anxieties, and rejects calls for more human involvement in design and production: it argues, against human special pleading, that 'creativity' rarely represents a large deviation from standard patterns, so humans are not needed for a system to be innovative. The cybernetician James Albus has said of creativity: 'We take a familiar behavioural trajectory, add a tiny variation, and claim we have discovered something completely new – a new dance step, dress style, song or idea.' He even wonders if true creativity 'ever happens at all . . . it may be argued that all creative acts and insights merely represent rearrangements of elements in experience.'[46]

Despite criticisms and alarums raised by expert objectors, this kind of reductive logic dominates AI thinking, and its engineers continue to steam ahead 'capturing knowledge' and 'rearranging elements in experience'. The first step in the machine displacement of human professionals (such as designers) is the standardization of their methodology. In the past professional work resisted this, but over time standard methods of adequate efficiency have emerged. Design, diagnosis, process control and flying are regarded as skills that are ripe for incorporation into expert systems.

Because computers are ideally suited to the manipulation of symbols (which some experts suggest is the fundamental activity of the 'information sector')[47] – far more suited than one of today's primitive robots to the manipulation of things – there is tremendous pressure for scientists to reduce all human knowledge and experience to symbolic form. Knowledge engineers, high on technology, and institution-bound, are reluctant to concede that *real* understanding requires the common sense that human beings have by virtue of having bodies, interacting skilfully with the material world, and being trained into a culture. AI experts are confident that most human skill can be codified into rules and heuristics, and immortalized on magnetic disks; they fail to ask whether this is actually desirable. The gap between design and experience is thus set to widen, and with it our alienation and anxiety.

There have been various attempts to pin down this phenomenon, to articulate the sense of 'cybernetic loss' that humans face in the information age. The French philosopher Jean-François Lyotard addressed the subject in the catalogue of an exhibition he organized in Paris called 'The Immaterial'.[48] He observed that, whatever the discipline used to approach the body – medicine, biology, biogenetics, diet, environment – it may now be analysed digitally according to a certain number of small (binary) constants; in short it is *dematerialized*. 'The modern view of the body and of the world was solid, but it was sad. I think we are going towards something that is infinitely complex, horribly hard to deal with, but much more fun. To look at the body through a scanner is to see it digitalized; access to the body is less direct, more mediated . . . this is the drama of the new-born era, the postmodern period.'[49]

The aim of 'The Immaterial' was, as the programme explained, 'to make you feel'. It sought to present analogues in experience for such intangible phenomena as biogenetics, synthetic aromas, and information networks based on miles of invisible wiring. 'Neither matter nor material is what it seems to be,' the visitor is told; 'we see nothing directly, outlines and surfaces are human perceptions, not concrete facts. The individual may feel lost, but in fact, in this new context, can become more free.'[50]

The proposition that the individual may be liberated by experiencing such uncertainty in contact with new tertiary technologies begs many questions – for example, will we all benefit equally, citizen and corporation alike, from their introduction and use? Who is to control all these autonomous systems? Are we supposed to welcome the advent of a technoscience which we cannot, by definition, understand? Is the machine, which modernism argued was an analogue of the rational mind, to become its replacement?

Design is not unique in facing these questions. Just as technology seems to be drifting out of control, knowledge itself slips out of our grasp, too, as science's classical foundations – order, simplicity and reason – are undermined by the new organizing principles of disorder, complexity and change. In science, as in design, 'we are both spectators and actors' as Niels Bohr put it.[51] Nothing is fixed, no knowledge is 'objective', everything is context. 'The guiding story of the Enlightenment, that knowledge can be gradually built up by careful observation of reality (from the superior standpoint of pure reason) is seen to be precisely that: a story.'[52] The result: a crisis of place, a crisis of knowledge, a crisis of identity.

The American artist Robert Irwin has talked about the artificial barriers which 'keep art from dealing with the universal experience of change', arguing that in rehabilitating non-objective art we may find one way to resolve the problem.[53] Although Irwin may be considered part of that modernist tradition which created art that had no apparent relation to the natural world, because abstraction was considered a 'new reality', he represents, too, a break with that tradition in his stress on the connectedness of art to the culture which nurtures it, and the consequent possibilities for involvement by those who view it. Irwin asks: 'If we are to continue taking the words "aesthetics" and "perception" as having a serious bearing on art, can we continue to hold the dialogue of art to be subsumable to the making of objects?'[54] Art, says Irwin, should be 'knowing in action', and the artist's job is to provide an opportunity to further that kind of knowing, to delegate a major share of the creative act to the observer.

In the practical applications of Irwin's ideas, a connection between his ideas about art and the germs of a distinctively postmodern design become apparent. His method is to set up environments that encourage the viewer to look around with the eye of an artist; this art is not finite, but conditional – conditional on the individual act of perception, or experience, which offers 'a level of aesthetic pleasure that heightens our sense of awareness – something that could be said of very few gallery shows'.[55] Other art to increase the 'permeability' of gallery walls includes the new sculpture, particularly strong in Britain, which takes space itself, rather than the materials used, as the stuff to be modelled and controlled. As the critic William Packer describes our experience of the new sculpture, 'The invitation is to go out with [the sculptor], to move through the same spaces and configurations of the landscape, to mark the fleeting evidence of human presence and passage, to savour a particular, personal experience.'[56] Performance art, new video, fashion, the craft revival, and of course the new music reflect this tendency to replace the modern spectator with the postmodern participant.[57]

A new abstract art and design for abstract, postmodern, experience? Perhaps, but it in the *process* implications of conditional art, rather than in the search for new forms and 'languages', that the real potential of the opening to art in design lies. In a world of simulacra and pseudo-events, in which past and future alike appear to have no reality, art may well provide a real and personal vision with which to fill the void. Postmodern design, in this context, far from being a skin-deep exercise in styling, becomes, with art, a latterday *Erlebniskunst*, an art of experience. Here, designing is no longer concerned with individual products, but with whole systems; it is not just about experts solving problems, but about collective participation; along with new science, it is not a rules-based game but a creative process, which can make products and places unique.

The trouble is that art, like design, is a system – not an idealized form of knowledge. Just as the design system includes factory production, economic interests, and the division of labour, so 'art' includes museums, economic interests, the cult of celebrity – features which some people say make art a latter-day replacement for the church. Making design more 'artistic' will not diminish the importance of its economic and social context, wherein the progressive nature and ambitions of history's early modernisms remain as valid now as they were a century ago.

REFERENCES

1 Jameson, Fredric, 'Postmodernism and consumer society', in *The Anti-Aesthetic*, ed. Hal Foster, Port Townsend, Washington, 1983
2 ibid.
3 Baudrillard, Jean, *Simulations. Semiotext(e)*, New York, 1983
4 Jameson, op. cit.
5 Habermas, Jürgen, 'Modernity – an incomplete project', in *Anti-Aesthetic*, op. cit. (1)
6 Foster, Hal, in *Anti-Aesthetic*, op. cit. (1)
7 Berman, Marshall, *All That Is Solid Melts Into Air*, London, 1983
8 Anderson, Perry, 'Modernity and Revolution,' *New Left Review* 144, London, 1984
9 Berman, op. cit.
10 Kwinter, Sanford, 'La Città Nuova, Modernity and Continuity', *Zone 1/2*, New York, 1986
11 Giedion, Siegfried, *Space, Time and Architecture*, quoted in Berman, op. cit.
12 Davis, Mike, 'The Postmodern City', *New Left Review* 151, London, 1985
13 Piore, Michael J., *The Second Industrial Divide*, New York, 1984
14 Tafuri, Manfredo, *Architecture and Utopia*, Boston, 1976
15 Benjamin, Walter, *Illuminations*, London, 1970
16 Tschumi, Bernard, 'The Discourse of Events', in *Themes 3*, Architectural Association, London, 1983
17 ibid.
18 Kwinter, op. cit.
19 Tafuri, op. cit.
20 Hatton, Brian, in *NATO, Gamma City Issue*, c/o Architectural Association, London, 1985
21 Berman, Marshall, 'City Life After Urbicide', *Village Voice*, New York, 1985
22 Guillaume, Marc, in *Zone 1/2*, New York, 1986
23 Koolhaas, Rem, in *Zone 1/2*, New York, 1986
24 Fitch and Company, Annual Report, London, 1985
25 Esslinger, Hartmut, 'Design in the Triad', paper given to 'Worldesign', 14th ICSID Conference, Washington DC, 1985
26 Sakashita, H., *Japan Design News*, Issue 3, Tokyo, 1984
27 Shinohara, Hiroshi, *Design Quarterly Japan*, Tokyo, 1985
28 Morello, Augusto, 'Design and the Age of Quality', *Design* magazine, London, April 1983
29 Goodall, Philippa, *The Home is Where the Heart Is*, unpublished paper
30 Alff, Wilhelm, quoted in W. F. Haug, *Critique of Commodity Aesthetics*, London 1986
31 Haug, op. cit. (30)
32 Berger, John, *The White Bird*, London, 1985
33 Timms, Edward, 'From Sensuousness to Sobriety', *Times Literary Supplement*, 14 September 1985
34 Vallin, Eugene, quoted in *Form Follows Function*, ed. Dennis Sharp, Milton Keynes, 1975
35 Galle, Emil, in *Form Follows Function*, op. cit. (34)
36 Foster, Hal, paper to Architectural Association, London, January 1987
37 Gibb, Julian, 'Design Primario', *Design* magazine, London, January 1985
38 ibid.
39 York, Peter, 'Style Wars', paper given to Aspen Design Conference, 1986
40 *Financial Times*, 5 February 1985
41 ibid.
42 Mandel, Ernest, *Late Capitalism*, London, 1980
43 Suzuki, Tessa Morris, 'Robots and Capitalism', *New Left Review*, 147, 1984
44 ibid.
45 *Processed World Magazine*, Issue 10, San Francisco
46 *Guardian*, 11 August 1983
47 Porat, M. U., *The Information Economy, Definition and Measurement*, Washington, 1977
48 Lyotard, Jean-François, *Les Immatériaux*, Paris, 1985
49 Lyotard, Jean-François, quoted in *Time* magazine, 15 April 1985
50 Lyotard, *Les Immatériaux*, op. cit.
51 Bohr, Niels, quoted in Lawson, Hilary, *Reflexivity, the Postmodern Predicament*, London, 1986

John Thackara

52 Lawson, op. cit. (51)
53 Irwin, Robert, *Being and Circumstance, Notes Towards a Conditional Art*, San Francisco, 1985
54 ibid.
55 Tomkins, Calvin, in *New Yorker*, 11 November 1985
56 *Financial Times*, 14 December 1986

— 2 —

The experience of
modernity

•

MARSHALL BERMAN

For most of my life, since I learned that I was living in 'a modern building' and growing up as part of 'a modern family', in the Bronx of thirty years ago, I have been fascinated by the meanings of modernity. I have tried here to open up some of these dimensions of meaning, to explore and chart the adventures and horrors, the ambiguities and ironies of modern life. In *All That Is Solid Melts Into Air* I move and develop through a number of ways of reading: of texts – Goethe's *Faust*, the *Communist Manifesto*, Dostoevsky's *Notes from Underground*, and many more; but also I try to read spatial and social environments – small towns, big construction sites, dams and power plants, Joseph Paxton's Crystal Palace, Haussmann's Parisian boulevards, St Petersburg prospects, Robert Moses' highways through New York; and, finally, reading fictional and actual people's lives, from Goethe's time through Marx's and Baudelaire's and into our own. I tried to show how all these people share, and all these books and environments express, certain distinctively modern concerns. They are moved at once by a will to change – to transform both themselves and their world – and by a terror of disorientation and disintegration, of life falling apart. They all know the thrill and the dread of a world in which 'all that is solid melts into air'.

To be modern is to live a life of paradox and contradiction. It is to be overpowered by the immense bureaucratic organizations that have the power to control and often to destroy all communities, values, lives; and yet to be undeterred in our determination to face these forces, to fight to change their world and make it our own. It is to be both revolutionary and conservative: alive to new possibilities for experience and adventure, frightened by the nihilistic depths to which so many modern adventures lead, longing to create and to hold on to something real even as everything melts. We might even say that to be fully modern is to be anti-modern: from Marx's and Dostoevsky's time to our own, it has been impossible to grasp and embrace the modern world's potentialities without loathing and fighting against some of its most palpable realities. No wonder then that, as the great modernist and anti-modernist Kierkegaard said, the deepest modern seriousness must express itself through irony. Modern irony animates so many great works of art and thought over the past century; at the same time it infuses millions of ordinary people's lives. My contribution here cannot resolve the contradictions that pervade modern life, but it should help us to understand them, so that we can be clear and honest in facing and sorting out and working through the forces that make us what we are.

The traditions of modernism

There is a mode of vital experience – experience of space and time, of the self and others, of life's possibilities and perils – that is shared by men and women all over the world today. I will call this body of experience 'modernity'. To be modern is to find ourselves in an environment that promises us adventure, power, joy, growth, transformation of ourselves and the world – and, at the same time, that threatens to destroy everything we have, everything we know, everything we are. Modern environments and experiences cut across all boundaries of geography and ethnicity, of class and nationality, of religion and ideology: in this sense, modernity can be said to unite all mankind. But it is a paradoxical unity, a unity of disunity: it pours us all into a maelstrom of perpetual disintegration and renewal, of struggle and contradiction, of ambiguity and anguish. To be modern is to be part of a universe in which, as Marx said, 'all that is solid melts into air'.

People who find themselves in the midst of this maelstrom are apt to feel that they are the first ones, and maybe the only ones, to be going through it; this feeling has engendered numerous nostalgic myths of a pre-modern Paradise Lost. In fact, however, great and ever-increasing numbers of people have been going through it for close to five hundred years. Although most of these people have probably experienced modernity as a radical threat to all their history and traditions, it has, in the course of five centuries, developed a rich history and a plenitude of traditions of its own. I want to explore and chart these traditions, to understand the ways in which they may obscure or impoverish our sense of what modernity is and what it can be.

The maelstrom of modern life has been fed from many sources: great discoveries in the physical sciences, changing our images of the universe and our place in it, the industrialization of production, which transforms scientific knowledge into technology, creates new human environments and destroys old ones, speeds up the whole tempo of life, generates new forms of corporate power and class struggle: immense demographic upheavals, severing millions of people from their ancestral habitats, hurtling them half way across the world into new lives; rapid and often cataclysmic urban growth; systems of mass communication, dynamic in their development, enveloping and binding together the most diverse people and societies; increasingly powerful national states, bureaucratically structured and operated, constantly striving to expand their powers; mass social movements of people, and peoples, challenging their political and economic rulers, striving to gain some control over their lives;

finally, bearing and driving all these people and institutions along, an ever-expanding, drastically fluctuating capitalist world market. In the twentieth century, the social processes that bring this maelstrom into being, and keep it in a state of perpetual becoming, have come to be called 'modernization'. These world-historical processes have nourished an amazing variety of visions and ideas that aim to make men and women the subjects as well as the objects of modernization, to give them the power to change the world that is changing them, to make their way through the maelstrom and make in their own. Over the past century, these visions and values have come to be loosely grouped together under the name of 'modernism'. I want to explore the dialectics of modernization and modernism.

In the hope of getting a grip on something as vast as the history of modernity, I have divided it into three phases. In the first phase, which goes roughly from the start of the sixteenth century to the end of the eighteenth, people are just beginning to experience modern life; they hardly know what has hit them. They grope, desperately but half blindly, for an adequate vocabulary; they have little or no sense of a modern public or community within which their trials and hopes can be shared. Our second phase begins at the great revolutionary wave of the 1790s. With the French Revolution and its reverberations, a great modern public abruptly and dramatically comes to life. This public shares the feeling of living in a revolutionary age, an age that generates explosive upheavals in every dimension of personal, social and political life. At the same time, the nineteenth-century modern public can remember what it is like to live, materially and spiritually, in worlds that are not modern at all. From this inner dichotomy, this sense of living in two worlds simultaneously, the ideas of modernization and modernism emerge and unfold. In the twentieth century, our third and final phase, the process of modernization expands to take in virtually the whole world, and the developing world culture of modernism achieves spectacular triumphs in art and thought. On the other hand, as the modern public expands, it shatters into a multitude of fragments, speaking incommensurable private languages; the idea of modernity, conceived in numerous fragmentary ways, loses much of its vividness, resonance and depth, and loses its capacity to organize and give meaning to people's lives. As a result of this, we find ourselves today in the midst of a modern age that has lost touch with the roots of its own modernity.

The modernist vision

If there is one archetypal modern voice in the early phase of modernity, before the American and French revolutions, it is the voice of Jean-Jacques Rousseau. Rousseau was the first to use the word *moderniste* in the ways in which the nineteenth and twentieth centuries were to use it; and he is the source of some of our most vital modern traditions, from nostalgic reverie to psychoanalytic self-scrutiny to participatory democracy. Rousseau was, as everyone knows, a deeply troubled man. Much of his anguish sprang from sources peculiar to his own strained life; but some of it derived from his acute responsiveness to social conditions that were coming to shape millions of people's lives. Rousseau astounded his contemporaries by proclaiming that European society was 'at the edge of the abyss', on the verge of the most explosive revolutionary upheavals. He experienced everyday life in that society – especially in Paris, its capital – as a whirlwind, *le tourbillon social*. How was the self to move and live in the whirlwind?

In Rousseau's romantic novel *The New Eloise*, his young hero, Saint-Preux, makes an exploratory move – an archetypal move for millions of young people in the centuries to come – from the country to the city. He writes to his love, Julie, from the depths of *le tourbillon social*, and tries to convey his wonder and dread. Saint-Preux experiences metropolitan life as 'a perpetual clash of groups and cabals, a continual flux of prejudices and conflicting opinions . . . Everyone constantly places himself in contradiction with himself', and 'Everything is absurd, but nothing is shocking, because everyone is accustomed to everything.' This is a world in which 'The good, the bad, the beautiful, the ugly, truth, virtue, have only a local and limited existence.' A multitude of new experiences offer themselves; but anyone who wants to enjoy them 'must be more pliable than Alcibiades, ready to change his principles with his audience, to adjust his spirit with every step'. After a few months in this environment,

> I'm beginning to feel the drunkenness that this agitated, tumultuous life plunges you into. With such a multitude of objects pasing before my eyes, I'm getting dizzy. Of all the things that strike me, there is none that holds my heart, yet all of them together disturb my feelings, so that I forget what I am and who I belong to.

He reaffirms his commitment to his first love; yet even as he says it, he fears that 'I don't know one day what I'm going to love the next.' He longs desperately for something solid to cling to, yet 'I see only phantoms that strike my eye, but disappear as soon as I try to grasp them'. This atmosphere – of agitation and turbulence, psychic dizziness and drunkenness, expansion of experiential possibilities and destruction of moral boundaries and personal bonds, self-enlargement and self-derangement, phantoms in the street and in the soul – is the atmosphere in which modern sensibility is born.

If we move forward a hundred years or so and try to identify the distinctive rhythms and timbres of nineteenth-century modernity, the first thing we will notice is the highly developed, differentiated and dynamic new landscape in which modern experience takes place. This is a landscape of steam engines, automatic factories, railroads, vast new industrial zones; of teeming cities that have grown overnight, often with dreadful human consequences; of daily newspapers, telegraphs, telephones and other rapid means of communication operating on an ever wider scale; of increasingly strong national states and multinational aggregations of capital; of mass social movements fighting these modernizations imposed from above with their own modes of modernization from below; of an ever-expanding world market embracing all, capable of the most spectacular growth, capable of appalling waste and devastation, capable of everything except solidity and stability. The great modernists of the nineteenth century all attack this environment passionately, and strive to tear it down or explode it from within; yet all find themselves remarkably at home in it, alive to its possibilities, affirmative even in their radical negations, playful and ironic even in their moments of gravest seriousness and depth.

We can get a feeling for the complexity and richness of nineteenth-century modernism, and for the unities that infuse its diversity, if we listen briefly to two of its most distinctive voices: Nietzsche, who is generally perceived as a primary source of many of the modernisms of our time, and Marx, who is not ordinarily associated with any sort of modernism at all.

Here is Marx, speaking in awkward but powerful English in London in 1856. 'The so-called revolutions of 1848 were but poor incidents,' he begins, 'small fractures and fissures in the dry crust of European society. But they denounced the abyss. Beneath the apparently solid surface, they betrayed oceans of liquid matter, only needing expansion to rend into fragments continents of hard rock.' The ruling classes of the reactionary 1850s tell the world that all is solid again; but it is not clear if even they themselves believe it. In fact, Marx says, 'The atmosphere in which we live weighs upon everyone with a 20,000-pound force, but do you feel it?' One of Marx's most urgent aims is to make people 'feel it'; this is why his ideas are expressed in such intense and extravagant images – abysses, earthquakes, volcanic eruptions, crushing gravitational force – images that will continue to resonate in our own century's modernist art and thought. Marx goes on: 'There is one great fact, characteristic of this our nineteenth century, a fact which no party dares deny.' The basic fact of modern life, as Marx experiences it, is that this life is radically contradictory at its base:

> On the one hand, they have started into life industrial and scientific forces which no epoch of human history had ever suspected. On the other hand, there exist symptoms of decay, far surpassing the horrors of the latter times of the Roman Empire. In our days everything seems pregnant with its contrary. Machinery, gifted with the wonderful power of shortening and fructifying human labour, we behold starving and overworking it. The new-fangled sources of wealth, by some weird spell, are turned into sources of want. The victories of art seem bought by the loss of character. At the same pace that mankind masters nature, man seems to become enslaved to other men or to his own infamy. Even the pure light of science seems unable to shine but on the dark background of ignorance. All our invention and progress seem to result in endowing material forces with intellectual life, and stultifying human life into a material force.

These miseries and mysteries fill many moderns with despair. Some would 'get rid of modern arts, in order to get rid of modern conflicts'; others will try to balance progress in industry with a neofeudal or neoabsolutist regression in politics. Marx, however, proclaims a paradigmatically modernist faith: 'On our part, we do not mistake the shrewd spirit that continues to mark all these contradictions. We know that to work well . . . the new-fangled forces of society want only to be mastered by new-fangled men – and such are the working men. They are as much the invention of modern time as machinery itself.' Thus a class of 'new men', men who are thoroughly modern, will be able to resolve the contradictions of modernity, to overcome the crushing pressures, earthquakes, weird spells, personal and social abysses, in the midst of which all modern men and women are forced to live. Having said this, Marx turns abruptly playful and connects his vision of the future with the past – with English folklore, with Shakespeare: 'In the signs that bewilder the middle class, the aristocracy and the poor prophets of regression, we recognize our brave friend Robin Goodfellow, the old mole that can work in the earth so fast, that worthy pioneer – the Revolution.'

Marx's writing is famous for its endings. But if we see him as a modernist, we will notice the dialectical motion that underlies and animates his thought, a motion that is open-ended, and that flows against the current of his own concepts and desires. Thus, in the *Communist Manifesto*, we see that the revolutionary dynamism that will overthrow the modern bourgeoisie springs from that bourgeoisie's own deepest impulses and needs:

> The bourgeoisie cannot exist without constantly revolutionizing the instruments of production, and with them the relations of production, and with them the relations of society . . . Constant revolutionizing of production, uninterrupted disturbance of all social relations, everlasting uncertainty and agitation, distinguish the bourgeois epoch from all earlier ones.

This is probably the definitive vision of the modern environment, that environment which has brought forth an amazing plentitude of modernist movements, from Marx's time to our own. The vision unfolds:

> All fixed, fast-frozen relations, with their own train of ancient and venerable prejudices and opinions, are swept away, all new-formed ones become antiquated before they can ossify. All that is solid melts into air, all that is holy is profaned, and men at last are forced to face . . . the real conditions of their lives and their relations with their fellow men.

Thus the dialectical motion of modernity turns ironically against its prime movers, the bourgeoisie. But it may not stop turning there: after all, all modern movements are caught up in this ambience – including Marx's own. Suppose, as Marx supposes, that bourgeois forms decompose, and that a communist movement surges into power: what it to keep this new social form from sharing its predecessor's fate and melting down in the modern air? Marx understood this question and suggested some answers, which we will explore later. But one of the distinctive virtues of modernism is that it leaves its questions echoing in the air long after the questioners themselves, and their answers, have left the scene.

If we move on a quarter of a century, to Nietzsche in the 1880s, we will find very different prejudices, allegiances and hopes, yet a surprisingly similar voice and feeling for modern life. For Nietzsche, as for Marx, the currents of modern history were ironic and dialectical: thus Christian ideals of the soul's integrity and the will to truth had come to explode Christianity itself. The results were the traumatic events that Nietzsche called 'the death of God' and 'the advent of nihilism'. Modern mankind found itself in the midst of a great absence and emptiness of values and yet, at the same time, a remarkable abundance of possibilities. Here, in Nietzsche's *Beyond Good and Evil* (1882), we find, just as we found in Marx, a world where everything is pregnant with its contrary.

> At these turning points in history there shows itself, juxtaposed and often entangled with one another, a magnificent, manifold, jungle-like growing and striving, a sort of tropical tempo in rivalry of development, and an enormous destruction and self-destruction, thanks to egoisms violently opposed to one another, exploding, battling each other for sun and light, unable to find any limitation, any check, any considerateness within the morality at their disposal . . . Nothing but new 'wherefores', no longer any communal formulas; a new allegiance of misunderstanding and mutual disrespect; decay, and the most superior desires gruesomely bound up with one another, the genius of the race welling up over the cornucopias of good and ill; a fateful simultaneity of spring and autumn . . . Again there is danger, the mother of morality – great danger – but this time displaced on to the individual, on to the nearest and dearest, on to the street, on to one's own child, one's own heart, one's own innermost secret recesses of wish and will.

At times like these, 'the individual dares to individuate himself.' On the other hand, this daring individual desperately 'needs a set of laws of his own, needs his own skills and wiles for self-preservation, self-heightening, self-awakening, self-liberation'. The possibilities are at once glorious and ominous. 'Our instincts can now run back in all sorts of directions; we ourselves are a kind of chaos.' Modern man's sense of himself and his history 'really amounts to an instinct for everything, a taste and tongue for everything'. So many roads open up from this point. How are modern men and women to find the resources to cope with their 'everything'? Nietzsche notes that there are plenty of 'little Jack Horners' around whose solution to the chaos of modern life is to try not to live them at all: for them, '"Become mediocre" is the only morality that makes sense.'

Another type of modern throws himself into parodies of the past: he 'needs history because it is the storage closet where all the costumes are kept. He notices that none really fits him' – not primitive, not classical, not medieval, not oriental – 'so he keeps trying on more and more', unable to accept the fact that a modern man 'can never really look well-dressed', because no social role in modern times can ever be a perfect fit. Nietzsche's own stance toward the perils of modernity is to embrace them all with joy: 'We moderns, we half-barbarians. We are in the midst of our bliss only when we are most in danger. The only stimulus that tickles us is the infinite, the immeasurable.' And yet Nietzsche is not willing to live in the midst of this danger forever. As ardently as Marx, he asserts his faith in a new kind of man – 'the man of tomorrow and the day after tomorrow' – who, 'standing in opposition to his today', will have the courage and imagination to 'create new values' that modern men and women need to steer their way through the perilous infinities in which they live.

What is distinctive and remarkable about the voice that Marx and Nietzsche share is not only its breathless pace, its vibrant energy, its imaginative richness, but also its fast and drastic shifts in tone and inflection, its readiness to turn on itself, to question and negate all it has said, to transform itself into a great range of harmonic or dissonant voices, and to stretch itself beyond its capacities into an endlessly wider range, to express and grasp a world where everything is pregnant with its contrary and 'all that is solid melts into air'. This voice resonates at once with self-discovery and self-mockery, with self-delight and self-doubt. It is a voice that knows pain and dread, but believes in its power to come through. Grave danger is everywhere, and may strike at any moment, but not even the deepest wounds can stop the flow and overflow of its energy. It is ironic and contradictory, polyphonic and dialectical, denouncing modern life in the name of values that modernity itself has created, hoping – often against hope – that the modernities of tomorrow and the day after tomorrow will heal the wounds that wreck the modern men and women of today. All the great modernists of the nineteenth century – spirits as diverse as Marx and Kierke-gaard, Whitman and Ibsen, Baudelaire, Melville, Carlyle, Stirner, Rimbaud, Strindberg, Dostoevsky, and many more – speak in these rhythms and in this range.

Impaired visions

What has become of nineteenth-century modernism in the twentieth century? In some ways it has thrived and grown beyond its own wildest hopes. In painting and sculpture, in poetry and the novel, in theatre and dance, in architecture and design, in a whole array of electronic media and a wide range of scientific disciplines that did not even exist a century ago, our century has produced a wealth of works and ideas of the highest quality. The twentieth century may well be the most brilliantly creative in the history of the world, not least because its creative energies have burst out in every part of the world. And yet, it seems to me, we do not know how to use our modernism; we have missed or broken the connection between our culture and our lives. Jackson Pollock imagined his drip paintings as forests in which spectators might lose (and, of course, find) themselves; but we have mostly lost the art of putting ourselves in the picture, of recognizing ourselves as participants and protagonists in the art and thought of our time. Our century has nourished a spectacular modern art; but we seem to have forgotten how to grasp the modern life from which this art springs. In many ways, modern thought since Marx and Nietzsche has grown and developed; yet our thinking about modernity seems to have stagnated and regressed.

If we listen closely to twentieth-century writers and thinkers about modernity and compare them to those of a century ago, we will find a radical flattening of perspective and shrinking of imaginative range. Our nineteenth-century thinkers were simultaneously enthusiasts and enemies of modern life, wrestling inexhaustibly with its ambiguities and contradictions; their self-ironies and inner tensions were a primary source of their creative power. Their twentieth-century successors have lurched far more toward rigid polarities and flat totalizations.

In *All That Is Solid*, I go on to indict nearly everybody in the twentieth century who has tried to theorize about modernity: philosophers, sociologists, aestheticians, poets, theologians, political theorists and activists, *et al.*, from Marinetti to McLuhan and Marcuse. I argue that their thinking tends to be flattened and polarized into what we might call modernisms of rejection and modernisms of acceptance.

A similar flattening of perspective can be found in twentieth-century ideas on architecture and design. At one pole, the modernism of rejection, we can locate Henry Russell Hitchcock and Philip Johnson's *The International Style*, published in 1932 under the auspices of New York's Museum of Modern Art. One of the main achievements of this book, which enabled it virtually to define the modern canon for the next forty years, was its own distinctive style: an Olympian voice that proclaimed with serene certainty and absolute authority what modernism was, and what is must be. (T.S. Eliot had been writing in this voice on literature since the early 1920s. Clement Greenberg would learn to use it on painting in the 1940s.) A modern building was built in 'the Style'; any deviations from it could only be inept, frivolous or corrupt. A building in 'the Style' is cubic, geometrically organized, constructed in steel, glass and reinforced concrete, regular in form, flat at the top and (with a few specified exceptions) pure white. It is to be conceived as a thing in itself, as if it were the only building in the world, and designed from the inside out, in terms of an abstract, idealized conception of its functions, with no concessions to the landscape or cityscape around it. Architectural and social history are dismissed as mere warehouses of forms that are hollow, played-out and dead. Preoccupation with the dead will divert the architect and designer from their lofty mission, which is nothing less than the salvation of the modern world. Hitchcock and Johnson emphasize Le Corbusier's dictum 'Architecture or Revolution', along with its corollary, 'Revolution can be avoided', if modern architects and designers are given the freedom and power to change the world.

Looking back at this modernism half a century later, we can admire the high seriousness, the moral purity and integrity, the strength of its will to change. At the same time, it is impossible to miss some ominous undertows: a lack of empathy, an emotional aridity, a narrowness of imaginative range. These modernists combine a celebration of the idea of the modern world with an almost total lack of feeling for the actual people in it.

One clear way in which this emerges is in the abuse that Hitchcock and Johnson heap on the most popular architectural form of the early 1930s, the urban skyscraper. They particularly disdain the skyscrapers that were springing up in midtown Manhattan even as they wrote: Chrysler, Empire State, General Electric, etc. It is apparently a fundamental violation of the modern canon for a building to be vertical; but if it must be, at least it should have the good taste not to *look* vertical. Alas, the skyscrapers that are springing up around the Museum lack the decency to mute or counteract their upward thrust: indeed, they seem to glory in it. The flamboyant and theatrical character of these buildings angers Hitchcock and Johnson to the point where they refuse to allow them even the dignity of the name 'modern', coining the derisive epithet 'modernoid' to put them in their place. Nor are they allowed to be called 'architecture', but only vulgar commercial entertainment. 'We are asked to take seriously the architectural taste of real estate spectators, renting agents and mortgage brokers!' They have no more patience with the Chrysler Building than Plato had with the shoemakers' and fishmongers' stalls in the agora. In retrospect, it is nice to see Americans denying the sacredness of market values; yet it seems that the real capitalist crime is to have conceived and built buildings that people actually enjoy. The rhetoric and sensibility here suggest a classical 'vanguard' movement that wants to liberate the people by protecting them from themselves.

In the 1930s the International Style was still a utopian dream. A generation later, it would materialize with overwhelming power. Late in the 1950s, the pioneers of 'the Style' and their now numerous followers obtained something like a mandate to rebuild America's cities. A few of their individual buildings, Mies's Seagram Building for example, were spectacular successes. But as their creations crystallized into full-blown environments, the limitations of their visions became dreadfully clear. Their manifestos and models had promised light and air, honesty and openness, fresh energy to engage the world, release from the dead weights of the past, vision that could transform new technologies into means of liberation, environments where modern men and women could feel at home. But when the buildings finally went up, and people began to live and work in them – from the Pan Am to the Pruitt-Igoe – the most general response was a sense of being more imprisoned, lost and alienated than ever before. This environment turned out to be open and honest only in the sense suggested by the *Communist Manifesto*: 'In a word, for exploitation veiled by religious and political illusions, the bourgeoisie has substituted naked, shameless, direct, brutal exploitation.' People who had enthusiastically embraced the premises and promises of modernism felt especially betrayed. The ever-growing row of grim steel and glass and concrete slabs along New York's upper Sixth Avenue looked like gigantic tombstones, at once marking the death of the city and mocking a generation of hopes that modernism could renew civic life.

By the late 1960s, there were plenty of people who felt that the International Style had become – or else had been all along – a gigantic rip-off of the modern public. At this point, the Museum of Modern Art, which had done so much to establish an orthodox modernist thesis, now stepped forward to proclaim a modernist Antithesis: Robert Venturi's *Complexity and Contradiction in Architecture*, published by the Museum (and introduced by Vincent Scully) in 1966. Venturi wrote with verve, wit and polemical brilliance. To the Miesian doctrine that 'Less is more', he retorted that 'Less is a bore.' He attacked 'the limitations of orthodox modern architecture and city planning, in particular the platitudinous architects who invoke integrity, technology or electronic pro-gramming as ends in architecture, the popularizers who paint fairy stories over our chaotic reality, and suppress those complexities and contradictions inherent in art and experience'. It was time to redefine the modern canon, and to open the floodgates to all the drama, rhetoric playfulness, irony, weirdness, inconsistency, multivalence, extravagance, that the votaries of 'the Style' had worked so hard to keep out. Against a modernism of exclusion and exclusive-ness, Venturi and MOMA were proclaiming a modernism that knew how to accept and embrace.

Venturi's programme for architecture paralleled the thinking of many diverse figures working in other media: John Cage, Lawrence Alloway, Marshall McLuhan, Leslie Fiedler, Susan Sontag, and many others. The sensibility they shared, sometimes called Pop, embraced popular culture from an intellectual and avant-garde perspective. It exhorted artists to 'Wake up to the very life we're living' (Cage) and to 'Cross the border, close the gap' (Fiedler) between culture and the totality of life. All this was part of the great wave of energy that animated the life of the 1960s. The modernists of the sixties confronted a culture that had become unbearably solemn, arid and closed; they opened it up to the immense variety and richness of things, materials, movements, images and ideas that the exploding 'global village' of the worldwide economic boom years was bringing forth. The best characterization of sixties modernism that I have ever heard was Jean-Luc Godard's phrase, 'the children of Marx and Coca-Cola'. But this was a precarious synthesis, and very few people anywhere were able to sustain it in their lives or in their work for long. What tended to happen in American modernism (some of which, by the 1970s, was calling itself postmodern) was that Marx got drowned in the flow of Coca-Cola: openness to the world metamorphosed imperceptibly into uncritical acceptance of everything that was there.

Re-reading Venturi in the 1980s, we can see that some of the problems that would emerge in this modernism were there from the start. On the one hand,

Venturi reasonably criticizes Miesian minimalism for 'separating architecture from the experience of life and the needs of society'. On the other hand, after echoing the lament of modern architects and planners that they really have very little power to 'shape the whole environment', he seems to propose, as a remedy, that they should simply stop worrying about the whole environment. Ironically, he says, the architect can be more effective if he restricts the effects he is aiming for, 'by narrowing his concerns and concentrating on his own job. Perhaps then relationships and power will take care of themselves.' Here, right before our eyes, Pop seems to be turning into Pangloss. Maybe this isn't quite the best of all possible worlds, but it comes close. 'Is not Main Street almost all right? Indeed, is not the commercial strip of a Route 66 almost all right?' Complexity and contradiction seems to be giving way to chamber-of-commerce celebration. 'As I have said, our question is: what slight twist of context will make them all right?' The sad irony here is that Venturi has been attacking the minimalist variety of modernism for giving up too much – and he is right. But radically to constrict the scope of modern architecture and design, from changing the world to making 'slight twists of context' in commercial strips, is to give up far more.

However, there is no way that Venturi or any of his readers could have dreamed how much further these professions (along with many others) would go in narrowing themselves over the next twenty years. By the mid-1980s, the one overriding concern of architects and designers seemed to be how best to ingratiate themselves with private and corporate developers, and to 'shape the whole environment' to fit developers' desires. My generation, disgruntled refugees from the 1960s, often blame these changes on the young. But it is worth noting that, here as elsewhere, it was the grand old men of modernism who led the way. Philip Johnson, who not so long ago was abusing the Chrysler Building for its commercial appeal, has spent the last decade flying around the world creating buildings and environments designed to make every Gerald Hines and George Klein feel like a king. His development offers priceless testimony of how modernism has come a long way.

(It is unlikely that Johnson would see any problem in this evolution – or, indeed, in any other – because he publicly prides himself on his nihilism. He proclaimed it enthusiastically on the BBC in 1965:

> To merely enjoy things as they are – we see an entirely different beauty from what [Lewis] Mumford could possibly see – What good does it do you to believe in good things? . . . It's feudal and futile. I think it much better to be nihilistic and forget it all. I mean, I know I'm attacked by my moral friends, but really, don't they shake themselves up over nothing?

This, of course, is one thing that enemies of modernism have always maintained: that it is nihilistic, hollow at its core, that it is indifferent to human values, believes in nothing, stands for nothing except doing whatever will work, whatever will play – or pay – whatever it can get away with.)

Backwards and forwards

In architecture and design, as in other areas, twentieth-century modernism has tended to lurch wildly back and forth between unpalatable poles, from pseudo-Olympian contempt for modern society and the people in it, to pseudo-Dionysian embraces of everybody and everything, from thesis to antithesis, unable to advance toward any sort of synthesis, or even to imagine what a synthesis might be.

One reason for this impasse is that, over the last half-century, ideas and arguments about modernism have been almost exclusively ideas and arguments about *style*. There has been a tacit suppression of all the crucial questions about what modern life means (or can mean) and how modern men and women should live. Modernists of the last fifty years have tended to limit their thought to the exterior of contemporary life, while the deepest and most urgent moral and political conflicts have been fought out over their heads. In this respect, ironically, we have regressed and fallen behind the great modernists of the nineteenth century, who saw the theme of modernity as a way to think and speak about all the overwhelming questions that permeate everyday life in the modern world.

I have been trying to bring some of the dynamic and dialectical modernisms of the past back to life. I believe that contact with the modernisms of the past can give us back a sense of our own modern roots, and expand our capacity for cultural and political renewal.

They can help us connect our lives with the lives of millions of people who are living through the trauma of modernization thousands of miles away, in societies radically different from our own – and with millions of people who lived through it a century or more ago. They can illuminate the contradictory forces and needs that inspire and torment us: our desire to be rooted in a stable and coherent personal and social past, and our insatiable desire for growth – not merely for economic growth but for growth in experience, in pleasure, in knowledge, in sensibility – growth that destroys both the physical and social landscapes of our past, and our emotional links with those lost worlds; our desperate allegiances to ethnic, national, class and sexual groups which we hope will give us a firm 'identity', and the internationalization of everyday life – of our clothes and household goods, our books and music, our ideas and fantasies – that spreads all our identities all over the map; our desire for clear and solid values to live by, and our desire to embrace the limitless possibilities of modern life and experience that obliterate all values; the social and political forces that propel us into explosive conflicts with other people and other peoples, even as we develop a deeper sensitivity and empathy toward our ordained enemies and come to realize, sometimes too late, that they are not so different from us after all. Experiences like these unite us with the nineteenth-century modern world: a world where, as Marx said, 'everything is pregnant with its contrary' and 'all that is solid melts into air'; a world where as Nietzsche said, 'there is danger, the mother of morality – great danger . . . displaced on to the individual, on to the nearest and dearest, on to the street, on to one's own child, one's own heart, one's own innermost secret recesses of wish and will.' Modern machines have changed a great deal in the years between the nineteenth-century modernists and ourselves; but modern men and women, as Marx and Nietzsche and Baudelaire and Dostoevsky saw them then, may only now be coming fully into their own.

Marx, Nietzsche and their contemporaries experienced modernity as a whole at a moment when only a small part of the world was truly modern. A century later, when the processes of modernization have cast a net that no one, not even in the remotest corner of the world, can escape, we can learn a great deal from the first modernists, not so much about their age as about our own. We have lost our grip on the contradictions that they had to grasp with all their strength, at every moment in their everyday lives, in order to live at all. Paradoxically, these first modernists may turn out to understand us – the modernization and modernism that constitute our lives – better than we understand ourselves. If we can make their visions our own, and use their perspectives to look at our own environments with fresh eyes, we will see that there is more depth in our lives than we thought. We will feel our community with people all over the world who have been struggling with the same dilemmas as our own. And we will get back in touch with a remarkably rich and vibrant modernist culture that has grown out of these struggles: a culture that contains vast resources of strength and health, if only we come to know it as our own.

It may turn out, then, that going back can be a way to go forward: that remembering the modernisms of the nineteenth century can give us the vision and courage to create modernisms of the twenty-first. This act of remembering can help us bring modernism back to its roots, so that it can nourish and renew itself, to confront the adventures and dangers that lie ahead. To appropriate the modernities of yesterday can be at once a critique of the modernities of today and an act of faith in the modernities – and in the modern men and women – of tomorrow and the day after tomorrow.

CITY
·
BUILDING
·
STREET

—3—
Place-Form and Cultural Identity

•

KENNETH FRAMPTON

We do not ask to be immortal beings, we only ask that things do not lose all their meaning.

Antoine de Saint-Exupéry

The vicissitudes of ideology: an Anglo-American perspective

We live in a paradoxical moment when, while we are perhaps more obsessed with history than ever before, we have, simultaneously, the feeling that a certain historical trajectory, or even, for some, history itself, is coming to an end. (See Gianni Vattimo, *La fine della modernità*, 1985).[1] This experience is so uncanny that we hardly know how to respond to it, for, faced with this apparent deliquescence of the modern world, we take comfort in the fact that the field of techno-science seems to be immune from this bewildering condition. Outwardly, scientists today appear to be just as modern now as Cavendish or Einstein did in their own time or, say, as Harvey and Volta did in the middle of the eighteenth century, a period which happens to coincide with the beginning of history in the modern sense. At the same time, and not only from a penchant for creature comforts, today's techno-scientists do not usually house themselves in modern environments. Like the man in the street, they gravitate towards a vaguely reassuring past, towards that suburban environment, the iconography of which is derived from a hypothetical agrarian culture which has disappeared forever. The humanists, on the other hand – that is to say, those whose vocation is to analyse and postulate the fundamental superstructure of the society – are the ones who find themselves enmeshed in the almost inexpressible aporias of the postmodern condition.

I am a member of that generation of so-called modern architects, who first came of age as active practitioners in the early sixties and whose concept of modernity (like that of the immediately previous generation) was already historically mediated; that is to say, unlike the pioneers of the inter-war period (1918-39) we did not conceive of ourselves as trying to engender an architecture, whose form was totally unprecedented. Instead we already saw our task as a qualified restoration of the creative vigour of a movement which had become formally and programmatically compromised in the intervening years. It was, of course, quite impossible to recapture the energy and the optimistic belief systems of this previous epoch, but none the less we could still conceive of ourselves as returning to a modern line in architecture, irrespective of the different forms that this might assume.

It is hard to say exactly when this mediated but still modern *modus operandi* began to falter, but I suppose it must have coincided, at least in England, with the realization (and partial deformation) of the long-term programme of post-war reconstruction and with the mediocre results of the new towns policy which culminated in 1972 with the inauguration of Milton Keynes. We had been, in any event, the last generation of students to entertain the projection of utopian urban schemes *in both a programmatic and a formal sense.* Thereafter, the emerging Megalopolitan reality instantly transformed such projections into historical non sequiturs, with regard to which one could no longer suspend even a modicum of disbelief. It is significant in this regard that Leon Krier's theoretical urbanism of the late seventies should focus, not without a touch of caricature, on a form of *anti-utopia*: that is to say, on the end of history in a certain sense. I am alluding to his campaign for the wholesale 'reconstruction' of the European city, in which the city would be reified in a kind of inaccessible past; frozen, as it were, at an ideal bourgeois moment, at some moment during the first half of the last century.

Throughout the sixties, Leslie Martin and his associates attempted to ground the practice of architecture in a normative typology. This approach was largely based on the architecture of two distinguished late modernists, Alvar Aalto and Louis Kahn, whose work seemed particularly appropriate to the British intellectual climate and its empirical traditions. The relevance of Martin's approach was to conceive of building as a background for life and thereby to limit its expressive scope.[2] It unconsciously recognized Walter Benjamin's aphorism that architecture, on the average, is appreciated in a state of distraction. In retrospect, it seems as if this normative attitude was replaced at the very end of the sixties by the British Productivist, or so-called High-Tech, School. This shift is decisive at many levels, for it represents a political and symbolic move away from the institutional and residential fabric of the society, towards the productive imperatives of neo-capitalism. Pragmatically and ideologically, the High-Tech School responded to the new levels of productive and communicational efficiency then being demanded by the expansion of the tertiary economy.

Aside from the Martin school, there is little doubt that by the mid-sixties, we were increasingly bereft of a *realistic* theoretical basis on which to work. Without the radical cultural and political programmes of the revolutionary modern movement, we had no alternative theory to the reductive efforts, made from the late fifties onwards, to fill this void with ergonomic design methods; a positivistic approach which was not without its distant connections to both the Martin school and the later Productivist line of Richard Rogers and Norman

Foster. Such methods, however, were soon to display their marked incapacity to synthesize building programmes of any complexity. The scientism of this attitude is evident from the ideological title changes suffered by prominent schools of architecture during this period, with one institution in particular passing through a brief period when it was known as a 'school of environmental studies'. The euphemistic use of the term 'environment', with its 'life-science' connotations is symptomatic of the time.

The redistribution of wealth brought about by the relative success of the post-war, neo-capitalist Welfare State, together with the capitalization of the unions and growth of the consumer society, were all factors which contributed to the universal campus crisis of the late sixties, euphemistically known, after the dramatic events which took place in Paris in 1968, as *les évènements de mai*. And while it is true to say that few lasting political changes were introduced by this all too brief moment of student radicalism, it none the less left behind a critical legacy which eventually manifested itself in terms of both left-and right-wing ideologies; on the one hand, Marxist feminism and various radical factions deriving from radical psychoanalysis and the critical theory of the Frankfurt School, on the other, the ambiguities of French structuralism and *les nouveaux philosophes*.

This mixed legacy, together with the subsequent real move to the right in many Western countries and a new-found capacity to sustain, through welfare provisions, unprecedented levels of mass unemployment (while still maintaining some semblance of consumerism), are, together with the perennial nuclear threat, all determining factors of a context in which the postmodern phenomenon begins to emerge. As far as architecture is concerned, the postmodern, as a ideological category, if not as a style, announces itself in three somewhat interrelated events.

The first of these was the publication of Charles Jencks' *The Language of Post-Modern Architecture* in 1977, a work which argued for a free-floating pluralist populist architecture, primarily conceived in terms of accessible imagery. The second event was an exhibition entitled *Transformations*, staged in 1979 by Arthur Drexler at the Museum of Modern Art, New York. While this exhibition presented a more comprehensive survey than Jencks' book, ostensibly displaying the vicissitudes of modern architecture over the past twenty years, it adopted a very similar rhetoric; above all, it omitted any graphic information, presumably on the grounds that the general public are unable to read plans. Like Jencks' *magnum opus* it featured a large number of photographs (also at the rate of one shot per building) including large, back-lit, coloured transparencies of the typical curtain-wall, high-rise office structure of the period, invariably sealed in tinted, clear or mirrored glass and shot in the late evening sun. The third event was the architectural section of the Venice Biennale of 1980; an exhibition whose underlying supposedly liberative, populist bias was evident from the outset. This exhibition, mounted by Paolo Portoghesi and given the mildly demagogic, if ironic, title *The Presence of the*

Past: the End of Prohibition, was precisely the occasion which prompted Jürgen Habermas to formulate his Theodor Adorno Prize address, given in Frankfurt in the same year under the title 'Modernity – An Incomplete Project'.[3]

By the early eighties it became clear that certain prominent figures in the American architectural establishment had been gradually moving towards a reactionary position for some time; certainly since the publication in 1966 of Robert Venturi's *Complexity and Contradiction in Architecture*, which was first issued, one should note, by the Museum of Modern Art.[4] This ambiguously critical position paper gave rise to forms of populist architectural collage, theoretically realizing Venturi's vision of 'the dumb and the ordinary' as an inexpensive and broadly understandable mode of building. This neo-Brechtian approach to architecture (made in this instance ironically complete by the use of outsize American flags to which Venturi, after Jasper Johns, was apparently so addicted) came to be popularized in the profession under the slogan 'Main Street is almost all right'; a brand of cultural populism which shifted to the right with the publication of *Learning From Las Vegas* in 1972, with its characterization of the exploitative Las Vegas Strip as a paradigm of popularly gratified desire. Again, as in Jencks' *The Language of Post-Modern Architecture*, the instruments of semiotic and communicational analysis were scientifically adduced, as a means of bestowing an apparent legitimacy on what was little more than a manipulative form of admass advocacy.

Since the early eighties this conservative tendency in American architecture has become more dominant, with the vestigially modernist strategy of populist collage giving way to cannibalized forms of eclectic historicism, ranging from Robert Stern's *arriviste* neo-Edwardian suburban essays patterned after Lutyens, to Helmut Jahn's outsized neo-Art Deco parodies in curtain wall construction and to the more general use of thin stone revetment to simulate, as inexpensively as possible, the past glories of Beaux Arts masonry.

There is an understandable tendency for this historicism to be restricted to external finishes, since American builder-developers tend to favour an ad hoc 'balloon-frame' approach to steel frame and sheet rock construction, thereby tending to eliminate both structure and volume as intrinsic forms of architectural expression. Under these conditions, the architect's task is reduced to the provision of a marketable image, once an optimal rental return has been assured by the general arrangement of the plan. Needless to say, the increasingly rapid theoretical amortization of building stock is an important factor in promoting this relatively inexpensive form of development.[5]

In the face of these successive devaluations I have increasingly felt the need, as a critic and teacher, to develop some form of alternative theoretical position with which to continue, albeit interstitially, with the critical practice of architecture; one which while avoiding superannuated avantgardism, would somehow be able to build on the liberative and poetic legacy of the pre-war modern movement.

It appeared to me in 1980, that a more sensitive and relevant form of architecture could be found on the periphery of the so-called developed world rather than in the apparent centres of cultural and communicational power, such as New York, London and Paris. I perceived that these peripheral nodes were able to sustain a more multi-layered complexity of architectural culture. The reasons for this were manifold, ranging from conditions of local prosperity to an assumed or traditional cantonal identity. I sensed that these interstitial cultural manifestations arose when there was desire and willingness on the part of architects and their clients to develop a self-conscious and local contemporary expression; one which, while remaining committed to the modernization process, would none the less be able to qualify the received consumerist civilization through a consciously cultivated 'culture of place'. It had seemed to me in the early sixties that these peripheral, incidental works, irrespective of where they occurred – be it Zurich, Lugano, Udine, Athens, Venice, Porto, Helsinki, Stockholm, Copenhagen, Madrid, Barcelona, Amsterdam, New Delhi or Mexico City – always manifested themselves through sensuous, concrete and tactile elements of either a topographic or tectonic nature. And so by degrees I found myself gravitating towards the ideal of a self-consciously cultivated 'regionalism' as a way of being able to continue with an architecture of resistance without falling into sentimentality, or into the false perpetuation of exhausted modern forms, or into the empty vagaries of historicism, placed at the service of optimized development.

Place-form and cultural identity

I declared my allegiance to this hypothetical line in 1982, with an essay entitled 'Towards a Critical Regionalism', which first appeared in *Perspecta 20* and which was then presented in a more didactic form, under the same title, in Hal Foster's *The Anti-Aesthetic*.[6] The term 'critical regionalism' was not my invention; it was coined by Alex Tzonis and Liliane Lefaivre in their essay on the work of Dimitris and Susana Antonakakis in 1981. In this essay, 'The Grid and the Pathway', Tzonis and Lefaivre recalled the ambiguous role played by *Schinkelschuler* architecture during the nineteenth century in the building of Athens and the founding of the Greek state. As they put it:

> Historical regionalism here had grown not only out of the war of liberation, it had emerged out of the interests to develop an urban elite set apart from the peasant world and its rural 'backwardness' and to create a dominance of town over country, hence the special appeal of historicist regionalism, based on the book rather than experience, with its monumentality recalling another distant and forlorn elite. Historical regionalism had united the people, but it had also divided them. [7]

They went on to caution against the reactionary potential of populist or historicist regionalism, particularly as this was to manifest itself in Germany, in the architecture of the Third Reich. This disturbingly regressive tendency no doubt accounts for our mutual attempts to qualify the term *regional* with the adjective *critical*, although what this might mean in specific terms is admittedly more difficult to define. This led me to insist that by Critical Regionalism I did not mean any kind of style, nor did I have in mind some form of vernacular revival. Instead, I wished to employ the term to allude to a hypothetical and real condition in which a local culture of architecture is consciously evolved in express opposition to the domination of hegemonic power. In my view, this is a theory of building which, while accepting the potentially liberative role of modernization, resists being totally absorbed by forms of optimized production and consumption. In this regard, it has a latent affinity with political policies favouring some measure of autarchy.

Apart from indicating its presence in contemporary practice, the prime ground for my theoretical elaboration of Critical Regionalism derives from Paul Ricoeur and above all, from his essay of 1961 entitled 'Universal Civilization and National Cultures'. I am indebted to Ricoeur not only because this distinction between civilization and culture is fundamental to any clear understanding of our present situation, but also because it affords the oppositional structure from which the rest of my argument follows. In my view, the constituent elements of architecture are to be seen as being determined by the way in which such oppositions are mediated through form.

For Ricoeur, universal civilization means universal technology, and he sees this as being inseparable from the long-term liberative aims of modernization. As he points out, no developing country is able to forgo for long the benefits of universal civilization. On the other hand, he remains acutely aware of the fragility of local culture; of its tendency to crumble in the face of a totally alien technology and the implicitly antithetical, often positivistic values that this often brings in its wake. For Ricoeur, writing in the early sixties, this dilemma is particularly dramatic and difficult in the case of newly de-colonialized countries. As he put it:

> Thus we come to the crucial problem confronting nations just rising from underdevelopment. In order to get on the road toward modernization, is it necessary to jettison the old cultural past which had been the *raison d'être* of a nation? . . . Whence the paradox: on the one hand, it [the nation] had to root itself in the soil of its past, forge a national spirit and unfurl this spiritual and cultural revindication before the colonialist's personality. But in order to take part in modern civilization, it is necessary at the same time to take part in scientific, technical and political rationality, something which very often requires the pure and simple abandon of a whole cultural past. It is a fact that every culture cannot sustain and absorb the shock of modern civilization. There is the paradox: how to become modern and to return to sources; how to revive an old, dormant civilization and take part in universal civilization.[8]

While this is a particularly crucial dilemma in most parts of the so-called Third

World, it does not take much reflection to recognize that, under today's conditions, almost all nations are developing nations and that, to markedly different degrees, this problem manifests itself throughout the contemporary world; and never more so, I would submit, then in the field of architecture

Architecture, however, possesses the intrinsic advantage of being a particularly resistant *métier*. This is perhaps never more evident than in the fact that all attempts to industrialize building production over the past forty years have met with only limited degrees of success, partly because the field is incapable of providing a sufficiently high level of repetition together with the requisite market to justify the large investment demanded by machine-tool production, and partly because the embedding of the product in the ground tends to retard the cycle of production and consumption favoured by modern industrial economy.[9] On all sides of the political spectrum every effort has been made to overcome this inherent resistance, above all in the many attempts made to construct high-rise residential fabric out of pre-cast concrete elements, usually to the ultimate detriment of both the fabric and its occupants. A comparable drive is evident in the current downtown, 'shrink-wrapped', mixed-use development now being realized on a mammoth scale in the United States. In both instances there is a discernible tendency to reduce architecture to a recalcitrant form of commodity, the quality of which is always severely limited by the need to justify the investment in *economic* terms, as though both 'left' and 'right' no longer possessed any other criteria by which to assess value.

As far as I am concerned, this recalcitrance of the *métier* vis-à-vis modernization is a blessing in disguise, since it provides the fundamental basis from which to cultivate a 'critical' architecture. It affords, above all, a hybrid situation in which rationalized production (even partially industrialized production) may be combined with time-honoured craft practices, provided that the scale of the investment remains sufficiently modest to permit idiosyncratic forms of disjunction and that the local culture retains a capacity to evaluate the results in terms which are not exclusively economic.

This is why I have conceived of my theory of a Critical Regionalism as a field of resistance, and in the passages that follow I have attempted to elaborate this theory in terms of foci conceived as points of opposition. These points seem to parallel, to some degree, the confrontation between civilization and culture alluded to by Ricoeur. Before elaborating this further, however, two additional qualifications have to be made.

Firstly, I have come to realize that the suffix *ism* presupposes style. This ending is therefore etymologically antithetical to the cultural syndrome I would like to evoke. I do not want to deny style, but at the same time I do not wish to imply its necessary presence in advance. On these grounds I have opted for the present title 'place-form and cultural identity'. Secondly, it is necessary to add that the term *resistance* has a number of connotations; first, the resistance of the *métier* itself in all its intrinsic aspects; second, the resistance of built form to the erosive force of time (that aspect of *work* which Hannah

Arendt once characterized as transcending individual mortality)[10] and last, but by no means least, the proposition that this cultural strategy implies a certain resistance to the forces of domination, wherever they may be found.

Five points for architecture of resistance

Each of the opposing pairs is to be seen as a site of confrontation within the overall conception and realization of architectural form. They should not be construed as positive and negative terms, in the sense of good or bad, but rather as irreducible poles which cannot overcome the state of tension which arises from their conjunction. They are arranged in pairs, after Ricoeur's opposition between *civilization* and *culture*; however, it cannot be claimed that they parallel this formation in a totally consistent way.

1 *Space/Place*   This opposition has perhaps been most clearly formulated by Martin Heidegger in his seminal essay 'Building, Dwelling, Thinking' of 1954, in which he opposed the Latin *spatium in extensio*, or regularly subdivided, theoretically infinite space, to the Teutonic concept of *Raum* as a phenomenologically bounded clearing or domain. His insight as to the importance of the boundary in this regard can hardly be improved upon. He writes of the Greek word *peras*: 'A boundary is not that at which something stops, but as the Greeks recognized, the boundary is that from which something begins its presencing.'[11] As opposed to this, modern urban development has favoured the proliferation of a universal, privatized, placeless domain; exactly that form of development, in fact, which was first enthusiastically recognized by the French geographer Jean Gottmann, who gave it the name Megalopolis.[12] And it was this same phenomenon which led the planner Melvin Webber to coin such terms as 'community without propinquity' or 'non-place urban realm' as slogans with which to rationalize the total loss of the civic domain in 'motopian' society.[13] It is significant, in this regard, that Webber was to assist in the initial formulation of the plan for Milton Keynes, which goes some way towards explaining why a one-kilometre-square grid was imposed over a very old and complex agrarian topography.

2 *Typology/Topography*   Typology is a term which admits both civilization and culture. In the first instance, it is clear that the building types of the Enlightenment – that is, the types initially propagated by the Ecole Polytechnique and the Ecole des Beaux Arts – were relatively open. They were gridded, rational matrices, capable of admitting a wide range of institutional programmes and universally applicable to almost any regular site. As opposed to this, the received types of the antithetical Arts and Crafts movement (cf. Gothic Revival) were culturally grounded in the real and/or mythic history of a particular place, as was even the case with the Veneto farmhouse of the sixteenth century, upon which Palladio superimposed his rationalist paradigms. If we add to this the regional and typological evolution of the Christian

basilica, in all its stages, we can see how a typologically given and its subsequent modification has been a basic procedure in almost all building culture. As such, it has invariably oscillated between the universality of civilization on the one hand, and the rootedness of culture on the other. Moreover, it may be argued that the terms 'architecture' and 'building' – the one, the representation of power *par excellence*, the other the ever unfinished metabolic provision of human shelter – are divided along comparable typological lines; with classical or regular paradigms tending to presuppose, and indeed to represent, power and with organic forms implying a more liberative and adaptable attitude.

Topography, on the other hand, is unequivocally site specific. It is, so to speak, the concrete appearance of rootedness itself. Nature is not only admitted at this juncture but is indeed the precondition for *topos* itself.

This opposition between typology and topography is potentially manifest at every level, from the integration of a new intervention with a pre-existing environment, to the ecological, climatological and symbolic aspects of the resultant *place-form*. As the Portuguese architect Alvaro Siza has put it: 'Architects don't invent anything, they transform reality.' This symbiotic transformation of a given topographic context is suppressed only where optimizing productive criteria are superimposed, such as the ruthless flattening out of the contours in a typical American suburban subdivision or, alternatively, where the building is conceived from the outset as a freestanding technical or aesthetic object. All high-rise constructions, over about eight floors, tend to become disjunctive in this regard, although it is obviously still possible to relate such works to existing topographic features of a comparable height and scale or, alternatively, to clusters of other high-rise structures. Apart from stylistic elements, one of the most striking features of unadulterated vernacular forms is the way in which they invariably harmonize with the rise and fall of the cultivated landscape.

3 *Architectonic/Scenographic* The term architectonic, and more specifically the Greek work *tekton*, alludes etymologically to the work of the carpenter and therefore not only to the maker of the primitive Greek temple, but also to the primordial role of the frame and the joint in the genesis of any built construction. It is hardly necessary to add that the term 'architect' itself derives from the term *archi-tekton*, meaning chief constructor. The generic term *architectonic* refers not only to the technical means of supporting the building, but also to the myth of the reality of this structural achievement; that is, an architectonic work should display in an appropriate way the manner in which the artifice interacts with nature, not only in terms of resisting gravity, but also in terms of its durability with regard to the erosive agencies of climate and time. This applies to all architectonic forms, irrespective of whether the element is a frame and hence strictly *tectonic* or alternatively made of bonded masonry or rammed earth and hence *stereotomic*. In either case, one should be able to

identify the primary architectonic element itself or, alternatively, the facing by which it is represented or by which it represents itself.

Scenography, on the other hand, comes from the Latin word *scena* and from *frons scenae*, meaning scene, and is thus essentially representational in nature. And while the architectonic and the scenographic may often be complementary, they can also be antithetical. It may be argued that they have had (and have always had) quite different affinities; the one arising out of building in the aboriginal primitive or Gothic sense of the term, the other being essentially identified with architecture, or, more precisely, with the Renaissance as a universal rationalizing drive.

Be this as it may, one can easily see how the current tendency to reduce built form to images or to scenographic representations alone (either in terms of actual building production or as a mode of beholding – this last being subject to the impact of high-speed film, advertising rhetoric and modern photo-litho processes) only serves to strengthen the scenographic or imagistic *reception/perception* of built form, as opposed to its intrinsic architectonic potential. As Marco Frascari reminds us, the suppression of constructional processes and the masking of framework (the ambiguous legacy of the balloon-frame) and the covering of the joints etc., serve to deprive architecture of its expressiveness, so that the architectonic significance of the work becomes obfuscated and mute. As Frascari puts it, the act of *construing*, interpreting, presupposes, as the common etymological root would indicate, the act of *constructing* in the first place.[14]

4 *Artificial/Natural* More than any other art form, building and architecture have an interactive relationship with nature. Nature is not only the topography and the site itself but also climate and light, to which architecture is ultimately responsive to a far greater degree than any other art. Built form is necessarily susceptible to an intense interaction with those two elements, and hence with time, in its diurnal and seasonal aspects.

All of this seems so self-evident as hardly to require stating, and yet we tend to forget how universal civilization, that is, universal technology, in the form of modern mechanical services (air-conditioning, artificial light etc.), tends towards the elimination of exactly those features which would otherwise relate the outer membrane of a given fabric to a particular place and a specific culture. Something similar may be claimed for the provision of natural light in relation to diurnal and seasonal change, as the antithetical example of the totally closed, climatically controlled, art gallery makes all too clear. It is, of course, well known that ultra-violet light has a deleterious effect on certain forms of art, but between the filtration and reflection of *direct* natural light and its total exclusion, there surely remains a certain scope for modulation and control. The exclusion of natural light deprives art, in experimental terms, of any form of interaction with the place in which it is situated.

One needs to add to this the potentially negative ecological impact of optimized mechanical services. I am alluding not only to excessive energy consumption and the pollution which results, but also to the way in which hermetically sealed, air-conditioned structures are incapable of responding to subtle and favourable variations in the outside climate. Once again built-form is deprived of its *inherently* mediatory capacity, such as the provision of natural shade (*brise soleil*), the admission of natural ventilation (louvres, shutters) and even the neutralization of seasonal extremes through changes in spatial occupation (roof v. cellar, etc.). Who has not experienced the perversity of being unable to open a window, during temperate weather, in an air-conditioned, hermetically sealed environment? To this must be added the technological indifference of air-conditioned structures to the climatological benefits which accrue to certain forms of layout rather than others. I am thinking of the climatological flywheel effect which is induced by the provision of enclosed courts (cooler in the summer, warmer in the winter). Lest this be construed as an anti-air-conditioning polemic, let me simply remind the reader of the need for balancing the benefits of universal civilization with the rooted forms of climatically inflected culture. A parallel may well be drawn between fully air-conditioned structures and forms of optimized agricultural production, particularly when recalling the recent research which has revealed that, apart from destroying the soil, pesticides are often uneconomic. It has been established that their use often entails an expense that is not justified by the value of the increased yield.

5 *Visual/Tactile* These two alternative modes of experiencing the environment address the way in which the architectural object is open to levels of perception other than the visual stimulus afforded by the artefact. Architecture possesses a unique capacity for being experienced by the entire sensorium; that is to say, sense pathways other than the optic nerve are involved in the experience of architecture. In most circumstances, even when they have been indifferently considered, materials and surfaces can be as much part of an overall tactile perception of architecture as its visual form. Air movement, acoustics, ambient temperature and smell, all these factors affect our experience of space.[15]

Most people surely recall becoming suddenly aware of the rake of a stair and the rhythm that this involuntarily imposes on the body. Some tread to riser relationships will be found awkward and others gracious, thereby affecting the momentum and sense of poise experienced by the being. If we include in this percept the materials with which the stair is surfaced, then clearly the overall experience will be a combination of both the surface finish and the going. Such an experiential capacity may be rendered particularly expressive of a certain hierarchical sequence. A typical example of this is the narrative promenade, created by Alvar Aalto, in the approach to the famous first-floor council chamber of Saynatsalo City Hall in Finland (1952). From the pavement level, the sequence is as follows: first, a wide, shallow flight of steps in fair-faced brickwork, open to the air; second, a narrow, enclosed, brick-lined stairway; third and last, the polished, light-weight timber floor of the council chamber itself. Where both brick stairs serve to stabilize the body's momentum through friction and where the second volumetrically encloses the being as it rises, the slippery, suspended timber floor of the honorific chamber demands an immediate effort on the part of the subject to maintain its balance. Moreover, after being constrained, the subject suddenly finds itself in a high and free volume, where the floor gives and creaks under the weight and movement of the body. The timber and the wax polish afford an array of sounds and smells of a totally different order from that obtaining in the approach stair. Finally, the volume itself responds, from moment to moment, to variations in the level of the ambient light.

Numerous other examples could be given, from Luchino Visconti's insistence on solid wood-block flooring in an Altona mansion which formed the principle setting for the film *The Damned* (so that the actors would be able to assume appropriate postures) to the attention that Jørn Utzon drew in 1962 to the cultural differentiations stemming from different forms of 'undercroft'; from say, the suspended timber platform generic to the architecture of the orient, to the solid masonry plateaux that are commonly found in Mesoamerica.[16] Suffice it to say that, in each instance, the biological privilege accorded to sight is complemented by strong tactile experiences. In a cultural and a historical sense, what is of significance here is the 'qualification' of the emphasis placed upon *rationalized sight* in Renaissance architecture. It is surely significant that perspective meant quite literally 'clear-seeing'. After the fifteenth century, the triumphant legacy of this intellectual construct would exercise a strong influence over the development of the occidental subject.[17] At its most reductive, this perspectival mode tends to put all the stress on the act of *formal representation*. Understandably this is achieved at the expense of tactile experience. Here, once again, one looks for a certain complementarity between the two poles, thereby permitting a critique of the visual in terms of the tactile and vice versa. The implication here is that the being as a whole has a greater capacity to resist than the well-known symbiotic link connecting visual stimuli to information rather than experience. One may remark here in passing on the current triumph of television and the general demise of architecture.

Conclusion: critical culture and the post-modern condition

The protagonists of Postmodernity, that is to say, those who are convinced that the period of High Modernity has ended, seem to fall, at least initially, into two groups; the neo-Historicists and the neo-Situationists. The first of these, who happen to be the least intellectual and the more prominent in the eyes of the popular press, are those who feel that the entire ideology and stylistic apparatus of the modern avant garde has been discredited and that no choice remains but to abandon this ostensibly inhuman and radical discourse, together with its style, and to return to tradition in every conceivable sense; from figuration and expressionism in painting to tonality and classical form in music, from kitsch historicism in architecture, to outright neo-conservatism in culture-politics and even in politics itself. The neo-Situationists (and I have termed them thus in order to imply that there may be direct or indirect links here to the *Situationist* movement of the fifties) seem to welcome the continuing escalation of modernization as an inevitable and fundamentally radical process; one which, despite its predominantly utilitarian and positivistic character, embraces a constantly varying and unstable mosaic and hence the latent, liberative conjunctions of the future.

Of the two groups it may be claimed that the second is the more consistent, for where the former is culturally and politically retrogressive it remains committed to the benefits of universal civilization. It seeks to combine the optimization of techno-science with reactionary culture-politics, exploiting the latter to soften and mask the harsh realities induced by the former. Where the neo-Conservatives are schizophrenic and culturally *anti-modern*, the neo-Situationists are more strictly *post-modern* in that through repudiating the utopian legacy of the Enlightenment (which some of them see as inseparable from political terror) they proclaim the end of 'master narratives', in all fields, including that of science itself. Both groups seem, in fact, to envisage an end of Enlightenment history; the former by embracing historicism and thereby reducing the cultural present to a perpetual and meaningless regurgitation of a petrified past, the latter by renouncing history as the master narrative *par excellence*. Both groups, for different reasons, distance themselves from the redemptive end of bourgeois history prophesied by Marx, and yet in both the master-narrative of techno-science seems to return through the back door; in the first case, by virtue of unabashed reactionary politics, in the second, by assuming an apparently acritical attitude towards the seeming autonomy of techno-science.

This acriticality towards techno-science has been and is still being attacked by the contemporary heirs of the Frankfurt School, above all, of course, by Jürgen Habermas, whose essay 'Technology and Science as Ideology'[18] remains in my view a seminal work. Inasmuch as Habermas returns us to the necessity of some form of decentralized democratic control over the autonomous processes of techno-science (which tend where they merge into applied science to reproduce themselves, irrespective of the consequences for either the species or the cosmos), the later Frankfurt School remains, in my view, the only valid basis upon which to develop a form of (post) modern critical culture. There is herein a comparable departure from the cult of the master narrative, for a cultural politics of this order patently assumes a certain decentralization of power in the constitution of the modern state. This approximates to what Habermas intends by his concepts of consensus and undistorted communication and this *may* explain, by way of extension, why a peripheral or *interstitial* architecture may still be capable of generating a more appropriate, sensitive and responsive physical environment, than that generally found today in the centres of hegemonic power.

Despite the spontaneous devolution of power, such as we have recently witnessed in Spain, it would be naïve, to say the least, to underestimate the staying power of the Jacobin state, along with its understandable interest in furthering the 'autonomous' domain of techno-science, together with its 'value-free' application. In this sense, I would submit, we are finally justified in calling for a culture of resistance, or more specifically, in our case, for a critical practice of architecture, which, without falling into sentimental primitivism, would resist the universal commodification of the modern world and in doing so react against the further centralization of power and control. Here the confrontation between universal civilization and rooted culture takes on a decidedly political potential.

However, to acknowledge the interstitial existence of such a resistant architecture and to develop a general theory by which to further its aims are two different things. While we may achieve the former, through the exercise of descriptive procedure and critical analysis, the latter demands a more funda-mental reappraisal of the limits of the field, from both an ontological and a normative standpoint. It is nothing less than this last which I have attempted in elaborating this theory of 'place-form and cultural identity'. It is evident that, in its present form, this theoretical schema owes much to the phenomenological amd existential traditions in Western thought, and to combine this mode of beholding with a political stance drawn from the critical traditions of the Frankfurt School is contradictory, to say the least. However, there remains the outline of an ill-defined terrain in which these two fields of critical discourse may be said to intersect and even to complement one another. While there are intimations of this in their mutual commitment to the liberative traditions of the modern world, perhaps this complementarity may be best sensed in the correspondence which appears to obtain between Habermas's idea of moder-nity as the 'unfinished project' and Heidegger's insistence on 'being as becoming'.

In attempting to formulate a critical theory of postmodern architectural practice, it is difficult to escape the implications of the current debate between Jürgen Habermas and Jean-François Lyotard, particularly the different stances that they each assume towards the future of 'progress' and the continuity of modernity as an unfinished enterprise. Two issues of fundamental consequence seem to divide these thinkers. The first concerns the different way in which they each conceive of the 'postmodern' as being a continuation and/or metamorphosis of the 'modern'. For Habermas the issue finally turns on the question as to whether or not the liberative programme of the Enlightenment can still be seriously entertained as a realizable aim? For Lyotard it is this aim itself which has to be renounced; see his book *La Condition post-moderne*.[19] The second concerns the way in which each philosopher conceives of 'value' as being determined by democratic discourse. Here the main difference arises from Habermas's insistence on the derivation of social and pragmatic value from what he regards as the 'finality' of consensus, with Lyotard categorically rejecting this concept for its latent totalitarianism. Paradoxically, both men subscribe to the principle that the self-realization of the species and the just and intelligent resolution of conflict can only be achieved in relation to specific, local conditions. Where Habermas predicates this resolution on the existence and maintenance of undistorted communication – an idea which, in my view, implies the evolution and proliferation of semi-autarchic or cantonal democracies, Lyotard leaves the issue of power and manner of its mediation disturbingly vague. He seems to suggest that the plurality of techno-science and the multiplicity of circumscribed language-games will jointly serve to perpetuate a condition of liberative anarchy.

Given the violent (or potentially violent) trajectory of occidental applied science and the various dominant interests which are served by its optimization, it is difficult to be sanguine about the claims which Lyotard makes for the autonomous plurality of techno-science. On the other hand, it is equally difficult to comprehend the importance which Habermas attaches to the principle of *final* consensus. Both Lyotard and Habermas, however, seem to be equally concerned with the determination of an 'end'; with the former renouncing (denouncing?) all forms of unified history and the latter maintaining a certain commitment to the Enlightenment ideal. Both seem to reject as 'irrational' the ahistorical–ontological future as envisaged in the thought of Nietzsche and Heidegger – the eternal return and the end of progress. Hence both seem to dispute, to an equal degree, the seminal role of ontology in the future evolution of critical theory and practice, while at the same time they both seem to ignore the Eurocentric and occidental bias of their discourse. For me the controversy ought to be focused somewhere here, that is, in the way in which the species-being conceives of its relationship to nature, including its own nature. In this context one questions whether the future will perpetuate the occidental *end-games* of limitless wastage and pollution or whether new dimensions of ethical practice will arise out of a new-found respect for the symbiotic limits of both being and cosmos. While nature is by definition dynamic rather than static, such a cultural symbiosis would imply an end of modernism *in se*, inasmuch as critical ecology would become the basis for limiting the aporia of occidental reason. Seen in this light, critical theory would have to define itself in terms of an organic practice wherein the myth of progress would encounter its natural limit. In such a prospect, conflict (including cultural-political conflict) would have to find its resolution in maintaining a 'homoeostatic' balance. Inasmuch as such a metabolic concept is dynamic, no consensus as to its detailed maintenance could ever be 'final' and yet within such a theoretical context, Habermas's 'condition–situation' remains as the fundamental ground within which a critical practice of architecture will have to find its material.

REFERENCES

1   See Vattimo, Gianni, 'Identità, differenza, confusione', *Casabella*, 519, December 1985, pp.42,43
2   See *Buildings & Ideas 1933 – 1983. From the Studio of Leslie Martin*, Cambridge, 1983. Among the more prominent members of Martin's office in the sixties were Colin St John Wilson and Patrick Hodgkinson. Although a typological point of departure was common to both Martin's practice and the research carried out under his auspices in the department of Land Form and Built Use Studies at Cambridge University, one needs to distinguish between the two. Where the former was pragmatic in its general orientation, the latter was logarithmic and abstract.
3   Habermas, Jürgen, 'Modernity – An Incomplete Project'. See *The Anti-Aesthetic: Essays on Postmodern Culture*, ed. Hal Foster, Port Townsend, Washington, 1983, pp. 3-15
4   Venturi, Robert, *Complexity and Contradiction in Architecture*, New York, 1966
5   The current American administration has seen to fit to reduce the period over which a built-investment may be amortized for purposes of assessing taxation liability. This tends to reduce the investor's interest in assuring the durability of the structure in relation to the initial capital investment.
6   Frampton, Kenneth, 'Towards a Critical Regionalism: Six Points for an Architecture of Resistance', in *The Anti-Aesthetic*, op.cit.(3), pp. 16-30
7   Tzonis, Alex, and Lefaivre, Liliane, 'The Grid and the Pathway: An Introduction to the Work of Dimitris and Susana Antonakakis', *Architecture in Greece*, 15,1981, pp. 164-178
8   Paul Ricoeur, 'Universal Civilization and National Cultures' (1961), in *History and Truth*, trans. Chas. A. Kelbey, Evanston, 1965. pp. 276-7
9   Pike, Alexander, 'Failure of Industrialised Building/Housing Programme', *Architectural Design*, Nov. 1967, p.507
10 Arendt, Hannah, *The Human Condition*, Chicago, 1958
11 Heidegger, Martin, 'Building, Dwelling and Thinking' (1954), in *Poetry, Language and Thought*, New York, 1971, p.154
12 Gottmann, Jean, *Megalopolis*, New York, 1961
13 Webber, Melvin, 'Order in Diversity: Community Without Propinquity', in *Cities in Space*, ed. Lowdon Wingo, Baltimore, 1963
14 Frascari, Marco, 'The Tell-The-Tale Detail', in *VIA 7*, Architectural Journal of the Graduate School of Fine Arts, University of Pennsylvania, 1984, pp 23-37. Frascari writes: 'Elusive in a traditional dimensional definition, the architectural detail can be defined as the union of construction, the result of the *logos* of *technè*, with construing, the result of the *technè* of *logos*.'
15 Leitner, Bernard, and Conrads, Ulrich, 'Acoustic Space. Experiences and Conjectures', in *Daedalos 17, Der hörbare Raum*, Berlin Architectural Journal, pp 28-45. In an issue devoted to acoustical space, this conversation between Leitner and Conrads is particularly revealing.
16 Utzon, Jørn, 'Platforms and Plateaux: Ideas of a Danish Architect,' in *Zodiac* 10, Milan, 1962, pp. 112-114
17 Leitner, op.cit., p.30: 'That is why oriental carpets with their lively ornamentation are not just pleasing to our eyes but also have important acoustic functions for the room as well as for our bodies – which should be one and the same. Carpets are meant to be walked on with bare feet, and it is via the soles of our feet that their quiet and tranquillity enters our body.'
18 Habermas, Jürgen, 'Technology and Science as Ideology' (1968), in *Towards a Rational Society*, Boston, 1970.
19 Lyotard, Jean-François, *The Post-Modern Condition: A Report on Knowledge*, Minneapolis, 1984. This 'neo-Situationist' work (my categorization) opens with a direct critique of Habermas's position. See also Stephen Watson, 'Jürgen Habermas and Jean-François Lyotard: Post-Modernism and the Crisis of Rationality,' in *Philosophy & Social Criticism*, no.2, vol,10, An International Disciplinary Quarterly Journal, Boston College, Cambridge, Mass., 1984.

—4—

A city is not a tree

•

CHRISTOPHER ALEXANDER

I

The tree of my title is not a green tree with leaves. It is the name of an abstract structure. I shall contrast it with another, more complex abstract structure called a semilattice. In order to relate these abstract structures to the nature of the city, I must first make a simple distinction.

I want to call those cities which have arisen more or less spontaneously over many, many years *natural cities*. And I shall call those cities and parts of cities which have been deliberately created by designers and planners *artificial cities*. Siena, Liverpool, Kyoto, Manhattan are examples of natural cities. Levittown, Chandigarh and the British New Towns are examples of artificial cities.

It is more and more widely recognized today that there is some essential ingredient missing from artificial cities. When compared with ancient cities that have acquired the patina of life, our modern attempts to create cities artificially are, from a human point of view, entirely unsuccessful.

Both the tree and the semilattice are ways of thinking about how a large collection of many small systems goes to make up a large and complex system. More generally, they are both names for structures of sets.

In order to define such structures, let me first define the concept of a set. A set is a collection of elements which for some reason we think of as belonging together. Since, as designers, we are concerned with the physical living city and its physical backbone, we must naturally restrict ourselves to considering sets which are collections of material elements such as people, blades of grass, cars, molecules, houses, gardens, water pipes, the water molecules in them etc.

When the elements of a set belong together because they co-operate or work together somehow, we call the set of elements a system.

For example, in Berkeley at the corner of Hearst and Euclid, there is a drugstore, and outside the drugstore a traffic light. In the entrance to the drugstore there is a newsrack where the day's papers are displayed. When the light is red, people who are waiting to cross the street stand idly by the light; and since they have nothing to do, they look at the papers displayed on the newsrack which they can see from where they stand. Some of them just read the headlines, others actually buy a paper while they wait.

This effect makes the newsrack and the traffic light interactive; the newsrack, the newspapers on it, the money going from people's pockets to the dime slot, the people who stop at the light and read papers, the traffic light, the electric impulses which make the lights change, and the sidewalk which the people stand on form a system – they all work together.

From the designer's point of view, the physically unchanging part of this system is of special interest. The newsrack, the traffic light and the sidewalk between them, related as they are, form the fixed part of the system. It is the unchanging receptacle in which the changing parts of the system – people, newspapers, money and electrical impulses – can work together. I define this fixed part as a unit of the city. It derives its coherence as a unit both from the forces which hold its own elements together and from the dynamic coherence of the larger living system which includes it as a fixed invariant part.

Of the many, many fixed concrete subsets of the city which are the receptacles for its systems and can therefore be thought of as significant physical units, we usually single out a few for special consideration. In fact, I claim that whatever picture of the city someone has is defined precisely by the subsets he sees as units.

Now, a collection of subsets which goes to make up such a picture is not merely an amorphous collection. Automatically, merely because relationships are established among the subsets once the subsets are chosen, the collection has a definite structure.

To understand this structure, let us think abstractly for a moment, using numbers as symbols. Instead of talking about the real sets of millions of real particles which occur in the city, let us consider a simpler structure made of just half a dozen elements. Label these elements 1,2,3,4,5,6. Not including the full set [1,2,3,4,5,6], the empty set [–], and the one-element sets [1],[2],[3],[4],[5], [6], there are 56 different subsets we can pick from six elements.

Suppose we now pick out certain of these 56 sets (just as we pick out certain sets and call them units when we form our picture of the city). Let us say, for example, that we pick the following subsets: [123],[34],[45],[234],[345],[12345], [3456].

What are the possible relationships among these sets? Some sets will be entirely part of larger sets, as [34] is part of [345] and [3456]. Some of the sets will overlap, like [123] and [234]. Some of the sets will be disjoint – that is, contain no elements in common like [123] and [45].

We can see these relationships displayed in two ways. In diagram A each set chosen to be a unit has a line drawn round it. In diagram B the chosen sets are arranged in order of ascending magnitude, so that whenever one set contains another (as [345] contains [34]), there is a vertical path leading from one to the other. For the sake of clarity and visual economy, it is usual to draw lines only between sets which have no further sets and lines between them; thus the line between [34] and [345] and the line between [345] and [3456] make it unnecessary to draw a line between [34] and [3456].

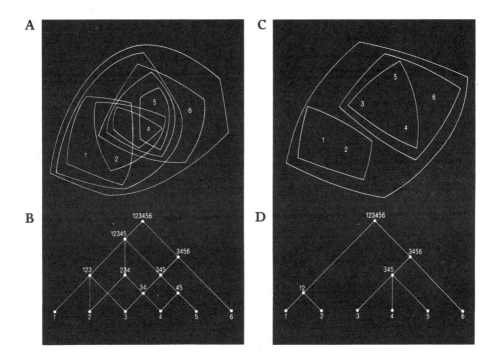

As we see from these two representations, the choice of subsets alone endows the collection of subsets as a whole with an overall structure. This is the structure which we are concerned with here. When the structure meets certain conditions it is called a semilattice. When it meets other more restrictive conditions, it is called a tree.

The semilattice axiom goes like this: *A collection of sets forms a semilattice if and only if, when two overlapping sets belong to the collection, the set of elements common to both also belongs to the collection.*

The structure illustrated in diagrams A and B is a semilattice. It satisfies the axiom since, for instance, [234] and [345] both belong to the collection and their common part, [34], also belongs to it. (As far as the city is concerned, this axiom states merely that wherever two units overlap, the area of overlap is itself a recognizable entity and hence a unit also. In the case of the drugstore example, one unit consists of newsrack, sidewalk and traffic light. Another unit consists of the drugstore itself, with its entry and the newsrack. The two units overlap in the newsrack. Clearly this area of overlap is itself a recognizable unit and so satisfies the axiom above which defines the characteristics of a semilattice.)

The tree axiom states: *A collection of sets forms a tree if and only if, for any two sets that belong to the collection either one is wholly contained in the other, or else they are wholly disjoint.*

The structure illustrated in diagrams C and D is a tree. Since this axiom excludes the possibility of overlapping sets, there is no way in which the semilattice axiom can be violated, so that every tree is a trivially simple semilattice.

However, in this chapter we are not so much concerned with the fact that a tree happens to be a semilattice, but with the difference between trees and those more general semilattices which are *not* trees because they *do* contain overlapping units. We are concerned with the difference between structures in which no overlap occurs, and those structures in which overlap does occur.

It is not merely the overlap which makes the distinction between the two important. Still more important is the fact that the semilattice is potentially a much more complex and subtle structure than a tree. We may see just how much more complex a semilattice can be than a tree in the following fact: a tree based on 20 elements can contain at most 19 further subsets of the 20, while a semilattice based on the same 20 elements can contain more than 1,000,000 different subsets.

This enormously greater variety is an index of the great structural complexity a semilattice can have when compared with the structural simplicity of a tree. It is this lack of structural complexity, characteristic of trees, which is crippling our conceptions of the city.

To demonstrate, let us look at some modern conceptions of the city, each of which I shall show to be essentially a tree.

Figure 1. Columbia, Maryland, Community Research and Development, Inc.: Neighbourhoods, in clusters of five, form 'villages'. Transportation joins the villages into a new town. The organization is a tree.

Figure 2. Greenbelt, Maryland, Clarence Stein: This 'garden city' has been broken down into superblocks. Each superblock contains schools, parks and a number of subsidiary groups of houses built around parking lots. The organization is a tree.

Figure 3. Greater London plan (1943), Abercrombie and Forshaw: The drawing depicts the structure conceived by Abercrombie for London. It is made of a large number of communities, each sharply separated from all adjacent communities. Abercrombie writes, 'The proposal is to emphasize the identity of the existing communities, to increase their degree of segregation, and where necessary to recognize them as separate and definite entities.' And again, 'The communities themselves consist of a series of sub-units, generally with their own shops and schools, corresponding to the neighbourhood units.' The city is conceived as a tree with two principal levels. The communities are the larger units of the structure; the smaller sub-units are neighbourhoods. There are no overlapping units. The structure is a tree.

Figure 4. Mesa City, Paolo Soleri: The organic shapes of Mesa City lead us, at a careless glance, to believe that it is a richer structure than our more obviously rigid examples. But when we look at it in detail we find precisely the same principle of organization. Take, particularly, the university centre. Here we find the centre of the city divided into a university and a residential quarter, which is itself divided into a number of villages (actually apartment towers) for

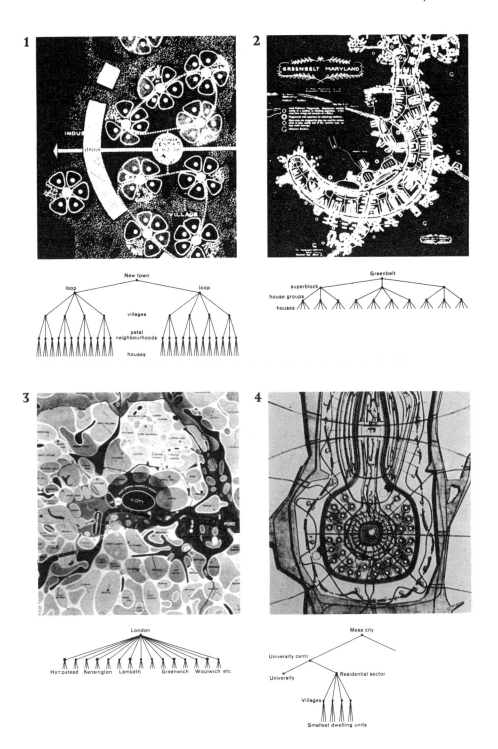

Christopher Alexander

5

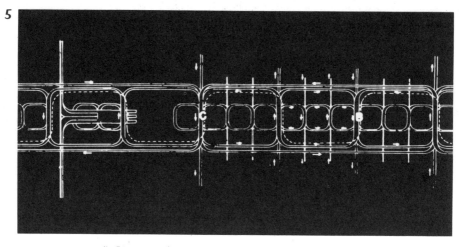

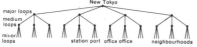

4000 inhabitants, each again subdivided further and surrounded by groups of still smaller dwelling units.

Figure 5. Tokyo plan, Kenzo Tange: This is a beautiful example. The plan consists of a series of loops stretched across Tokyo Bay. There are four major loops, each of which contains three medium loops. In the second major loop, one medium loop is the railway station and another is the port. Otherwise, each medium loop contains three minor loops which are residential neighbourhoods, except in the third major loop where one contains government offices and another industrial offices.

Figure 6. Chandigarh (1951), Le Corbusier: The whole city is served by a commercial centre in the middle, linked to the administrative centre at the head. Two subsidiary elongated commercial cores are strung out along the major arterial roads, running north-south. Subsidiary to these are further administrative, community and commercial centres, one for each of the city's 20 sectors.

Figure 7. Brasilia, Lucio Costa: The entire form pivots about the central axis, and each of the two halves is served by a single main artery. This main artery is in turn fed by subsidiary arteries parallel to it. Finally, these are fed by the roads which surround the superblocks themselves. The structure is a tree.

Figure 8. Communitas, Percival and Paul Goodman: Communitas is explicitly organized as a tree: it is first divided into four concentric major zones, the innermost being a commercial centre, the next a university, the third residential and medical, and the fourth open country. Each of these is further subdivided: the commercial centre is represented as a great cylindrical skyscraper, containing five layers: airport, administration, light manufacture, shopping and

—72—

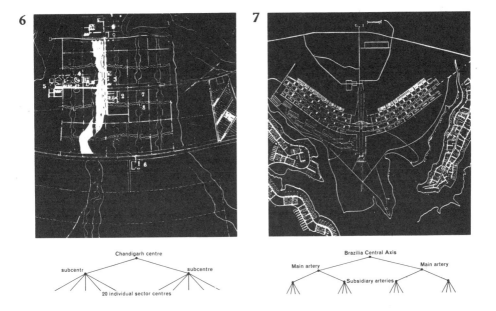

6 Chandigarh centre
subcentr   subcentre
20 individual sector centres

7 Brazilia Central Axis
Main artery   Main artery
Subsidiary arteries

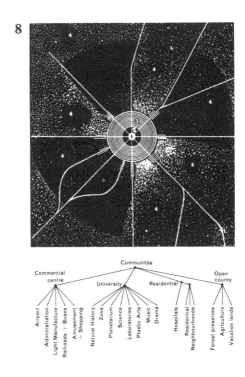

8 Communitas

Commercial centre   University   Residential   Open county

Airport
Administration
Light Manufacture
Railroads + Buses
Amusement + Shopping
Natural History
Zoos
Planetarium
Science
Laboratories
Plastic Arts
Music
Drama
Hospitals
Residential Neighbourhoods
Forest preserves
Agriculture
Vacation lands

9

amusement; and, at the bottom, railroads, buses and mechanical services. The university is divided into eight sectors comprising natural history, zoos and aquariums, planetarium, science laboratories, plastic arts, music and drama. The third concentric ring is divided into neighbourhoods of 4000 people each, not consisting of individual houses, but of apartment blocks, each of these containing individual dwelling units. Finally, the open country is divided into three segments: forest preserves, agriculture and vacationlands. The overall organization is a tree.

Figure 9. The most beautiful example of all I have kept until last, because it symbolizes the problem perfectly. It appears in Hilberseimer's book *The Nature of Cities*. He describes the fact that certain Roman towns had their origin as military camps, and then shows a picture of a modern military encampment as a kind of archetypal form for the city. It is not possible to have a structure which is à clearer tree.

The symbol is apt, for, of course, the organization of the army was designed precisely in order to create discipline and rigidity. The photograph on the right is Hilberseimer's own scheme for the commercial area of a city based on the army camp archetype.

Each of these structures, then, is a tree. Each unit in each tree that I have described, moreover, is the fixed, unchanging residue of some system in the living city (just as a house is the residue of the interactions between the members of a family, their emotions and their belongings; and a freeway is the residue of movement and commercial exchange).

However, in every city there are thousands, even millions, of times as many more systems at work whose physical residue does not appear as a unit in these tree structures. In the worst cases, the units which do appear fail to correspond to any living reality; and the real systems, whose existence actually makes the city live, have been provided with no physical receptacle.

Neither the Columbia plan nor the Stein plan for example, corresponds to social realities. The physical layout of the plans, and the way they function suggests a hierarchy of stronger and stronger closed social groups, ranging from the whole city down to the family, each formed by associational ties of different strength.

In a traditional society, if we ask a man to name his best friends and then ask each of these in turn to name their best friends, they will all name each other so that they form a closed group. A village is made up of a number of separate closed groups of this kind.

But today's social structure is utterly different. If we ask a man to name his friends and then ask them in turn to name their friends, they will all name different people, very likely unknown to the first person; these people would again name others, and so on outwards. There are virtually no closed groups of people in modern society. The reality of today's social structure is thick with overlap – the systems of friends and acquaintances form a semilattice, not a tree (Figure 10).

In the natural city, even the house on a long street (not in some little cluster) is a more accurate acknowledgement of the fact that your friends live not next door, but far away, and can only be reached by bus or car. In this respect Manhattan has more overlap in it than Greenbelt. And though one can argue that in Greenbelt, too, friends are only minutes away by car, one must then ask: since certain groups *have* been emphasized by the physical units of the physical structure, why are just these the most irrelevant ones?

II

The units of which an artificial city is made up are always organized to form a tree. So that we get a really clear understanding of what this means, and shall better see its implications, let us define a tree once again. Whenever we have a tree structure, it means that within this structure no piece of any unit is ever connected to other units, except through the medium of that unit as a whole.

The enormity of this restriction is difficult to grasp. It is a little as though the members of a family were not free to make friends outside the family, except when the family as a whole made a friendship.

In simplicity of structure the tree is comparable to the compulsive desire for neatness and order that insists the candlesticks on a mantelpiece be perfectly straight and perfectly symmetrical about the centre. The semilattice, by comparison, is the structure of a complex fabric; it is the structure of living things, of great paintings and symphonies.

It must be emphasized, lest the orderly mind shrink in horror from anything that is not clearly articulated and categorized in tree form, that the idea of

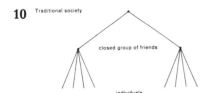

10 Traditional society

closed group of friends

individuals

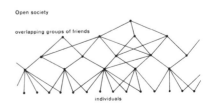

Open society

overlapping groups of friends

individuals

11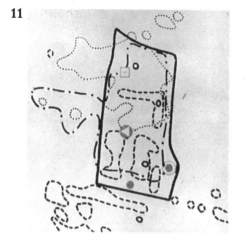

12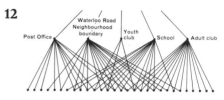

13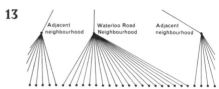

overlap, ambiguity, multiplicity of aspect and the semilattice are not less orderly than the rigid tree, but more so. They represent a thicker, tougher, more subtle and more complex view of structure.

Let us now look at the ways in which the natural, when unconstrained by artificial conceptions, shows itself to be a semilattice.

A major aspect of the city's social structure which a tree can never mirror properly is illustrated by Ruth Glass's redevelopment plan for Middlesbrough, England, a city of 200,000 which she recommends be broken down into 29 separate neighbourhoods. After picking her 29 neighbourhoods by determining where the sharpest discontinuities of building type, income and job type occur, she asks herself the question: 'If we examine some of the social systems which actually exist for the people in such a neighbourhood, do the physical units defined by these various social systems all define the same spatial neighbourhood?' Her own answer to this question is *no*.

Each of the social systems she examines is a nodal system. It is made of some sort of central node, plus the people who use this centre. Specifically she takes elementary schools, secondary schools, youth clubs, adult clubs, post offices, greengrocers and grocers selling sugar. Each of these centres draws its users from a certain spatial area or spatial unit. This spatial unit is the physical residue of the social system as a whole, and is therefore a unit in the terms of this discussion. The units corresponding to different kinds of centres for the single neighbourhood of Waterloo Road are shown in Figure 11.

The hard outline is the boundary of the so-called neighbourhood itself. The white circle stands for the youth club, and the small solid rings stand for areas where its members live. The ringed spot is the adult club, and the homes of its members form the unit marked by dashed boundaries. The white square is the post office, and the dotted line marks the unit which contains its users. The secondary school is marked by the spot with a white triangle in it. Together with its pupils, it forms the system marked by the dot-dashed line.

As you can see at once, the different units do not coincide. Yet neither are they disjoint. They overlap.

We cannot get an adequate picture of what Middlesbrough is, or of what it ought to be, in terms of 29 large and conveniently integral chunks called neighbourhoods. When we describe the city in terms of neighbourhoods, we implicitly assume that the smaller elements within any one of these neighbourhoods belong together so tightly that they only interact with elements in other neighbourhoods through the medium of the neighbourhoods to which they themselves belong. Ruth Glass herself shows clearly that this is not the case.

Next to Figure 11 are two representations of the Waterloo neighbourhood. For the sake of argument I have broken it into a number of small areas. Figure 12 shows how these pieces stick together in fact, and Figure 13 shows how the redevelopment plan pretends they stick together.

There is nothing in the nature of the various centres which says that their catchment areas should be the same. Their natures are different. Therefore the units they define are different. The natural city of Middlesbrough was faithful to the semilattice structure of the units. Only in the artificial-tree conception of the city are their natural, proper and necessary overlaps destroyed.

Consider the *separation of pedestrians from moving vehicles*, a tree concept proposed by Le Corbusier, Louis Kahn and many others. At a very crude level of thought this is obviously a good idea. Yet the urban taxi can function only because pedestrians and vehicles are not strictly separated. The cruising taxi needs a fast stream of traffic so that it can cover a large area to be sure of finding a passenger. The pedestrian needs to be able to hail the taxi from any point in the pedestrian world, and to be able to get out to any part of the pedestrian world to which he wants to go. The system which contains the taxicabs needs to overlap both the fast vehicular traffic system and the system of pedestrian circulation. In Manhattan pedestrians and vehicles do share certain parts of the city, and the necessary overlap is guaranteed (Figure 14).

Another favourite concept of the CIAM theorists and others is *the separation of recreation from everything else*. This has crystallized in our real cities in the form of playgrounds. The playground, asphalted and fenced in, is nothing but a pictorial acknowledgment of the fact that 'play' exists as an isolated concept in our minds. It has nothing to do with the life of play itself. Few self-respecting children will even play in a playground.

14

Play itself, the play that children practise, goes on somewhere different every day. One day it may be indoors, another day in a friendly gas station, another day down by the river, another day in a derelict building, another day on a construction site which has been abandoned for the weekend. Each of these play activities, and the objects it requires, forms a system. It is not true that these systems exist in isolation, cut off from the other systems of the city. The different systems overlap one another, and they overlap many other systems besides. The units, the physical places recognized as play places, must do the same.

In a natural city this is what happens. Play takes place in a thousand places – it fills the interstices of adult life. As they play, children become full of their surroundings. How can children become filled with their surroundings in a fenced enclosure? They cannot.

A similar kind of mistake occurs in trees like that of Goodman's Communitas or Soleri's Mesa City, which separate the university from the rest of the city. Again, this has actually been realized in the common American form of the isolated campus.

What is the reason for drawing a line in the city so that everything within the boundary is university, and everything outside is nonuniversity? It is conceptually clear. But does it correspond to the realities of university life? Certainly it is not the structure which occurs in nonartificial university cities.

There are always many systems of activity where university life and city life overlap: pub-crawling, coffee-drinking, the movies, walking from place to place. In some cases whole departments may be actively involved in the life of the city's inhabitants (the hospital-cum-medical school is an example). In Cambridge, a natural city where university and city have grown together gradually, the physical units overlap because they are the physical residues of city systems and university systems which overlap (Figure 15).

Let us look next at the hierarchy of urban cores realized in Brasilia, Chandigarh, the MARS plan for London and, most recently, in the Manhattan Lincoln Center, where various performing arts serving the population of greater New York have been gathered together to form just one core.

Does a concert hall ask to be next to an opera house? Can the two feed on one another? Will anybody ever visit them both, gluttonously, in a single evening, or even buy tickets from one after going to a performance in the

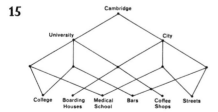

other? In Vienna, London, Paris, each of the performing arts has found its own place, because all are not mixed randomly. Each has created its own familiar section of the city. In Manhattan itself, Carnegie Hall and the Metropolitan Opera House were not built side by side. Each found its own place, and now creates its own atmosphere. The influence of each overlaps the parts of the city which have been made unique to it.

The only reason that these functions have all been brought together in Lincoln Center is that the concept of performing art links them to one another.

But this tree, and the idea of a single hierarchy of urban cores which is its parent, do not illuminate the relations between art and city life. They are merely born of the mania every simple-minded person has for putting things with the same name into the same basket.

The total separation of work from housing, started by Tony Garnier in his industrial city, then incorporated in the 1929 Athens Charter, is now found in every artificial city and accepted everywhere where zoning is enforced. Is this a sound principle? It is easy to see how bad conditions at the beginning of the century prompted planners to try to get the dirty factories out of residential areas. But the separation misses a variety of systems which require, for their sustenance, little parts of both.

Finally, let us examine the subdivision of the city into isolated communities. As we have seen in the Abercrombie plan for London, this is itself a tree structure. The individual community in a greater city has no reality as a functioning unit. In London, as in any great city, almost no one manages to find work which suits him near his home. People in one community work in a factory which is very likely to be in another community.

There are therefore many hundreds of thousands of worker–workplace systems, each consisting of individuals plus the factory they work in, which cut across the boundaries defined by Abercrombie's tree. The existence of these units, and their overlapping nature, indicates that the living systems of London form a semilattice. Only in the planner's mind has it become a tree.

The fact that we have so far failed to give this any physical expression has a vital consequence. As things are, whenever the worker and his workplace belong to separately administered municipalities, the community which contains the workplace collects huge taxes and has relatively little on which to spend the tax revenue. The community where the worker lives, if it is mainly residential, collects only little in the way of taxes and yet has great additional burdens on its purse in the form of schools, hospitals, etc. Clearly, to resolve this inequity, the worker–workplace systems must be anchored in physically recognizable units of the city which can then be taxed.

It might be argued that, even though the individual communities of a great city have no functional significance in the lives of their inhabitants, they are still the most convenient administrative units, and should therefore be left in their present tree organization. However, in the political complexity of a modern city, even this is suspect.

Edward Banfield, in his book *Political Influence*, gives a detailed account of the patterns of influence and control that have actually led to decisions in Chicago. He shows that, although the lines of administrative and executive control have a formal structure which is a tree, these formal chains of influence and authority are entirely overshadowed by the ad hoc lines of control which arise naturally as each new city problem presents itself. These ad hoc lines depend on who is interested in the matter, who has what at stake, who has what favours to trade with whom.

This second structure, which is informal, working within the framework of the first, is what really controls public action. It varies from week to week, even from hour to hour, as one problem replaces another. Nobody's sphere of influence is entirely under the control of any one superior; each person is under different influences as the problems change. Although the organization chart in the Mayor's office is a tree, the actual control and exercise of authority is semilattice-like.

Now, why is it that so many designers have conceived cities as trees when the natural structure is in every case a semilattice? Have they done so deliberately, in the belief that a tree structure will serve the people of the city better? Or have they done it because they cannot help it, because they are trapped by a mental habit, perhaps even trapped by the way the mind works – because they cannot encompass the complexity of a semilattice in any convenient mental form, because the mind has an overwhelming predisposition to see trees wherever it looks and cannot escape the tree conception?

I shall try to convince you that it is for this second reason that trees are being proposed and built as cities – that is, because designers, limited as they must be by the capacity of the mind to form intuitively accessible structures, cannot achieve the complexity of the semilattice in a single mental act.

Let me begin with an example. Suppose I ask you to remember the following four objects: an orange, a watermelon, a football and a tennis ball. How will you keep them in your mind, in your mind's eye? However you do it, you will do it by grouping them. Some of you will take the two fruits together, the orange and the watermelon, and the two sports balls together, the football and the tennis ball. Those of you who tend to think in terms of physical shape may group them differently, taking the two small spheres together – the orange and the tennis ball and the two large and more egg-shaped objects – the watermelon and the football. Some of you will be aware of both.

Let us make a diagram of these groupings (Figure 16). Either grouping taken by itself is a tree structure. The two together are a semilattice. Now let us try and visualize these groupings in the mind's eye. I think you will find that you cannot visualize all four sets simultaneously – because they overlap. You can visualize one pair of sets and then the other, and you can alternate between the two pairs extremely fast, so that you may deceive yourself into thinking you can visualize them all together. But in truth, you cannot conceive all four sets at once in a single mental act. You cannot bring the semilattice structure into a

16

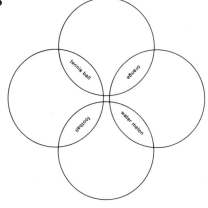

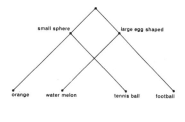

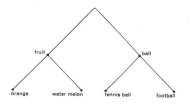

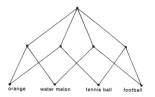

visualizable form for a single mental act. In a single mental act you can only visualize a tree.

This is the problem we face as designers. While we are not, perhaps, necessarily occupied with the problem of total visualization in a single mental act, the principle is still the same. The tree is accessible mentally and easy to deal with. The semilattice is hard to keep before the mind's eye and therefore hard to deal with.

It is known today that grouping and categorization are among the most primitive psychological processes. Modern psychology treats thought as a process of fitting new situations into existing slots and pigeonholes in the mind. Just as you cannot put a physical thing into more than one physical pigeonhole at once, so, by analogy, the processes of thought prevent you from putting a mental construct into more than one mental category at once. Study of the origin of these processes suggests that they stem essentially from the organism's need to reduce the complexity of its environment by establishing barriers between the different events that it encounters.

It is for this reason – because the mind's first function is to reduce the ambiguity and overlap in a confusing situation and because, to this end, it is endowed with a basic intolerance for ambiguity – that structures like the city, which do require overlapping sets within them, are nevertheless persistently conceived as trees.

17

 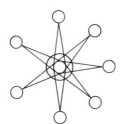 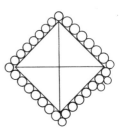

The same rigidity dogs even perception of physical patterns. In experiments by Huggins and myself at Harvard, we showed people patterns whose internal units overlapped, and found that they almost always invent a way of seeing the patterns as a tree – even when the semilattice view of the patterns would have helped them perform the task of experimentation which was before them.

The most startling proof that people tend to conceive even physical patterns as trees is found in some experiments of Sir Frederick Bartlett. He showed people a pattern for about a quarter of a second and then asked them to draw what they had seen. Many people, unable to grasp the full complexity of the pattern they had seen, simplified the patterns by cutting out the overlap. In Figure 17, the original is shown on the left, with two fairly typical redrawn versions to the right of it. In the redrawn versions the circles are separated from the rest; the overlap between triangles and circles disappears.

These experiments suggest strongly that people have an underlying tendency, when faced by a complex organization, to reorganize it mentally in terms of non-overlapping units. The complexity of the semilattice is replaced by the simpler and more easily grasped tree form.

You are no doubt wondering by now what a city looks like which is a semilattice, but not a tree. I must confess that I cannot yet show you plans or sketches. It is not enough merely to make a demonstration of overlap – the overlap must be the right overlap. This is doubly important because it is so tempting to make plans in which overlap occurs for its own sake. This is essentially what the high-density 'life-filled' city plans of recent years do. But overlap alone does not give structure. It can also give chaos. A garbage can is full of overlap. To have structure, you must have the right overlap, and this is for us almost certainly different from the old overlap which we observe in historic cities. As the relationships between functions change, so the systems which need to overlap in order to receive these relationships must also change. The recreation of old kinds of overlap will be inappropriate, and chaotic instead of structured.

One can perhaps make the physical consequences of overlap more comprehensible by means of an image. The painting illustrated is a work by Simon Nicholson (Figure 18). The fascination of this painting lies in the fact that, although constructed of rather few simple triangular elements, these elements unite in many different ways to form the large units of the painting – in such a way indeed that, if we make a complete inventory of the perceived units in the painting, we find that each triangle enters into four or five completely different kinds of unit, none contained in the others, yet all overlapping in that triangle.

Thus, if we number the triangles and pick out the sets of triangles which appear as strong visual units, we get the semilattice shown in Figure 19.

Three and 5 form a unit because they work together as a rectangle; 2 and 4 because they form a parallelogram; 5 and 6 because they are both dark and pointing the same way; 6 and 7 because one is the ghost of the other shifted sideways; 4 and 7 because they are symmetrical with one another; 4 and 6 because they form another rectangle; 4 and 5 because they form a sort of Z; 2 and 3 because they form a rather thinner kind of Z; 1 and 7 because they are at opposite corners; 1 and 2 because they are a rectangle; 3 and 4 because they point the same way as 5 and 6, and form a sort of off-centre reflection; 3 and 6 because they enclose 4 and 5; 1 and 5 because they enclose 2, 3 and 4. I have only listed the units of two triangles. The larger units are even more complex. The white is more complex still and is not even included in the diagram because it is harder to be sure of its elementary pieces.

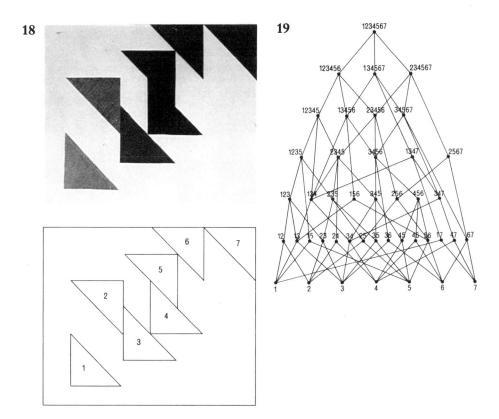

18

19

The painting is significant, not so much because it has overlap in it (many paintings have overlap in them), but rather because this painting has nothing else in it except overlap. It is only the fact of the overlap, and the resulting multiplicity of aspects which the forms present, that makes the painting fascinating. It seems almost as though the painter had made an explicit attempt, as I have done, to single out overlap as a vital generator of structure.

All the artificial cities I have described have the structure of a tree rather than the semilattice structure of the Nicholson painting. Yet it is the painting, and other images like it, which must be our vehicles for thought. And when we wish to be precise, the semilattice, being part of a large branch of modern mathematics, is a powerful way of exploring the structure of these images. It is the semilattice we must look for, not the tree.

When we think in terms of trees we are trading the humanity and richness of the living city for a conceptual simplicity which benefits only designers, planners, administrators and developers. Every time a piece of a city is torn out, and a tree made to replace the semilattice that was there before, the city takes a further step toward dissociation.

In any organized object, extreme compartmentalization and the dissociation of internal elements are the first signs of coming destruction. In a society, dissociation is anarchy. In a person, dissociation is the mark of schizophrenia and impending suicide. An ominous example of city-wide dissociation is the separation of retired people from the rest of urban life, caused by the growth of desert cities for the old like Sun City, Arizona. This separation is only possible under the influence of treelike thought.

It not only takes from the young the company of those who have lived long, but worse, it causes the same rift inside each individual life. As you pass into Sun City, and into old age, your ties with your own past will be unacknowledged, lost and therefore broken. Your youth will no longer be alive in your old age – the two will be dissociated; your own life will be cut in two.

For the human mind, the tree is the easiest vehicle for complex thoughts. But the city is not, cannot and must not be a tree. The city is a receptacle for life. If the receptacle severs the overlap of the strands of life within it, because it is a tree, it will be like a bowl full of razor blades on edge, ready to cut up whatever is entrusted to it. In such a receptacle life will be cut to pieces. If we make cities which are trees, they will cut our life within to pieces.

—5—

Architecture and Cognac
•
RICHARD BOLTON

The architect has been working late. The day has been demanding, like other days: there have been budgets to review, plans to revise, important cross-continental phone calls to make. With deliberation, the architect smooths over technical problems, mechanical errors, bureaucratic snafus. Meticulously, almost relentlessly, the architect constructs; with rule and square, urban life is brought under control. Throughout it all, the architect remains cool and self-assured. His work has brought him success, and all of its accoutrements are his: the advertisement showcases his polished appearance, his easy access to communications (the telephone outrageously springing from his loins), his well-equipped office in a prime location. Who can blame him if he rewards himself at the end of the day with a toast to his own efforts, with an ice-cold cognac, shared with an attractive co-worker?

Beyond the architect's window, night has fallen, and the city appears to reverse itself. The sheer and inhospitable glass walls of daylight hours disappear and are replaced by the yellow lights of office interiors. The city nears the condition of pure architecture: just as the exteriors disappear, so do the inhabitants; the city is reduced to a luminous and seemingly infinite grid. To find the content of the social, we are forced to look through this filter of architecture; we discover a social reality that is ambiguous, empty, like the architectural spaces themselves – a social reality with the confusing topology of a Klein bottle, with no consistent interior or exterior. 'The social'. A vague expression for a vague reality. What might the social be? At best, we can arrive at only a general formula: the social = the sum of each illuminated window.

What motivates the present-day architect? The successful and comfortable architect in our advertisement approaches architecture very differently from his modernist predecessors. We need only recall the hard-headed modern architect of the film *The Fountainhead*: an architect towering over his building, scrutinizing creation. His withering gaze said it all – the desire to merge utopian vision and material object was never greater; never was an architect more disappointed in a building's inability to fulfil this desire. The architect's rage and idealism demanded the destruction of the building. Social reality, guilty by association, fell victim to the same fate: the social could exist only as the architect wanted it to be, and only *if* the architect wanted it to be.

For our architect in the advertisement, rage and egoism are things of the past, replaced by a search for status and pleasure. The failure of modernism has given rise to malaise, confusion and reactionary agendas; it seems that architecture has chosen this time to ignore its social commitments, instead withdrawing into the world of the corporation. The architect has become a part of the corporation's public relations team, joined to the logic of production and consumption. Our advertisement assumes as much: the architect is a plausible spokesperson for luxury products because the architect is a member of the corporate class. He already speaks for the system through his own work – the building is just one more luxury commodity.

So there appears to be a vast difference between modern and current practice, between these two mythologies of architecture. Modernism stood *against* prevailing authority, demanding critical responsibility and moral rage. Current practice stands *with* those in power, encouraging acquiescence to the status quo. This difference is important; but beneath it, both approaches share something crucial: the abstraction of the social. In both cases, this abstraction is undertaken in an attempt to *control* the social. In modernism, despite all discussion of social change, architecture understood the audience only as a *mass*. The audience was represented as raw material, waiting to be transformed – designed – into the universal city. The social existed only as a site of contest and triumph for the architect. On the other hand, in current practice, the social is controlled by ignoring it completely, by casting the social out to find its way amidst infinite planes of gridded lights. Although many enthusiasts of post-modernism have argued differently, current practice introduces no new radical possibilities; it marks only the exhaustion of the modern. Fundamentals remain the same: the goal of design remains the creation of order; the city is still apprehended as a geometric plan and as a space of surveillance. The concept of the Panopticon continues to inform architectural practice. Our advertisement hints at this: high in the air, the city is laid out for the architect; this view provides a sense of control. The drawing on the architect's board tells us something further. This generic plan promises a building just like those already found within the luminous vista beyond the window. The architect has sustained urban uniformality; city future and city present mirror one another. The present-day architect may determine the city, and the city may belong to him, but this is true only as long as the architect reflects the status quo. The modern architect, like Faust, saw the entire world as a theatre for his development. Now the architect puts this mythology of domination to work for the benefit of his corporate clients.

But architecture's role in maintaining the status quo cannot be understood simply by pointing to its choice of clients. The very basis of architectural practice has changed. In the past, architecture identified with religion, or science, or engineering; today another equation is apparent: architecture = advertising. For it is advertising that is the dominant form of discourse in contemporary life, and architecture and all other forms of cultural production have been recast by this fact. Victor Hugo predicted that the book would bury the building; in fact, the mass media have. Just as the photograph introduced to Malraux the possibility of a museum without walls, the environment of the mass media *in toto* may take over all styles of building.

Our advertisement addresses this shift of power from architecture to the mass media. Of course, at first glance, the advertisement calls forth the power of architecture. First of all, it speaks to the (actual or potential) members of the architect's class: those who are (or who want to be) wealthy, educated, powerful, privileged. But it calls up a far deeper level of the myth of architecture: architecture's position as the fundamental determinant of modern experience. The building is at the centre of representational practice for the first half of the twentieth century; architecture attempted to synthesize within itself many different forms of cultural expression; it attempted to provide these diverse practices with a common basis for formal experimentation – a universal semiotics of form. And, of course, this desire for totality was extended to everyday life: architecture worked to build a totally controllable environment. Through boulevard, grid and suburb, architecture defined and organized the social.

But now, through sheer omnipresence, it is advertising that is at the centre of representation. And although our advertisement acknowledges architecture's determining role, we might say that the advertisement proposes to pick up where architecture has left off. For advertising actually does not need to borrow any authority from architecture – the advertisement here pays homage to a mode of representation it has *surpassed*. The tables have been turned, and architecture now works to form itself after the image of advertising. Even the endless grid of the city cannot compare with the astonishing density of the advertising environment. Experience is no longer fabricated from the catalogue of geometry; it is fashioned from the archive of advertising. All messages, all meanings have been invaded by advertising; all realities verge on the stereotypical.

Yet the authority that supports these stereotypes is invisible. Like the contemporary city, the media seem without centre or boundaries; everywhere, but *from nowhere*. The media present to us a decentralized system, seemingly full of disruptions; on the surface of the media, discontinuities abound. But differences are entertained only to be made entertaining. The discontinuities presented in the media are in fact deeply stereotypical – there are no disruptions of the magnitude of Cubism, Dada or Surrealism. Discontinuities play an important managerial role in late capitalism, offering a controlled version of the contradictions of the time. Beneath these discontinuities, a centralized system of order still exists. No resistance is offered to the underlying uniformity of experience, no challenge is made to the advancing homogenization of social life.

These discontinuities are in fact crucial to commodity production. We are offered a parade of choices, a parade of promotional competitions, a parade of spectacles; these do not merely distract us from crisis and conflict, they absorb the conflict, strive to replace it. It is this process of social control that architecture has borrowed from advertising. Present-day architecture turns our attention to the discontinuities of surface, distracting us from the institutional authority that forms architecture. Postmodern pastiche, architectural 'quotation' – architecture portrays experience and history in the same way as the media do, as an archive of stereotypes. Like advertising, architecture offers a simulation of difference while upholding the power of the same.

Let us return to the advertisement, to obvious content we have not yet discussed. In addition to the architect's drawing, it presents us with another 'plan', another 'development' – this one between man and woman. The male designs, while the female 'has designs'; the mediation of sexual difference proceeds through a string of exchanges, through an economy of gesture and pose: exchange denied (the phone call), exchange proposed (the cognac), exchange accepted (the glance). This difference might be explained as a (typical) contrast between nature and culture: eros meets architect. One possible fantasy: clothing removed, lights extinguished . . . secretly, within a darkened space on the grid, the female returns the male to nature. Perhaps. Nature and the erotic female *are* often portrayed as sources of anarchy, as threats to the system of order. Once tamed, however, they offer the possibility of sublime experience. They are placed in the service of culture – they *fuel* culture. The female in the advertisement is presented at the second step in the myth. She is a member of the professional class, somehow a servant to the architect, presenting her sexuality *in his language*. As such, she does not offer a return to nature, but the sustenance of culture. Difference is treated as a divertissement that will leave the existing power structure unchallenged.

The female and the city both fall within the domain of the architect; both are formed in his language, so much so that we can consider the female as a symbol for the city. The social, indistinct as an elegant illuminated grid, is more clearly personified by the erotic female. That is, the social is cast as the *other* in the way that the female and nature often are. The social: pushed into oblivion by urban planning and by the abstraction of the city, denied existence by the constant barrage of the media, it is now the site of wild speculation, of possible anarchy – the site where all that has been repressed may return. And so the architect, and the advertiser, fear the social. Their systems of representation profess to free the social but must instead deny the social, attempt to 'civilize' it. The social, like nature, must be constructed as a commodity which can be mined, refined, stored, distributed, controlled; like the erotic, it must be portrayed as a force to repress and channel, that will be allowed to energize the system of identity and power, but not be allowed to subvert it.

Understanding the change in architecture depends upon a recognition of the general conditions of production in late capitalism. As Baudrillard has noted, symbolic production has overtaken all other forms of commodity production –

the object itself is less significant than the semiotic value attached to it. Value is not determined by need, but by the demands of symbolic exchange. *Objects* are not bought and sold, *signs* are. These signs may in fact exist as everyday consumer objects; they may also be the results of symbolic production in entertainment, mass media, art, design and architecture.

Advertising is an important form, perhaps the most important form, of symbolic production. In advertising, the object is laden with semiotic meaning. Objects *depend* upon the system of simulation; they are merely three-dimensional manifestations of a sign which exists more perfectly in the fantasy of the media. The media give life to the object by breathing exchange value into the sign. This is not only done by the rendering the object receives in the advertisement. Advertising works more generally as an *institution*, bringing order to representation, establishing the parameters of discourse, forming a method for reading all experience. And advertising has accomplished these goals so remarkably that other media have followed its example.

Architecture is one case in point. Architecture has become a *form* of advertising in several significant ways. First, it has allowed the building to be transformed into a public relations spectacle. The building draws attention to the corporation throughout its production: from arguments over zoning, through the competition over the building's design, through the actual con-struction of the building, to the final promotion of the building in popular and trade publications, and the analysis of the building in architectural criticism and history. The corporation attempts to establish its needs at every step. Secondly, architecture has devised the entire urban environment as a rhetorical expression of the economic and political system. Buildings and 'public space' join to communicate the grandeur and permanence of the corporation, its city and its nation. And finally, and most important for this essay, architecture has amplified the phenomenological impact of advertising; it has added to 'advert-ising-effect'. The information society, late capitalism, advanced urban life, postmodernism – call it what you will, the present is marked by the loss of the object, by the invisibility created by communication, by the electronic and photographic distribution of images, information and capital. Objects are merely vehicles used to reach some rarified semiotic state. In architecture, this circumstance is evident in the exaggerated 'hyperspaces' (Jameson) of current buildings – gigantic interiors full of confusion, distracting surfaces, mirrored walls. In all of these instances of invisibility, architectural or mass-media, the social is literally lost. The individual is overwhelmed by an incomprehensible flood of signs, surfaces and space. The sensuality of information takes over: experience fills with rapidly changing images, swirls, glass and light; the fetish of surface dissolves the contradictions of experience. Drunkenness is not an inappropriate metaphor, and the intersection of cognac, architecture and advertising makes further sense: postmodernism and capitalism join to form an inebriated state of consciousness.

Advertising also forms reality by the way it inserts itself into messages, and into experience generally. Advertising *interrupts*, either by intruding upon the message and breaking it apart, or by positioning itself adjacent to the message and competing with it. This interruption is a *fait accompli*: we are forced to take our information and advertising together. They are interwoven, jumbled up, blurred; each adopting the style of the other – news reportage, entertainment and commercials threaten to become indistinguishable. Faced with this totality of discourse, and recognizing how little control we have over it, we begin to treat advertising as an unavoidable fact of life – as nature, as some kind of permanent reality.

'Advertising-effect', with its phantasms and interruptions, generates the fetishism of the sign: before the void of social life dances the ideal simulation. This is evident in our advertisement: rarefied cognac in the foreground, posed against the indistinct public realm beyond. The sign *must* be ösed against emptiness, for a more specific account of the social would diminish the sign, would complicate consumption. Is the sign an abstraction based upon a reality, or is it a reality formed from an abstraction? It is impossible to tell; simulation must destroy this very dichotomy. Neither a 'representation' of the social, nor an 'abstraction' of it, simulation confuses both. One thing is certain: simulation requires a system of authority. Without a system that controls meaning, we might discover 'a rubble of distinct and unrelated signifiers' (Jameson). Or worse: we might fall into the empty social and be lost forever.

Architecture strives to duplicate the construction of sign and object in advertising, borrowing the processes of 'advertising-effect'. Postmodern eclecticism and pastiche apply interruption to history; the buildings themselves intrude upon urban life, demanding our adaptation. Glamorous (even if ironic) signs adorn the surfaces of buildings; high-tech materials and fantastic arcades transform the building into a fantasy of simulation. Beyond the formal distinctions that separate 'late modern' and 'postmodern' lie more important similarities: both practices approach the building as a vehicle for ahistorical experience, for spectacle and effect, for the uncritical support of corporate authority.

The claim might be made that the approach to representation described here contains a political intention, pushing experience beyond the normal bonds of representation. In early modernism, this may have been true. Breaking apart representation was felt to lead to freedom, to the liberation of social possibility. Technology (in the form of mass production, engineering, photography, cinema, etc.) was lionized as an appropriate tool for this liberation, but as it became apparent (for reasons too numerous to discuss here) that such liberation would not be accomplished easily, and perhaps not at all, technology became a fetish object, and would assist in the construction of other fetish objects. Technology was no longer seen as a social practice. Instead, it provided distractions from the failure of its own utopia. Utopia came to be displaced into technological simulation, eliminating the pragmatics of implementation, eliminating the need for an analysis of its failure.

Perhaps technology has always encouraged this displacement from social praxis to artificial utopia. The joy of dislocation, the trajectory of the unmapped body, the rich hallucinogenic mirage of the *image*; the high building, the reach into heaven – fantasy has mingled with technological possibility even since the Enlightenment. Throughout the development of Western technological consciousness, the metaphysical search for the sublime has been joined to the technological search for domination; the transcendental and the Fascist have been interwoven. What is manifest (in different ways) in Le Corbusier, Mies, Speer and Portman is latent in the fantasies of Piranesi, Ledoux and Bentham. Who are those who could exist within 'big hotels, railway stations, immense roads, colossal ports, covered markets, brilliantly lit galleries, freeways, demolition and rebuilding schemes'? Marinetti's technologically-induced fantasy of the Futurist audience echoes centuries of desires.

Postmodernism is in many ways the final exaggeration of such modernist aspiration. Much postmodern culture is merely 'decadent' modernism; no longer able to sustain the fantasy of utopia, we cynically remain tied to its shell of illusions. Postmodernism might be better named as 'fin-de-moderne', or even 'capitalist baroque'. The spectacular and disorienting city stands as the final form of, for instance, Tatlin's *Monument to the 3rd International*. The 'line of advance of a free humanity' depicted in this monument (to quote Tatlin) has been replaced by the advancing credit line of the Visa card, and by the spiral of inflation in Third World countries. Gropius claimed to be working toward 'the new structure of the future . . . which will one day rise towards heaven from the hands of a million workers like the crystal symbol of a new faith'. As our advertisement tells us, this structure has risen. High in the city, the architect sits at its helm, hanging up the phone, drinking cognac as he unbuttons his assistant's blouse.

To begin again: our hard-working architect, after a long day dividing up the wilderness of the social, is confronted by the wilderness of desire: the female. This scene seems accessible to the magazine audience; the advertisement *appears* to set up a hierarchy of control that begins with the individual reader and then moves to the architect, to the woman and finally to the city beyond. But this accessibility does not empower the reader/voyeur; instead it marks an impersonality that implies the insignificance of any specific member of the audience. The advertisement works to construct a universal featureless audience. The reader is constructed just as the city is; the audience on either 'side' of the architect is cloaked in anonymity. Even the woman is made anonymous through stereotype. The city audience might glimpse the scene through the window, just as the reader catches the scene through the page, but all view a scene they cannot engage. They witness a disembodied image, a transcendental glow provided by the process of simulation. The authority of the architect, the authority of the advertiser, is projected through the powerful independence of this simulation. The image seeps into the surrounding urban darkness.

The death of the social . . . has it come to this? Do the members of the audience truly compose what Baudrillard called 'that opaque but equally translucent reality, that nothingness: the masses'? We have been describing the rhetoric of the system, a rhetoric that attempts to form power on one side, and anonymity and powerlessness on the other. Has this rhetoric succeeded? Long denied a voice, has the social disappeared? Is individualism also a fantasy, our differences mere phantasms?

Has the city murdered the social? Even in modernism, despite all considera-tion of social function, architecture sought to impose a model of the audience as a *mass*. This abstraction allowed the architect to concentrate undisturbed upon the city, to proceed with little thought of the social, economic or political differences within the audience. In fact, the architect could ignore lived experience entirely. This situation continues to the present day. The public, considered passive, is played upon by the skilful hands of the architect and the corporation. Like the cognac bearer in the advertisement, the desires of the public are named through language that belongs to the powerful.

The public is allowed to exist only as the sum of corporate interests; one must look for the public at the intersections of ownership. 'Public space' is but a montage of areas dominated by the corporation, areas that the public is allowed to trespass upon by day. 'Public discourse' is the corporate controlled speech of the media. 'Participation' means participating in the corporation. Corporations fight with each other over control of space, information, reality. Architecture and the media help to hide these battles. The disorientations of simulation mask the drunkenness of power.

Of course, the social is *not* empty, and history is not over. Economic and political conflicts do exist in that hazy realm of the social, no matter how completely it is rewritten by corporate rhetoric. But there is no social that awaits liberation; the social is something that must be *built*. If we are to invent social experience beyond that which exists in the media, we must contest the institutional representation of the public. We must identify the rhetoric of power and capital, the false consciousness that is *intended*, and separate it from any actual description of the audience. We have come to understand that reality does not exist outside representation (at least, it is not *discernible* outside representation). This means that if the corporation controls the means of representation, then the audience can exist only as the corporation allows. This state of affairs can only be countered by finding the disjunctions within corporate reality, and by turning these disjunctions into disruptions. In this way can opposition be formed. The public may indeed be an institutional formation; we must then strive to change the institution. Representation must be transformed from the privately owned discourse of the corporation into a public arena of conflict; this will allow 'the public' and 'the social' to take many different *specific* forms. The various factions of the audience will begin to discover ways to name themselves.

Postmodernism could become this oppositional practice, this challenge to the institutional authority built by modernization. Postmodernism properly should be the search for new possibilities for representation, both pictorially *and* politically. It need not be characterized by eclecticism and pastiche, or the cynical duplication of 'advertising-effect'. Instead, postmodernism can strive to disrupt the monologue of power. For this to happen in architecture, the architect must challenge advertising – that is, the corporate control of representation. But this cannot be done by reasserting a modernist separation from mass culture – architecture must critically *engage* the power of the corporation, its public relations and 'advertising-effect'. The corporate control of reality and identity needs to become the *subject* of architecture, which is to say, architecture must be rewritten as a social practice. To this end, the architect cannot generalize the audience, or even assume to know the audience. Rather than construct the public as an anonymous mass, architecture must search out ways to encourage the self-invention of the audience. Rather than using difference as a marketing strategy, or as a form of social control, architecture can allow the manifestation of difference to challenge the corporate construction of a uniform society. And rather than treating history as an archive of stereotypes, architecture can help instil a sense of history in everyday life, as well as the unfolding of history to come. In short, design must encourage growth and change, rather than the maintenance of order. Architecture can help confront the institutions that control the city, that limit reality for the sake of profit and power, or it can continue to aid these institutions. It is not an easy choice, for this problem remains: today, criticism of the institution must be formed using the institution's money; and the institution is unlikely to encourage such a challenge to itself. The question arises: is architecture so joined to corporate reality, so enmeshed in the logic of symbolic production, that it cannot offer any challenging alternatives? Is critical architecture even possible?

We return once more to our cognac advertisement. It speaks to and attempts to form the public. It offers a definition of civilization: private pleasure mixed with private power; enjoyment added to isolation. The viewer – the audience – looks from the outside into the glowing page of the magazine. Floating at the top of the page above the architect stands the corporation – a voice from the outside, offering definition and stability. Banished to the endless space beyond, divorced from power, divorced from representation, participating through passivity and voyeurism, is the audience. The masses. Found at last, living within a system administered by the architect, formulated and promoted by the advertising department.

— 6 —

Street signs
•
NIGEL COATES

'Crazy silhouettes of twisted steel from piles of broken masonry, memorials to the chaos of the old town. A fine building in ruins and we turn away sadly. But we should be thankful for much of the destruction – challenging opportunity confronts us.'

Ralph Tubbs, catalogue to the show 'Living in Cities', 1942

Modern life as TV

No architect will be the slightest surprised if attacked by other guests at dinner. I speak from experience. Suddenly the heads turn, as if I am personally responsible for the daily misery of whole neighbourhoods. The general view seems to be that all architects are irresponsible, uptight professionals who have manipulated people and the cities they live in. Given the state of most cities on these islands, one is tempted to agree and change the subject.

'You architects are all the same,' spat one such instant adversary at a recent dinner-party. 'And you teach as well. What right do you have to interfere with other people's minds?' The attacks began to be tinged with hysteria, probably in response to my remarks on the value of ugliness.

The other standard architectural conversation is less negative but equally shortcircuiting: in the wake of what the American critic Hal Foster calls 'reactionary postmodernism', the Battle of the Styles still focuses on Toytown classic. Despite the talk, the fact is that most new buildings in Britain are indescribably bland, because, when the chips are down, invention is assumed to cut value, not create it.

This relegates architecture to the level of a bewildering TV documentary, equal to those on the other popular subjects of unemployment and the forthcoming nuclear holocaust. Off the air, most recent building has adopted nostalgia and pastiche, such as the hypermarket shed with a fake tiled roof. At best the public is treated to mirrored office blocks, which hide any real architectural issues as if behind reflecting sunglasses. And the planners are worse, having enforced the modernist policy of functional segregation to the point that the public has *demanded* nostalgia. Hence the fantasy worlds of

Nigel Coates *Bongo Half-built Tokyo 1986* Photo by Ned Flex

Covent Garden, and timeshare holiday villages in the vernacular Mediterranean style. It is hardly surprising that well-meaning fashion and interiors magazines are willing to publish Quinlan Terry's cardboard cutouts of the way things used to be . . . On the whole, the audience longs for urban innocence, because any other prospect is too frightening.

Is it becáuse the language of architecture became so difficult to speak? For public and client alike, the problem could be that the old language of modernism and 'progress' is the only one they know, but it has gone stale, leaving the business of making new buildings with as much chance to invent as second-hand car dealing.

Architects must take their share of the blame. Throughout the twentieth century, they have projected themselves as missionaries of taste. At the outset, no doubt, new buildings signified belief in the new age: when battles to be fought were against slums and disease, shiny, uncomplicated housing blocks must have been welcome intruders in the Babylonian quagmire of styles. But by the mid-sixties, when the old ideological crusades of modernism actually seemed to have been won, the architectural visions of this century finally took shape identically in suburbs from London to Moscow. The home in particular had become a formula, capable of being repeated, labelled and stacked; and inside every one of them the main source of illumination was the television set.

Rather than being a means to organize manufacturing, cities had become a focus for consumption; they had ceased to be networks of spaces, situations and events, and consequently had lost their dimension of public life in flux, which broadly speaking is the subject of Marshall Berman's book *All That Is Solid Melts Into Air*. In a section titled 'Modernism in the Streets', he argues that chaos was once an essential quality of the urban experience.

> The city development of the last forty years, in capitalist and socialist countries alike, has systematically attacked, and often successfully obliterated, the 'moving chaos' of nineteenth-century urban life ... The old modern street, with its volatile mixture of people and traffic, businesses and homes, rich and poor, is (*now*) sorted out and split up into separate compartments.[1]

Whether for political or economic reasons, the rationalized cities we now build rely on packaging and neutralizing events, rather than encouraging their free-form diversity: *experiences* of the city do not mix with maps or plans. No wonder the conservationists triumphed, with their vision of counterfeit memories. Fortunately we could never arrive at the predicted Nirvana of homogeneity. The actual result of the machine age has been to segregate and separate: one lives in a product, one spends for products, one *is* a product; yet there is neither a positive ideal of consumption to hold all these together, nor a public dimension to life which can overcome them.

Certainly in Britain, two further phenomena have changed everybody's life fundamentally. The first of these sprang from being *without*: the now national institution of under-employment, or unemployment, has undermined confidence individually and collectively. The second is the stratum of software. Technology and communication have created excess – excess space, excess meaning, excess processing.

At first we left our jobs, the streets, our cities, either to go abroad or to close ourselves inside our mortgaged three-roomed flat, sink into an armchair and watch television. Outside, the once proud and symbolic city landscape was left, an abandoned stage safely viewed through the frame of the cathode ray tube. Baudrillard, the elliptical media philosopher, describes the scenario:

> Today it is the very space of habitation that is conceived as both receiver and distributor, as the space of both reception and operations, the control screen and terminal which as such may be endowed with telematic power – that is, with the capability of regulating everything from a distance, including work in the home and, of course, consumption, play, social relations and leisure. Simulators of leisure or of vacations in the home – like flight simulators for airplane pilots – become conceivable.[2]

As a result, we think, work, play, differently now. The floppy disc has replaced the book; the telephone has barred the visitor; the credit card has done away with money; video has recorded the movie; taped music has become more real than live performance; advertising has sublimated the product; and as Baudrillard has shown, the television is the new measure of our perceptions.

In other words, daily life is less clear-cut than it was postwar. It has been banalized and yet elevated into the software age of signs and images, of competing fragments operating within a newly universalized fluid of communication. Yet despite these tendencies towards robotic reduction, we are not necessarily nearer to the brink of collective breakdown. We learn to compensate, by adopting the vocabulary we are faced with. Down every path, we take change in our stride – on TV, in advertising, in music, in a lifestyle split into a myriad rhetorical enlargements.

Ironically, the distancing from the self caused by unemployment, software lifestyle and the media has actually *supplied* culture with its curious existential inversions, and thus the means of turning the institutional signs of the city inside-out and upside-down. As the city decays, the giro cheque is of limited joy – so people find new models, new lifestyles, new interests and new ways to present themselves; now people adopt lifestyle stances. Some people, particularly young people, discredit television-as-truth because they want to do something for themselves, however makeshift.

In Britain it has become a characteristic of the 1980s for culture to grow from its differences. Instead of progress, we tend to heroicize what is normally hidden, to play up the differences, to encourage a society in a simultaneously primitive and advanced state of flux, in which adopted narratives and roles are able to reactivate the otherwise empty social stage, which television as a phenomenon (but not as a language) appeared to have forced us to abandon. In fact we have adopted the artificial in place of the real, and learned to make use of this new 'reality'. Now we can all make TV programmes and handle computers. We assemble and recontextualize the spare parts of culture to suit our own expression of identity. The old cultural compartments, patterns and processes have been deprogrammed from the constraints of a manufacturing based society towards one which manipulates excess. Resources are available to all by accident – whether in the form of the city wasteland or the computer console. Architects, on the other hand, have remained strangely isolated from these changes: perhaps they don't have television sets. The fact is that the *way* we live has changed for good, and architecture must respond with a thorough rethink.

Narrative in architecture

The architects' favourite cocktail of function and appearance has lost its appeal. We need to re-examine the way architecture is designed, what it contains, and the way it works. Conventionally, architecture constitutes the hardware of the city. It provides the backbone for the city's efficiency and its symbolic prowess. Traditionally, architecture has ordered chaos, and created an enlarged iconography for the society that has produced it. The common good has been its reason for being.

Today, the common good is harder to define, and is hardly the issue anyhow.

Culture now has a software dimension equally as important as its hardware. Processes which were at one time as real as bricks and stucco are now practically speaking invisible. Electric cables, telephone lines and radio waves carry a huge proportion of what makes modern environments work. In the software age architecture is required to do less, even though what goes on in and around it is more varied than ever before.

This leaves the purpose of architecture open to redefinition. Meaning and conventional function need not necessarily be linked. Buildings need to coax people back into working with them rather than against them . . . they need a time dimension, a mental dimension . . . or what we could call *narrative*. The practice of architecture needs to drop its production-line thinking – to adopt layering and random access. It has to learn how to dramatize and emphasize; in short, how to build on the nature of experience.

The idea that architecture can operate in a reflective or literary dimension is not new: if anything it always has, outside the confines of the twentieth century. So why has it not happened in this century, not even in the disguise of postmodernism?

Part of the answer lies in the way architects are taught to design. Even now, designing is done to a formula handed down from the early days of the Modern Movement, when the process of design actually mimicked the process of production. You are told to start with the facts dictated by the brief, and turn them into a plan; by a process of repeated overlay, the design takes shape as an orthogonal organization of rooms and structure. The appearance of the thing is only dealt with at the end – and even then merely in the two-dimensional form of 'elevations', most of which can convey next to no idea of the built result. Any reference to the body, the feel of the place or what it alludes to, are firmly left out. And this is not because they are not communicated, they are simply absent from the design process at any stage. No wonder most students of architecture have sunk into a romance of Rapidograph neoclassicism.

What, then, can change the means, and thus the results, of architecture? Modernism itself was of course a challenge to its predecessors, and with it was born the whole concept of the 'avant-garde'. When battles were being fought over the future of both art and architecture, one avant-garde onslaught followed another. Iconoclastic disruptions, such as those of the Futurists, the Surrealists and Dadaists (all of whom aimed to produce an art-minded, self-determining middle class), worked because they could be clearly heard from within the homogenous compound of mainstream thought. Now we are at a similar crossroads, and yet iconoclastic lunging towards the future does not seem to be the solution. Curiously, the culture of architecture now lags behind society, whereas previously the reverse was true.

It was against this critical background that the architectural group NATO (of which I have been a member since it began in 1983) was formed. At first, rather than tackling design via real building, it presented its ideas in its magazine and on the gallery wall. It employs what it calls *narrative method,* and narrative architecture, in the form of drawings, is what it produces. NATO (Narrative Architecture Today) set out to invest design with narrative fragments that enrich and pull apart the experience of buildings. Avoiding utopian trajectories, it set out to emphasize the 'absurdity of the way things are'. It aimed to create a liberalized and radicalized view of buildings which is not confined to the taste of architects. Its images, references and codes are deliberately chosen to bring out an architectural dimension from the totality of city surroundings – from the city's moments of exquisite high culture to its backyards of decay. Essentially NATO works with a programme of signs and processes which, unlike those of postmodernism, embrace the idiosyncrasies of modern life with pleasure.

On the basis of NATO's cultural stocktaking stance, an art dimension to its work is implicit. However, this has more to do with a way of thinking than with whether a drawing is pretty, unbuildable, or more at home in an art gallery than in the pages of the *Architect's Journal*. Its efforts are extreme because they are exemplary, and as such must carry themselves beyond the restrictions of mere drawing. Our purpose was to disturb prevailing views, even at the risk of anger. Sometimes the rift between what is built and what is right for the time is so broad that effort must be concentrated into the gallery and the magazine, as the Futurists, Dadaists and Suprematists understood.

Compared with the theoretical work of the seventies, the focus of our *narrative architecture* shifts from the sphere of the designer's statement towards *architecture-in-use*. We site the implicit reverse futurology in the work of the moviemaker, the TV or video producer, and transfer it to architecture by investing the building in the drawing with a vision of it in use, as if it had actually been built and were full of people using and abusing it. Eisenstein clarifies the director's method; before he starts filming, he must visualize his film as *real*, but more than this he must know how to disassemble his vision into its constituent parts, how to use his medium, that of film, to convey his total intention. In his words:

> Before the inner vision, before the perception of the creator, hovers a given image, emotionally embodying his theme. The task that confronts him is to transform this image into a few basic *partial representations* which, in their combination and juxtaposition, shall evoke in the consciousness and feelings of the spectator, reader, or auditor, that same initial general image which originally hovered before the creative artist.[3]

Similarly, *narrative architecture* states this fundamental need to describe the *mise-en-scène* of buildings to overlap the complementary layers of situation, action, perception and form, and so discover more about a building before it is built. The drawing has to contain a filmic hypothesis and at the same time bring this back into the moment of the creative process. Sometimes this means drawing key pictures of the action even bigger than the building – in other words manipulating the content of the drawing dialectically, critically and synthetically. When designing we need to create a complete picture of architecture in action, and not just a blueprint. The first drawings will have to be three-dimensional and sensual. They must grasp the feeling of being in and moving through the building, so scale is more phenomenological than actual. Dealing with real scale comes later.

Here Venturi has supplied some critical background. In his key text *Complexity and Contradiction in Architecture*, he made a famous case for everyday imperfection in architecture. 'Meaning can be enhanced by breaking the order; the exception points up the rule. A building with no "imperfect" part can have no perfect part, because contrast supports meaning. An artful discord gives vitality to architecture.'[4] Not to be caught out, he qualified these liberalizations with a warning: 'You can allow for contingencies all over, but they cannot prevail all over.' His calls for imperfection did not nearly encompass all the software 'complexity', or the 'narrative', of modern life. He repeats Le Corbusier's dictum 'There is no work of art, without a system.'

Of course there must be structure to our manoeuvres, but the current city situation is a far cry from Le Corbusier's. Non-architectural sources prove to be of far more use – art theory, structuralism or linguistics. One of the key narrative concepts, that of the *re-use of the existing* as radical strategy, has ancestry in Russian Formalist literary criticism. In the pursuit of an accessibility to literature in line with the revolution, Shklovsky, Tomashevsky and others developed the device of 'defamiliarization' – an idea which symbiotically connects the ordinary and the extraordinary. 'I (Tomashevsky) consider the device of *defamiliarization* to be a special instance of artistic motivation . . . The old and habitual must be spoken of as if it were new and unusual. One must speak of the ordinary as if it were unfamiliar.'[5]

Many artists working in the early eighties used defamiliarization (and refamiliarization) to engage the 'reader'. Then painting reclaimed the limelight from the conceptualists, largely because of the lessons of McLuhan, Barthes and other structuralists had been digested well enough for a new explosion of expression to be linked to the manipulation of everyday signs. The artists that formed what the Italian art critic Achille Bonito Oliva called the *trans-avant-garde* took up methods based on the reassembly of the existing dismantled. Just as for the Russian Formalists, complexity was born from simplicity, almost from banality.

The territory of the building in its context has to be pared down into a system of fragments in motion. Then, and only then, can a building be conceived as a field of processes, interactions and symbols in balance – if the goal is architecture that lays bare a higher unity in which experience and the place can truly interact, the conventional notion of architectural unity has to be blown apart, just as Oliva's artists had done with the subject layers of their paintings:

> The sensitivity of the work calls the echoes of the outside back into the field
> of language and bends patterns and spatial and temporal accident to the

purposes of art . . . This process is favoured by the shattering of the unitary conception of the work, a projection of the shattering of any unitary vision of the world.[6]

In architecture, the possibilities are even greater than in painting, because buildings actually exist in a three-dimensional reality in which the user can genuinely react, in the fullest space-time dimensions of hot, cold, day, night – in the events and processes of the city.

But sensitivity, however three-dimensional, is dead without irony. Architecture must regain a sense of humour, but critically. Oliva explains why:

> Irony, as a passion that liberates itself through detachment, accentuates the lateral character of the language and introduces the possibility of a further pleasure, that of a work which does not deprive the spectator of his own presence and narrative ability.[7]

In *narrative architecture*, irony is the magical ingredient which throws the meaning of the building back towards the spectator. Since the *raison d'être* of any building is to create a system of functioning entities, it can adopt this ironic stance by overlapping straightforward functions with decoys that elevate or distort them. In other words, the conventional 'narrative' (or function) of a building can cross-fertilize with a system of non-essential narratives, the function of which is simultaneously to destabilize the objectivity of the building and to synthesize it with its contiguous entities, the body and the city.

Thus *narrative architecture* has consolidated a 'trans'-architectural design vocabulary which aims to transfer the creative condition to the users themselves using exactly the means Oliva might describe, combining figurative overstatement with the deliberate regression of authorship; in doing so it uses logic and irrationality in equal measures, even if, to the architectural establishment, it seemed arbitrary, superficial and, worst of all, unbuildable. A checklist of techniques for *narrative architecture* might read as follows:
To confront design from a subjective author/reader point of view is critical . . . Rather than avoiding sterotypes, narrative architecture uses them, and shifts and explodes hierarchies and systems of power . . . Design should be approached by anticipating the full force of the architecture in use. Therefore drawings must be three-dimensional, sensual and interactive. The more so if they are computer aided . . . Social circumstances must be read as space and language, thus forming them into architectural 'elements' . . . Narrative architecture looks for local legend, and researches the archaeology of culture . . . Stress the precultural state; primitivism is at the base of social experience . . . To exploit the possible tension or sympathy between them, search out structural similarities between events, images and spaces . . . Motion is the key to narrative – existing motion can be stressed by adding more. It reorganizes permanence and ephemerality . . . Narrative exploits excess meaning and the fact that in real space it is a function of necessity . . . Figures from foreign situations and

cultures help make cultural leaps in narrative space–time . . . Narrative architecture is not about telling stories, but about amplifying the situation . . . Narrative architecture scribes and circumscribes itself within the ordinary. It works as a kind of symbolic software . . . Narrative architecture questions the immobile status of the object – it stresses the becoming or dematerializing of the object, as ruin, as yet to be built, as makeshift . . . Narrative uses order and type, but deconstructively. Types of 'situation' challenge the order that lies within real architecture . . . Narrative architecture capitalizes on TV/film/ advertising languages, because they operate by provoking the reader's intimacy, and thus use the key image-in-process techniques of continuity, cut, shock, repetition – the rhetoric of modern life . . . Narrative architecture never obliterates the existing world, but exploits and overlays it. It is an architecture of reverberation between the known and the unknown . . . It works within a broader definition of space as prerequisite for architecture and events alike . . . Narrative architecture uses the flux condition of the total city and the parallel organ of the total body and its many parts in motion as the bed of design . . . Define the characters and their relationships more distinctly than the plot. Ultimately the plot is only written in the course of actual events . . . Use adaptation and transformation as fundamental tools . . . Objets trouvés et déformés.

Join up the dots and reveal an approach to design which is procedural, but leaves plenty of room for irrationality. The key to the puzzle might be the word 'caprice'. The English critic Brian Hatton has suggested that there is a parallel between the 'capricci' of Venetian painters of the eighteenth century and NATO drawings. He sees in NATO that 'madness is the method'. 'Only by metamorphosing the madness of life into the magic of architecture,' he says 'are we going to get real cities, and not the monofunctionally zoned zombie/ gnomescapes that the unholy alliance of the market and misunderstood modernism has produced in our midst.'[8]

There is another sense in which the method of madness can be harnessed, namely its sheer psychic energy in the context of a richly stimulating chaos: consider the creativity born of bomb sites, or the ruins in places like the South Bronx, where the richness and intensity of small-group life has animated, even inspired, what Marshall Berman calls a 'post-urbicidal frenzy'. Hence NATO does not set out to create the creativity but, like Cage and Eno in music, creates the conditions and preoccupations by means of which everyone may participate.

Hence narrative architecture can learn from the psychological schisms, signs and patterns – the social narratives – of the times, and see them in parallel with madness and sanity. Therein lies the possibility of reinvesting architecture with an oscillation between banality and creation at the level of the *use* of the city. In Britain, we watch the demise of great industries leaving on the one hand, barren landscapes and many lost people, and, on the other, a chance to experiment with the excesses that, until now, have had no space to move.

Street and culture

It seems that, as a reaction to Baudrillard's TV condition, the public sought to split itself into tribes that challenge one another with their looks and habits. Consumer society took up its 'lifestyle' as a counterfeit politic. Style, as Peter York pointed out in his book *Style Wars*,[9] became a question of opposition, of each group stressing its differences.

Some people still watched television, but style-conscious groups looked again at the 'chaotic scenes' of the open city spaces. They went back to the broken buildings and the back yards, back to the streets. And it was in the streets, otherwise abandoned by the prevailing urban refusal, that underprivilege itself grew into a stylistic attitude. Street-wise, street-culture, street-style gradually shaped a common lifestyle. Street-culture hallmarks were DMs and torn jeans. Its products were witty amalgams of the found and the forged. They spelt out an eccentric heroism that said 'keep moving'.

There were 'baroque' chairs made out of ladles and woks. There were brooches made out of compasses and springs. There were radios in plastic bags. Street culture always looked up and down, forwards and backwards: it amplified the present by exposing a slippage between the origin and the goal.

In the art schools interest abandoned the studios: from the production of art *per se*, a newly purposeful breed of art object took up its meaning within the everyday scenario. In the streets, people born and bred in earlier subcultures got bored with hanging out. They too could be artists or designers. They had the time if not the money. They were deliberately ambivalent about good and bad, beauty and ugliness, they cultivated their difficulty in choosing between Beauty and the Beast.

In Britain, Thatcher's years in government have caused a flagging of interest in directly political issues, but a hardening of self-determination. The now stable black economy was inevitable: that art and subculture would combine was more surprising. Inadvertently, television, and the media in its spectacular dimension, created a narrative software which, when detached from the one-way control of transmission and reception, could provide a narrative medium of everyday subversion at ground level.

For the first time an 'avant-garde' was practising in parallel with society at large, with protagonists who had learned from the technologized void they had been brought up in. Finally, competing subcultures had found a common ideological space within which to develop a *narrative* commodity, an artefact which embraced everyday contradictions, instead of trying to solve them as traditional 'Design' had done. For previous subcultures, 'commodity' had been a dirty word.

By the mid 1980s the street had become the context for design, making the scene of cultural action rather than the frame for the mythological youth identity of films like *West Side Story* or bands like the Sex Pistols. In a 1982 edition of *ZG* magazine on the theme 'Street Vision', Rosetta Brooks dismisses street culture as follows:

> It was on the streets the adolescents first established their sexual identities. In the past, the first step outside the Oedipal regime was onto the streets. But the combined forces of authoritarian surveillance and the super-surveillance of the mass media, in illuminating the dark recesses of street life, produced the independent sub-cultures and their codes of behaviour, reducing street culture to myth.[10]

Yet elsewhere the issue anticipates the commodity dimension of street culture – in the sculpture of Bill Woodrow, and in the consideration of Graffiti as art. A watershed is indicated, embodying the traditional subculture 'refusal' of prevailing circumstances, yet for the first time suggesting how the classic concepts of subculture, such as *bricolage* can be applied to the artefact, whether clothing, or furniture or room, and not just to the pose. Dick Hebdidge has pointed out how subcultures such as reggae or punk were typically created in response to specific historical conditions. 'This response,' he stresses in his book *Subculture*, 'embodies a Refusal: it begins with a movement away from the consensus.' In the end all subcultures express a fundamental tension between those with power and those without it. Then, to home in on the tension, subcultures convert the parts rather than the whole, and reassemble them to make a new whole capable of sublimating the source. The *bricolage* process of assembly entails a deliberate aberration, to release an originality from the use of utterly ordinary material.

> The concept of *bricolage* can be used to explain how subculture styles are constructed. In *The Savage Mind*, Lévi-Strauss shows how the magical modes utilized by primitive peoples (superstition, sorcery, myth) can be seen as implicitly coherent, though explicitly bewildering, systems of connection between things which perfectly equip their users to 'think' their own world.[11]

What has either been discarded or held sacred by those in power, he says, provides the ideal material for most subculture factions. In the context of street-*design*, and here I include NATO, the city itself provides the perfect resource, with its combination of monuments and broken buildings. Hebdidge explains how what is 'found' occurs in the mythology of every subculture group; that unlike the traditional iconoclastic position of an avant-garde, it uses the excesses of the prevailing situation to create its own vocabulary:

> The objects chosen were, either intrinsically or in their adapted forms, homologous with the focal concerns, activities, group structure and collective self-image of the subculture. They were 'objects in which [the subcultural members] could see their central values held and reflected'.[12]

This explains why the fashion side of street-design harnessed a kind of street-level creative spirit that was not immediately visible with that strength in any other form. The body is, after all, the most readily available territory of expression. Via a shower of new magazines, it brought from nowhere a whole stable of new personalities who based their work on eccentricity. A lot of Vivienne Westwood's work was about distorting fashion stereotypes, like making a jacket inside out, or putting a cut-up Marks and Spencer's skirt on a boy, or leaving the tacking in the clothing when it was finished. This kind of fashion was able to mark out a creative territory which was neither hierarchical nor conventionally snobbish. She, and others like her, produced an effective refiguring of the culture of the body, and at the sort of soft end of lifestyle which had nothing to do with being tied to buildings, or doing the right thing in the right place.

Some of these ideas apply directly to architecture, but not in the sense that architecture should become a fashion commodity. Street-culture reverts to individual expression, and to the handling of culture at a transparent level, the influence of which has pervaded all culture. Strictly speaking, we could not have made a subcultural architecture in any form other than NATO – it dealt with the creative possibilities of an avant-garde condition in architecture. It was a magazine, and not entire cities or actual buildings. Now the coincidence between these ideas and society at large makes these ideas achievable. But rather than representing the disposability of fashion, what is important about narrative architecture, when it does eventually get built, is that it should emphasize the moment in which it is perceived, whether it is 1988 or 1998. In fashion terms, one can play with the notion of 'classic', discarding its old bourgeois connotation. Now, it means a useful fragment that can be put together with others, so retaining the transitory sensibility without falling into the trap of style.

In areas other than architecture, street-culture narratives have returned to the mainstream they were derived from. They are on television, in the way we think when dealing with the computer screen, in a desire to experiment continually with language. Even the commercial culture of the street has assimilated the narrative sensibilities of overlay and reassembly of the sign. Magazine and billboard advertising, for example, has learned to hide the product in an elaborate narrative, or pseudo-filmic context. It makes commercial sense to diminish the distance between the producer and the consumer. Inadvertently, the street as the territory of messages coincides with the street as the market place for ideas.

Now that people have written books about street-culture, its lessons are learned. One of these is that street-culture has had practically no effect on the street itself. It has certainly lined plenty of pockets, but never those of architects. NATO functioned perfectly within the street-culture context because, although it dealt with the commodity of the building, it could never have remained independent except by functioning on the periphery. Since street-culture is in its final consolidating phase, we are in a position to look at its effect, and at the new possibilities it has created, at first at the level of a fashion adjunct, in the form of shops, bars or nightclubs, but later at the city.

Street language

It may have looked as though the 'moving chaos' of the street has gone, but in fact the movement has come back by accident. The popular imagination has been busy elsewhere, reading little fluorescent dots on cathode ray tubes, but quietly streets have become new corridors of urban software, with tills in the walls, teeming merchandise in the windows, and magical electronic billboards on top of buildings.

Buildings cannot survive without streets; they indicate one another, and serve one another. The street encompasses a fundamental principle of space. Whether a lane or an avenue, the participant (pedestrian, cyclist, jogger, driver, passenger, dog, postman, fireman, jaywalker, tramp . . .) is confronted by the choice to follow signs of movement – or to deviate from this, to dive into a building. Instincts are at work in every street, however urban – they are movement, choice, access, display, buy, sell. Far from being another bland component of the city, the street is its most essential and most ambiguous spatial unit. Hatton explains the street 'As encounter between people and things: the street is the primal site of exchange, the buying and selling of commodities, and transformations of value arising from there. It is the locus of the unstable alterations of subject and object, of window-gazing and hustling, vacancy and haste, dreams and demand, self-abnegation and self-regard. To be "on the street" is a euphemism for basic prostitution.'[13] In other words the street is not just narrative, but an open framework for the drama of everyday life.

This explains why the street is a favourite set on stage. In Renaissance theatre, as for the Roman models on which it was improving, drama took place amid urban architecture which, when organized to suit the perspective principle of the stage, naturally adopted the form of the street. Indeed, movements on the stage grow from the same basic principles of space. Actors must enter and exit laterally – painted flats of buildings allow them to appear as if from doors or alleyways. The visible action occurs towards the gaze of the audience, along the path of the street's axis of communication.

In the real city, the street is the key dynamic model for the play between public and private, static and mobile, restraint and release. As Hatton says, 'Disorder renders the street undwellable, but overorder makes it a charade or museum of function and surveillance.'[14] It exhibits a narrative framework which is neither purely symbolic nor purely representational: its layering of a whole spectrum of objects in flux provides the perfect extant framework for narrative architecture. Think of the movement between: traffic islands, traffic, road markings, cyclists, route signs, parked cars (some with clamps), plastic cones, kerbstones, barriers, traffic wardens, lampposts, letter boxes, zebra crossings, pedestrians, street signs, hoardings, postcard stands, shop windows, shop signs, doors, window boxes, windows, walls, air curtains, curtains, welcome mats, cash desks, displays, umbrella stands, visitors' books, lavatories, sofas, drinks cabinets, armchairs . . . a real log fire.

Unlike most architects, the Futurists capitalized on this blurring of objects in the city scenario. They seized on the street as the stage for a twentieth-century vision of dynamic social exchange. But from Le Corbusier onwards, architects and planners have tended to see the street as a menace, and consequently did their best to enlarge it and fence it in. From being the space of interaction and exchange, architects have seen streets merely as 'roads', geared towards the separation of buildings from the business of travelling to and from them, thus distancing public and private realms even further from each other. As Baudrillard said: 'In a subtle way, this loss of public space occurs contemporaneously with the loss of private space. The one is no longer a spectacle, the other no longer a secret.'[15] The street, it seems, is an empty stage.

The American sociologist-architect, Christopher Alexander, says 'a city is not a tree'. Even the most mildly sociological analysis of the city reveals that it is a network of shifting conditions, events, encounters, patterns of communication and processes. Cities should exist to nurture the life taking place in and around them. Life no longer consists of the simple categories of type and task invented in the nineteenth century, and later to be used as the basis of the twentieth-century programme of functional division.

It is difficult to accept that many architects now hanker after a pre-industrial rationalized streetscape. The Leo Kriers and the town hall planners of this world share the view that cities need tidying up into an ersatz version of the past, in which everybody knows his place, and knows what was what. Even Venturi seems quaintly liberal, however much he has taught us about architecture with his lessons on Las Vegas billboards.

Baudrillard's observations on the advertising landscape now work better as points of departure than as the warning he intended:

The body, landscape, time all progressively disappear as scenes. And the same for public space: the theatre of the social and theatre of politics are both reduced more and more to a large soft body with many heads. Advertising in its new . . . dimension invades everything, as public space (the street, monument, market, scene) disappears. It realizes, or, if one prefers, it materializes in all its obscenity; it monopolizes public life in its exhibition . . . It is our only architecture today: great screens on which are reflected atoms, particles, molecules in motion. Not a public scene or true public space but gigantic spaces of circulation, ventilation and ephemeral connections.[16]

Fashion, at least in the British sense, is a clue to this advertising/software attitude, because, at the scale of the body, it performs in the quasi-street spaces of the shop and the nightclub. And in one night club held in spaces borrowed from the city, its railway arches or its faded dancing halls, fashion and architecture join to perform the ultimate narrative of the street:

'Leaning against a column, casually emphasizing my body with its stillness, I enjoy being prey for passing eyes. When I walk, catching the glances of those who watch, I enact my movie as I please. Statue and stroller need one another as camera needs film.'[17]

But shop design has undoubtedly become the first real territory for architecture to flex its muscles in the 'street' idiom, because shops do not pretend to solve the century's disillusion with architecture. Besides, the owner of a shop is usually more prepared to take risks than a bank looking for a new home in the City.

A fashion shop builds around the clothes, to become both an advertisement for them and a complete little world in which the story behind the clothes becomes a space to explore. Any shop is a stage with the street as its audience. Somehow it must throw what is inside outwards to be caught by the passer-by; it must exploit and play with the building it is part of, yet simultaneously create a desire to be inside it. Shop design must transgress the division between interior and exterior; business depends on it.

With delight I recall the World's End shop (opened 1982, closed in 1984) on St Christopher's Place, London. A sort of NATO prototype, it played with its form as a set of spaces, and overlaid decoy signs, like the mud cut-out map of the world with dirty tarpaulins behind it suspended over the window, so that a critical *bricolage* resulted. Its partner shop[18] at the far end of the Kings Road, which opened in 1980, still sports a huge clock, the hands of which race backwards, and inside the floor tilts as if at sea.

Similar intelligence was at work in Demob in Beak Street, Soho until its final immolation. There the war was not yet truly over: again the allusion to the world, this time in the form of an enormous lit globe which sat in the window behind the sort of expanded metal grilles you would expect to see in Belfast. Inside, the fittings from the previous shop were clearly visible, and in fact revered: among the tweed skirts and flannel turnups, a chrome tea-urn reared from a terrazzo servery. Walk on, past Workers for Freedom (a fashion sweatshop), past Johnsons (a Gothic enlargement of Teddy Boy mythologies), past One Off (Dr Frankenstein's furniture cave), past Jones in Covent Garden (an exercise in turning new material into scrap). Past Freuds, Site, The World.

Ironically, the left-over street has been taken up as the space in which the contemporary English sensibility for cultivated individualism can fester – where fashion, time off, the media, consumption, production and the tribal urban instinct all gel. On the deserted stage of the street, anything can happen.

In the street, a new layer of machinery is needed to cultivate this kind of creative slippage – to allow what began as subculture to bed itself into the grain of the city. Then the narrative method will focus, not just within the marginal territory of an avant-garde, but as practice. It will analyse the hidden structures (the soft structures) of the street as found, and deconstruct them as if converting the situation into coherent overlapped fragments of film. It will stimulate the desires of the crowd on the pavement, and the people that live and work in the street. It will aggregate symbolic rallying points in between the old order components, like the walls and the pavements. It will encourage decoded activities by laying new codes irregularly over old ones . . . it will force the street to become the source of language rather than its final resting place.

Body building

> NATO's Gamma-City is a get-up-and-go starter pack based on typical sites and probable events. It scrambles uses and meanings . . . it bends stereotypes . . . it uses double levels . . . fictions are used politically. Its city is made active again, putting back the movement that Modern Movement Man forgot about . . . Why Gamma? Because gamma-rays emit spontaneously. They radiate strong short radio waves, effecting built mutations.[19]

Until now architecture has been unable to take up a directly critical expression. Now it can, because society at large is on the verge of assimilating what used to be called the 'avant garde' into its vernacular language, not as building, but as lifestyle. Now a building can take up a deliberately commentative stance at the same time as performing its pragmatic functions. Therefore NATO's show 'Gamma-City', held at the Air Gallery in 1985, was not so much predictive, as an archaeology-projected and a futurology-reversed into the present. This drawing back of the temporal bowstring corresponds exactly to the way narrative architecture performs on buildings. It adds on (or lances through) new elements which are deliberately chosen to advance rhetorically the spectrum of meaning. It treats new architecture as a kind of 'clothing' (or surgery?), so that the old architecture shows through.

Already most European cities perform this metamorphosis unprompted. In a city like London, new buildings, railways and roads never quite obliterate what went before them. Tall buildings pierce through the old skyline, and flyovers are unperturbed by the terraced houses beneath. Some architectural situations use this palimpsest consciously, not quite as narrative, but very nearly. As we have seen, shops depend on the freedom to overide the mores of conventional architectural practice. They apply an acute spatial and imagistic psychology to their shells – their 'architecture' and their windows perform a narrative role for their stock, helping to transgress the 'security' of the shop window.

Other types of buildings only need a nudge. Although often closer to kitsch than to narrative, pubs, bars and brasseries are on the way. Night clubs already have a narrative spirit, the more so when they take place in old factories or hard times sex clubs. The list can be extended easily, to the school, the park, the bus stop, the warehouse, the home . . . and of course the street. Ultimately these categories will slide into one another, and all buildings perform at least two functions at once. Suddenly, from nowhere to go there will be everywhere, even to the subculture *images noires*. To the dole office, council houses, police stations, factories, office blocks . . . even to Buckingham Palace. Cities will entwine their functions and their metaphors. There will be less and less difference between the city and the airport . . . All buildings will be doubles. Witness the extraordinary new 'art' of scaffolding on conversion building sites. Since the beginning of the eighties, there have been incredible displays of steel poles, tarpaulins, plastic rubbish chutes, cranes and skips.

This was the spirit of Gamma-City's gallery takeover. With scaffolding on the outside, and elements from the street, like the zebra crossing, extending inside, it planted a terrain of flux around the viewer. With its loose system for dividing the conditions of the city into *market place* and *boudoir*, it interlaced full-sized objects designed for imaginary inhabitants of Gamma-City (or London if you like) with riotously three-dimensional drawings showing the Gamma effect on a sample range of London streets and living-rooms.

The accompanying manifesto proclaimed: 'Our cities are museums of the old order of logical compartments, yet undone and overlaid so often that movement has crept back in by accident.' By looking at what exists, we found our goals already alive, but hidden in the ordinary. 'Gamma-City architecture looks for clues under stones . . . near railway stations, beneath motorways or on the seventeenth floors of tower blocks.' We found city *situations* which were all too ready to be converted. We advised a subtle application of energy, archaeology, irrationality and even elegance. Then these ordinary sites could become 'Gamma situations', and as such would be capable of tipping the balance towards visibility. Gamma-City's six-point charter read as follows:

Think of an intermediary architecture on that edge between people's lives and the given city, city furniture poised to refurbish rather than rebuild.

Unpick the situation until bare signs show through, then expand them and spread them out to make space really work as a trigger for experience.

The interweaving of diverse function should be seen as positive. Hence look upon tangled road-rail junctions, building sites and converted factories as Gamma-places built by accident.

Build in fictional gestures and narrative sidesteps, because peripheral ingredients can upgrade reality when thrown in with it.

Customize situations with new means and new technologies, not as futurology, but as taking stock. Tape decks, discdrives and VTRs have outgrown their status as commodities. They're spare parts of the architecture of our daily lives.

Use materials to exploit their differences. Bend them, stretch them, paint them and erode them, use their contortions to build impulse into dynamic form. We want sensual architecture, architecture which stimulates.

The suggestion is to treat the street as an applicable architectural principle. In Gamma-City, the model of the street underwrites all architectural experience, and, as such, can be transferred into any spatial situation. At a certain point, read the street as a sign for the discourse of events, as a model of dramatic continuity within which narrative is anticipated.

The street also renews its parallel with television, or more specifically with video – especially in its computer graphics mode. Together, existing architecture and experiential codes form the soundtrack, to which the moving image can be added as the layer which brings out the narrative. Promotion videos are an afterthought to the song, and can seem illustrative, indeed trivial. The fact is they succeed in creating a total 'reality' based on representation. They create a fluid artificial space closer to architecture than to film, because they are not purely finite or sequential. They engage repetition and overlay, the ordinary and the subliminal. This urban video condition is already upon some cities, particularly in Japan. There buildings and streets are so intertwined that it is hard to define either. It won't be long before their lifts have traffic lights. The streets have piped music and ten times more signs than necessary to advertise what goes on in the rooms behind them.

Curiously, my first opportunities to build narrative architecture arose in Japan rather than in Britain, although not necessarily because the clients there are more enlightened. In terms of ideas, they tend to believe in the output of the West more wholeheartedly than we do. Perhaps because buildings there grow like weeds (there is the money to water them), disbelief is suspended. Only in Tokyo was I able to hang an aircraft wing over a café window two storeys high, thus realizing an idea in a pre-NATO project drawn in 1981; only there has it been possible to graft entire scenarios on to cafés and shops, in order to elevate their basic purpose into a fluid narrative dimension, and do better business.

In Britain, street-culture has already duplicated the city, and made a video narrative out of it, but not at the scale of architecture. Fashion shops and quirky one-night clubs and cafés have started to connect, forming many simultaneous city software systems linked by streets, cables and satellite dishes. In this we see potential accord between electronic representation and an almost archaic desire for expressive theatricality. The fortunate fact is that the compacting of functions which technology allows makes space for the theatrical dimension. At last we can play with the symbolic in architecture without worrying about it being dismissed as decoration.

Signs on the screen

Baudrillard's conclusion is that 'We are no longer a partner of the drama of alienation; we live in the ecstasy of communication. And this ecstasy is obscene':

> Today there is a whole pornography of information and communication, that is to say, of circuits and networks, a pornography of all functions and objects in their readability, their fluidity, their availability, their regulation, in their forced signification, in their performativity, in their branching, in their polyvalence, in their free expression.[20]

It is exactly this ecstasy which I applaud, if, that is, it can be freely experimented with by all of us. The role of architecture must be central, not because architecture is directly political, nor could it ever be, but because it is the duty of architecture to provide a usable laboratory with some decent equipment. The poverty of architecture has lasted long enough. This play with the erratic dimensions of perception is part of everybody's life – to the extent that our sense of space has changed fundamentally. Space, in the old architectural definition, relied on objects and how they looked. Space now synthesizes form, information and perception. It involves completely new rituals, like using VDUs and floppy discs. It relies on *hidden* information at every level.

And since we live in a software world, the challenge for architecture is completely new. On the one hand, it must sympathize with the software/underemployment/self-expression mix of conditions; on the other, it must expand the environment into a system of dramatized cultural markers that create a narrative pressure on the software space between them. Real-life architecture must dismantle its finite stance, by simultaneously aggregating and disintegrating. It must learn to deal with processes as well as products.

The first buildings to have emerged from NATO's programme are not just about the physical components of environments, but about the processes, signs and software which circumscribe the programmes that define the way we act, communicate and use the world. Once you start looking at environments as soft, you have to contrast design in the mechanical age (and this applies, obviously, as much to buildings as it does to products and technical systems), to design in the information age, which is concerned not so much with 'result' as with the *process of use*.

We architects cannot for ever avoid integrating this dynamic structure into the way we work, but to do so we will need some fairly radical 'deprogramming'. The process of design must anticipate the result by working within the same conceptual territory as the desired result. Oliva's explanations of *trans-avant-garde* art forecast the same attention to process:

> In the new attitude that sees art as a process, the world is arbitrarily defrozen from its verticality and placed on a horizontal plane, on which the imagination of the artist [*or the architect*] is exercised individually.[21]

If you are an architect you must be a new kind of Renaissance man – moviemaker, social forecaster, artist, inhabitant – and learn to switch roles as a key aspect of designing. You must learn to tap schizophrenia at all levels, in terms of thinking and drawing, in terms of imagining events and designing buildings fit to stage them. You must never be trapped by style. The architect who follows one aesthetic is dead. The expression must grow out of the situation. Replace style with attitude.

The way cities work has changed for good, and so has the professional role of architecture. From now on none of us, and yet all of us, will be professionals. Play with excess, but keep it sharp. The story of the street is usable allegory. But life itself is the real architecture, so let's use it.

Nigel Coates

REFERENCES

1 Berman, Marshall, *All That Is Solid Melts Into Air*, New York, 1982, p.168.
2 Baudrillard, Jean, 'The Ecstasy of Communication', in *Postmodern Culture* (ed. Hal Foster), Port Townsend, Washington, 1983, p.128.
3 Eisenstein, Serge, *The Film Sense*, London, 1943, p.33.
4 Venturi, Robert, *Complexity and Contradiction in Architecture*, New York, 1966, p.47.
5 Tomashevsky, Boris, 'Thematics', in *Russian Formalist Criticism* (ed. Lee Lemon and Marion Reis), Nebraska, 1965, p.85.
6 Oliva, Achille Bonito, *Avanguardia Transavanguardia*, Milan, 1982, p. 150.
7 Ibid., p.148.
8 Hatton, Brian, 'Who is Sylvia, What is NATO?', in ZG, No 13, Political Fictions.
9 York, Peter, *Style Wars*, London, 1980.
10 Brooks, Rosetta, 'Between the Street and the Screen', in ZG, No 6, Street Vision.
11 Hebdige, Dick, *Subculture, the Meaning of Style*, London, 1979, p.103.
12 Ibid., p.132.
13 Hatton, Brian, 'Ghosts in the Glass', in ZG, No 6, Street Vision.
14 Ibid.
15 Baudrillard, op. cit., p.130.
16 Ibid., p.129.
17 Coates, Nigel, 'New Clubs at Large', in AA Files Vol. I, No 1 Autumn 1981.
18 'World's End', Kings Road, was designed by Powell-Tuck Connor & Orefelt.
19 Coates, Nigel, 'Gamma-City Manifesto', *NATO Magazine No.3*, c/o Architectural Association, London, 1985.
20 Baudrillard, op. cit., pp. 130-1.
21 Oliva, op. cit., p.147.

PRODUCT
·
ORNAMENT
·
CRAFT

—7—

The search for a postmodern aesthetic

•

PETER FULLER

In a notorious passage, Adolf Loos, that most philistine of architects, declared that ornament was a crime. He argued that the greatness of the Modern Age lay in its 'inability to produce a new form of decoration'. Nor was this view in any way exceptional. Until recently, anti-ornamentalism has remained one of the key dogmas of the modern movement in art and design. I believe that the destruction of ornament within the Modernist movement was one of the cultural crimes of our age. Ornament is, as Joan Evans wrote, a *speculum minus* of human life, 'darkly reflecting the web of man's thought and feeling'. But we cannot simply *will* a new system of sound ornament into being and apply it to our goods and buildings. For its destruction revealed the underlying emptiness of the aesthetic, ethical and spiritual life of that age. No arbitrary 'New Ornamentalism' can fill that void.

Of course, much has changed since Loos' day; indeed the concerns of Loos, and many of his contemporaries, seem almost quaint in the era of the new electronics. None the less, I believe that many of the most significant and destructive Modernist assumptions are built in to those design movements which are commonly described as 'Post-Modernist'. A genuinely 'postmodern' design aesthetic will not be possible until those assumptions have been examined, and eradicated. Indeed, the constructive tasks facing designers today are, as I hope to demonstrate, essentially *conservationist* and *recuperative*.

There are those who will no doubt say that the position I am about to elaborate is nostalgic and 'reactionary'. In fact, it involves recognition of the necessity of change from the antiquated aesthetic system of Modernism. For today, Modernism has lost any claim it may once have possessed to modernity. It finds itself in the position of an ageing dictator whose power, influence and credibility have already failed, and from whom international support has fallen away. Modernism resembles a teetering oligarch in another way, too. It has always tended to re-interpret the past from its own perspective, even when that has necessitated the most wilful of misrepresentations. Before we can point in the direction of a genuinely 'postmodern' aesthetic, we must attempt to unravel those inbuilt distortions. Here, I intend to advance the process by taking a fresh look at Nikolaus Pevsner's *Pioneers of Modern Design*. First published in 1936, this text has been through several editions and revisions; it has provided the staple introduction to the history of modern design for students in Britain for half a century. In many ways, *Pioneers* was a gospel of the Modern Movement and, like other gospels, it attempts rather more than the telling of a story.

Pevsner begins his book by quoting Ruskin – 'Ornamentation is the principal part of architecture' – and ridicules the 'battle of the styles' which flowed out of such ideas. Nonetheless it soon becomes apparent that *Pioneers* is itself a move in a battle for a style. Pevsner explains that the 'chief aim' of his book is 'to prove that the new style, the genuine and legitimate style of our century, was achieved by 1914'. Its genuineness and legitimacy, of course, sprang from the summit of neither Mount Olympus nor Mount Sinai; none the less Pevsner makes it clear that this century's style, like that of any other, was in no sense simply 'functional', but rather issued forth from faiths and beliefs:

> The Modern Movement in architecture, in order to be fully expressive of the twentieth century, had to possess . . . the faith in science and technology, in social science and rational planning, and the romantic faith in speed and the roar of machines.

One of the main theoretical problems facing Pevsner was to show how all that was 'progressive' in nineteenth-century design pointed irreversibly towards this one genuine and legitimate style. He began by considering the case of William Morris, whom he declared to have been 'the true prophet' of the twentieth century, because Morris believed that art should not be for a few, but for all:

> We owe it to him that an ordinary man's dwelling-house has once more become a worthy object of the architect's thought, and a chair, a wall-paper or a vase a worthy object of the artist's imagination.

Here, Pevsner maintained, we have the 'fundamental meaning' of Morris's life and work. But Morris was unfortunately held back by something which Pevsner describes as his 'historicism'; Morris 'remained committed to nineteenth-century style and nineteenth-century prejudices'. He suffered, in Pevsner's view, from an unfortunate 'hatred towards modern methods of production' and tended to look back to the medieval world, rather than forwards towards the 'progressive' era of complete mechanization. Surprisingly, Pevsner argued that in certain respects Charles R. Ashbee surpassed the 'intellectual Ludditism' of Morris and arrived at a 'genuinely progressive attitude' towards the machine. Surprisingly, because Ashbee is best known as the founder of the Guild and School of Handicraft, which flourished in the medieval town of Chipping Campden in the Cotswolds. Even Morris found Ashbee's Arts and Crafts attitudes hard to stomach. But Pevsner maintains that in his later life Ashbee underwent a change of heart and that:

> The first axiom of his last two books on art, published after 1910, is that

'Modern civilization rests on machinery, and no system for the encouragement or the endowment of the teaching of the arts can be sound that does not recognize this.'

However, Pevsner explained that there was 'an immense difference' between the sort of grudging acknowledgement of machinery to be found in Ashbee (or Lewis Day and John Sedding) and 'the wholehearted welcome' which he believed it received in the writings of the leaders of the next generation – none of whom, Pevsner announced almost triumphantly, was English. He went on to argue that the first architects to admire the machine and to understand its essential character and its consequences in the relation of architecture and design to ornamentation were two Austrians, two Americans and a Belgian: Otto Wagner, Adolf Loos, Louis Sullivan, Frank Lloyd Wright and Henri van de Velde. Although 'decisively stimulated in their thoughts by England' these pioneers progressed beyond the English in their hostility to ornament, their refusal of medievalism, enthusiasm for The Machine and 'progressive' recognition that, in van de Velde's words, engineers were 'the architects of the present day'.

None the less, in America, and 'in most European countries as well', the theory of Modernism was isolated: only a few scattered individuals had the perspicacity to recognize that engineering had displaced architecture, and the machine had transcended the vexatious problem of style. 'To achieve a wide movement promoting these new ideas,' Pevsner comments, 'is undeniably the merit of German architects and writers' – like Hermann Muthesius, proponent of 'standardization'; Alfred Lichtwark, apostle of the *Neue Sachlichkeit*, the new objectivity in art and design; and Paul Schultze-Naumburg, author of *Kulturarbeiten* (who later became a leading Nazi theorist on art and design). These Germans fully grasped the beliefs that informed Modernism: they were the true practitioners of the only 'genuine and legitimate style of our century' because they sincerely believed not only in science, but also in 'social science and rational planning', and they were moved by the glamour of technology and 'the roar of machines'.

Thus, Pevsner reasoned:

Morris had started the [Modern] movement by reviving handicraft as an art worthy of the best men's efforts, the pioneers about 1900 had gone further by discovering the immense, untried possibilities of machine art . . . Morris laid the foundation of the modern style; with Gropius its character was ultimately determined.

Predictably, Pevsner was critical of movements like Art Nouveau, which seemed to him to be decorative deviations from the clear mainstream of architectural 'progress' towards the century's 'legitimate' style. 'Art Nouveau,' he declared in *The Sources of Modern Architecture and Design*, 'is indeed very largely a matter of decoration . . . and it is furthermore largely a matter of surface decoration.' Gaudi, who was not discussed in the first edition of *Pioneers*, occupied the aberrant position 'of the individualist-craftsman, the outsider, the lonely, do-it-yourself inventor'. It was just such 'individualism' which, in Pevsner's view, tied Art Nouveau 'to the century at whose end it stands' and rendered it guilty of 'resisting the needs and declining the responsibilities of the new century'. But his ultimate objection to the decorative schemes of Art Nouveau was thoroughly Ruskinian, or at least moralistic. 'Art Nouveau,' he complained, 'can only be appreciated on purely aesthetic grounds – and its products might well be called unprincipled.' Indeed, Pevsner believed that Muthesius's 'victory' on the standardization question would rapidly have been demonstrated internationally, 'if the outbreak of the First World War had not disrupted European unity and held up cultural progress'.

As it was, of course, the arrow of 'progress' was taken up by Walter Gropius, who had worked out a memorandum on standardization and mass production of small houses as early as 1909. For Gropius's achievement, Pevsner's praise knew no bounds: the *Pioneers* ends with a notorious comparison between the 'Model Factory' which Gropius and Meyer exhibited at the Werkbund Exhibition in Cologne in 1914, and the discovery of the Gothic arch.

The rhetoric of Pevsner's *Pioneers* was reflected in the writings of his 'progressive' contemporaries in Britain, such as Herbert Read, and J. M. Richards. 'The machine,' wrote Read, 'has rejected ornament; and the machine has everywhere established itself. We are irrevocably committed to a machine age.' Richards explained that modern buildings were not enriched with conventional ornament because their parts were made by machines, 'and applied ornament is not the machine's method of beautification.' For many years Pevsner's historical account was accepted without criticism; writers as diverse as Ray Watkinson and Gillian Naylor tended to see William Morris and the Arts and Crafts movement as proto-modernists, significant as precursors of the twentieth century's machine aesthetic.

But Naylor is among those who have recently changed their minds. Not surprisingly, perhaps, for the closer we examine Pevsner's case concerning Morris, the less substance it seems to have. It really makes no more sense to see Morris as a 'pioneer' of Modernism than to proclaim R. H. Tawney as a 'pioneer' of monetarism. (Tawney laid the foundation of modern economics; but he would not necessarily associate himself with the policies of Margaret Thatcher and Ronald Reagan.) The view I want to put forward here is in many ways the inverse of Pevsner's. Achievement in design in the later nineteenth century depended upon the capacity to resist the relentless onslaughts of the machine. This Morris, and Ashbee, were able to do in large part because they conserved aspects of the continuing Gothic tradition, and refused to allow mechanization to displace aesthetic production. In so far as British design has achieved anything in this century, its strength has lain at least as much in its *conservationism* as in its modernity. Similarly, the strength of the American 'pioneers' lay in the extent to which they were not simply engineers.

The trouble with the German design which Pevsner regards as thoroughly modern was that it broke entirely with that earlier tradition: if Pevsner's thesis concerning the cultural 'braking' effects of World War One is correct, then perhaps we have more to thank that appalling conflagration for than ever we believed possible.

For example, Pevsner contrasts Morris's chintz called 'Honeysuckle' with a design for a silk shawl, exhibited at the Great Exhibition, by the now forgotten E. Hartneck, a Frenchman. Pevsner claims that the dependence of Morris on past styles has been overrated; there is, he says, a 'fundamental novelty' to 'Honeysuckle', exemplified in its clarity and sobriety. He insists that this 'revival of decorative honesty' counts for far more than any 'connection with bygone styles'. On the other hand, he dismisses the shawl as a 'thoughtless concoction', and as merely 'bad imitation vulgarizing eighteenth-century licence'.

But there are problems with this line of reasoning. Pevsner can be excused for misdating Morris's chintz, which in the first edition of *Pioneers* he placed in 1883, since the chronology of Morris's patterns remained obscure until the late 1950s. It is surprising, however, that he did not correct this error in later editions of the book. In 1959, Peter Floud published his pioneering paper 'Dating Morris Patterns' in *The Architectural Review*. Floud did not specifically discuss 'Honeysuckle', but as a result of his researches this chintz has been definitively dated 1876 – the year when, it so happens, Morris also made his first designs for woven fabrics. Morris had just been appointed an examiner of students' work in the South Kensington Museum; thanks to Floud we now know not only that he took advantage of the opportunity to study the medieval textiles there, but which examples he studied, and when.

Floud demonstrated how between 1876 and 1883 most of Morris's chintz designs were based on rigid 'turn-over' patterns – where the motifs form precise mirror images on either side of a vertical axis. He argued that, in the period 1876 to 1883, Morris abandoned the 'naturalism' of his earlier work in favour of 'the use of conventional symbols derived from a study of historic textiles'. The strength of 'Honeysuckle' seems to derive from the way in which it combines Morris's earlier direct observation of nature with the awakening of his re-discovery of medieval tradition.

There was nothing *progressive*, let alone prophetic, about this design, and no way in which it prefigured, or foreran, the ethics or aesthetics of Modernism, which by Pevsner's own account have precious little to do with 'decorative honesty' anyway. Indeed, even in relation to designers of his own day, Morris's approach to pattern-making was self-consciously conservative, and (in an aesthetic sense) reactionary. (Floud appears to have believed – in my view quite unjustly – that Morris's pattern-making work *declined* from 1876 onwards.) While 'Honeysuckle' openly flaunts the glories of *naturalism* and *tradition*, the work of younger designers such as Lewis Day and Christopher Dresser was becoming increasingly abstract. They were designing for industrial production:

Morris may well have intended 'Honeysuckle' to teach them a thing or two about the value of what they were abandoning. Nor could Pevsner have defended himself with the argument that 'Honeysuckle' shows a peculiar appropriateness between its decorative forms and the materials used. For, as Floud himself observed, the 'turn-over' type of pattern which Morris exploits here was 'particularly suitable for weaving but not for block-printing'. A chintz is, of course, block-printed and it is unlikely that Morris would have designed one in this way if he was not really, at that time, rather more interested in woven textiles.

As Floud wrote elsewhere, Morris's best patterns 'have a classic, timeless, quality which cuts across the normal concepts of changing fashion'; but if we attempt any analysis of what, beyond individual genius, gave rise to that quality we are led in precisely the opposite directions to those which design was to take in the twentieth century.

Indeed, Pevsner's position would have been more consistent if he had proposed Hartneck's Great Exhibition shawl as an early example of the emerging machine aesthetic. The suggestion is not a facetious one: the design for the shawl is typical of the sort of thing which spread throughout Europe with the arrival of the Jacquard loom, and the designer-card-cutter. The decorative dishonesty of this work (which is not to be denied) eventually convinced many that, in Richards's phrase, 'ornament is not the machine's method of beautification'. Those interested in the ornamental crafts, like Morris, recognized the necessity of a conservative aesthetic position; whereas Modernists began to perceive that the future of machine production lay with an anti-ornamentalist 'functionalism'. In other words, Henry Cole (whom Pevsner constantly jibed against) and *not* William Morris 'laid the foundation' of the style whose character was 'ultimately determined' by the later Gropius.

The problem is Pevsner's assumption in *Pioneers* that the kernel of Morris's ideas was his affirmation of art for all; and his insistence that Morris's actual craft practices – involving the revival of medieval tradition, 'natural' materials and suspicion of mechanical production – were just a disposable 'historicist' husk which could be thrown away without any real danger to the underlying theory. But Morris believed that a machine could make anything – except a work of art. When he wrote *News From Nowhere*, his utopian romance, machines entered into it only as a hidden source of power; but hand-made decoration abounded. Morris made one of the inhabitants of his dream paradise explain: 'The energies of mankind are chiefly of use to them for [ornamental] work; for in that direction I can see no end to the work, while in many others a limit does seem possible.' He would not have regarded the replacement of aesthetic work by mechanical production as a fulfilment of the 'decorative honesty' of 'Honeysuckle'; he would have seen it as 'art for no one', rather than 'art for all'.

Similarly, Pevsner's identification of Ashbee as the figure who made the decisive break from a Morrisian 'historicism' is based on the misinterpretation of a single phrase, rather than on serious assessment of his life's work. As Alan Crawford puts it in his recent study of Ashbee:

> But in the end, the Pevsnerian view, the view which concentrates attention on the 'forward-looking' elements in Ashbee's work is inaccurate, unbalanced and unsympathetic. It is inaccurate because Ashbee did not change his fundamental convictions in 1911; there was no abandoning of the Arts and Crafts, no adopting of the Modern Movement at that time; and if advocates of this view would take the trouble to read the first chapter of *Should We Stop Teaching Art*, from which they so regularly quote, they would see that in pronouncing the axiom 'Modern Civilization rests on Machinery . . .', Ashbee, so far from abandoning the Arts and Crafts Movement, was actually stating its *raison d'être* as clearly as he could.

Crawford declares that Ashbee, for better or worse, was 'no less than a full-blown, drastic, Romantic anti-Modernist, shaking his cultured fist at the birth of the modern world'. He recognizes this interpretation may be pretentious, but adds that it probably touches Ashbee at more points than does Pevsner.

And so, despite the mythology of the *Pioneers*, it is important to emphasize that the best aspects of British design in the later nineteenth century were essentially *conservative*, and even reactionary. They were inspired by a sense of tradition and a vision of nature, and owed little or nothing to concepts of technological 'progress'. The weakest design was, again and again, produced by those who had most enthusiastically espoused the idea of a machine aesthetic.

Nor is it just a matter of Pevsner's distorting the real nature of the British achievement. What he says about the second generation, the 'pioneer' Americans, is also misleading. For, as with Ashbee, Pevsner's assessments of, say, Louis Sullivan and Frank Lloyd Wright, depend far more on verbal asides than on what they actually did as architects and designers. Thus, for example, he puts a good deal of emphasis on a quotation from Sullivan, to the effect that ornament 'was mentally a luxury, not a necessary' and that 'It would be greatly for our aesthetic good, if we should refrain entirely from the use of ornament for a period of years in order that our thought might concentrate acutely upon the production of buildings well formed and comely in the nude.' Similarly, Sullivan's sometime associate Frank Lloyd Wright is praised for his remarks about the 'emancipation' of the craftsman 'in humbly learning from the machine'. Later we are told that Wright's 'outstanding importance lies in the fact that nobody else had by 1904 come so near to the style of today in his actual buildings'. (The style 'of today' was always for Pevsner the most 'progressive', i.e. the best.)

But Pevsner is conspicuously uncomfortable when dealing with the profusion of ornament which constituted such an important part of Sullivan's actual work:

> How Sullivan came to evolve these curious tangles of tendrils, cabbagy,

scalloped leaves and coral reef growths remains a mystery. Can they really rest on no more promising ground than Gray's *Botany*? Or can one dimly recognize behind them the cabbagy forms of Gothic Revival foliage? Another look at Burges's fireplace might be advisable.

He simply ignored Frank Lloyd Wright's equally complicated, though very different, decorative systems. He claimed that in his dismissal of handicraft and ornament, Wright's position in 1901 was 'almost identical with that of the most advanced thinkers on the future of art and architecture today'. Pevsner was, of course, right to imply that the ornamental systems of Sullivan and Wright distinguished their work from the full-blown 'Modernism' of the twentieth century; but a large part of their greatness as architects rather than engineers lay in their retention and development of this 'reactionary' ornament.

Sullivan's ornament depended not only on its relationship to *natural forms* ('curious tangles of tendrils, cabbagy, scalloped leaves . . .') but also on its self-conscious 'historicizing', on the medievalism of the nineteenth-century *English* Gothic Revival, perhaps even on William Burges.

Wright's dependence on Ruskin and Morris was deep, and often acknowledged. Although his own decorative schemes were often (but not always) rectilinear, they bear a self-evident similarity not only to those of Charles Rennie Mackintosh, but also to Charles Ashbee's. Indeed, Ashbee's influence on Wright was confirmed through their close personal friendship. Wright invited Ashbee to contribute a preface to his *Ausgeführte Bauten und Entwurfe*, in which Ashbee wrote:

> We may differ vitally in manner of expression, in our work, in our planning, in our touch, in the way we clothe our feeling for proportion, but although our problems differ essentially, we are altogether at one in our principles.

It is, I think, absurd to claim that Wright's importance lay in the extent to which his work led to the aridity of the International Style. The truth is rather that, whatever he may have said, Wright was a most reluctant and ambivalent Modernist: the greatness of his architecture depended upon the fruitful tension between his 'full-blown, drastic, Romantic anti-Modernism' and modernity.

There were, of course, those among Pevsner's *Pioneers* whose aesthetic positions were much less creatively equivocal, especially, perhaps, the Austrians and Germans he names. For example, Pevsner frequently refers to Adolf Loos as a *Pioneer* who was well aware of the British contribution, but who was determined to 'progress' further towards the 'legitimate' style of the twentieth century. Unlike Morris, Ashbee, Sullivan and Wright, Loos did indeed largely dispense with ornamental and decorative systems, not only in theory, but also in practice.

But it is instructive to consider the *reasons* Loos gave for his objections to ornament. In the first place, he did not like it because, he said, it was erotic. He regarded all forms of decoration as sexually regressive or 'polymorphously perverse', in the Freudian sense. Ornament, he thought, was characteristic of those groups whose sexual and sensual pleasures were of such a messy kind that they could not conform to the social requirements of the modern world. Ornament was symptomatic of children, who liked to scribble on lavatory walls; of criminals – 'there are prisons in which eighty per cent of the prisoners are tattooed'; 'degenerate aristocrats' – who persisted in their unfortunate preferences for rouge, frills and powdered periwigs; and for 'primitive' people, like the Red Indian and the Papuan who, according to Loos, tattooed 'his skin, his boat, his rudder, his oars; in short, everything he can get his hands on'.

But Loos delivered an equally swingeing but much less frequently quoted objection to ornament on economic grounds. He believed that ornamental work was simply 'wasted labour':

> Lack of ornament means shorter working hours and consequently higher wages. Chinese carvers work sixteen hours, American workers eight. If I pay as much for a smooth box as for a decorated one, the difference in labour time belongs to the worker. And if there were no ornament at all – a circumstance that will perhaps come true in a few millennia – a man would have to work only four hours instead of eight, for half the work done at present is still for ornamentation.

Pevsner persistently implied that the British had proved unable to 'progress' fully out of medievalist historicism into a Loosian, anti-ornamental Modernism because of the peculiarities of their cultural history:

> So long as the new style had been a matter which in practice concerned only the wealthier class, England could foot the bill. As soon as the problem began to embrace the people as a whole, other nations took the lead, nations that lived no longer, or had never lived, in the atmosphere of the *ancien régime*, nations that did not accept or did not know England's educational and social contrasts between the privileged classes and those in the suburbs and the slums.

In one sense, Pevsner was right: the reluctance of the British to embrace the machine aesthetic of incipient Modernism was a product of its cultural history. Indeed, despite the proselytizing of Pevsner, Read, Richards and co., Modernism never caught on in any exclusive sense in Britain. Fortunately, Lutyens was always more influential than Loos.

Pevsner is not the only commentator to have noticed that British history presents a paradox: the first nation to progress from feudalism to capitalism, the first to undergo an industrial revolution, Britain none the less underwent no violent confrontation between an *ancien régime* and an emergent bourgeois class. As a result its ruling elite retained a rural and aristocratic complexion, despite the convulsions of industrialization.

This peculiar history has often been associated with the persistence of English cultural pastoralism, to which all manner of ills have been attributed by commentators on both the left and the right. For example, Perry Anderson of the *New Left Review* once argued that this history inhibited the development of a radical and progressive bourgeois culture in Britain. (Such a culture was, he argued, only artificially inserted into our national life through the processes of immigration of European intellectuals, among whom he names Pevsner.) This absence of an intellectual centre, in Anderson's view, inhibited the development of an indigenous Marxism. Martin J. Wiener on the other hand, in his book *English Culture and the Decline of the Industrial Spirit*, tried to explain Britain's alleged recent failure in the manufacturing industries on the grounds that the British middle classes were, from the beginning, absorbed into 'a quasi-aristocratic elite, which nurtured both the rustic and nostalgic myth of an "English way of life".' He complained that this process led to an unfortunate transfer of interest and energies away from the creation of wealth, and to 'a pattern of industrial behaviour suspicious of change, reluctant to innovate, energetic only in maintaining the status quo'.

I do not wish to dispute the Anderson–Wiener description of Britain's historical development: but whether we regard the effects of that conjuncture as an inhibition on 'progress' (of a 'left' or 'right' variety) or as ultimately positive will depend upon our vision of the past, beliefs about the present and hopes for the future. Anderson once saw the future of socialism as being dependent upon the cutting of this cultural knot; similarly, Wiener argued that Margaret Thatcher's 'most fundamental challenge' might lie in her ability to change this 'nostalgic' frame of mind. Nor are these merely theoretical positions; today, *all* political parties are committed to the idea that 'progress' is synonymous with an increase in the quantity of produced goods. No ethic has more force than the appeal to the expansion of the productive process. For Margaret Thatcher, design can be said to succeed, or to fail, in so far as it affects, or fails to affect, what the Design Council recently described as, 'the success of British industry in today's highly competitive markets'. There are no indications that Britain's Labour Party radically dissents from this position. Needless to say, politicians in the West promoting productivity, often through the use of design, show no concern for the *pleasure* (whether sexual or otherwise) of the producers, nor, come to that, of consumers, nor yet much concern for the environment within which productive work is carried out and manufactured goods ultimately find their place.

I believe, however, that the strength of British design in the nineteenth century resulted from the continuation of aristocratic, rural and 'historicizing' components – let us say of the 'Gothic' tradition – or rather on their combination with, and reaction against, the immense forces of industrial and market growth. Far from being negative or 'historicist', this resilient 'Gothicism' was a positive affirmation of definite, yet threatened, values. Ruskin and Morris would have agreed with Loos that ornament could not be justified on utilitarian or market-economic grounds. But though neither of them knew much about oriental art, they certainly would not have regarded, say, the sixteen hours spent by Chinese carvers on a single box as 'wasted labour'. For Ruskin, ornament was that dimension which brought meaning and value to the man-made object; and for Morris, ornament testified to the 'joy in labour' of the producers. Sound ornament was, for both of them, the sign and guarantee of the spiritual dimension of human work and of the creativity of those who toiled. As such, it could have no price.

The question, for the *Pioneers*, came down to whether these – or something like them – were the human values, for which you stood; or whether you put your trust in 'science and technology, in social science and rational planning, and the romantic faith in speed and the roar of machines'. If you chose the latter, of course, then the temples at which you worshipped (if worship it could be called) would look rather different: they would be designed to express values which celebrated material production, and were 'progressive', plebian, dehumanizing and mechanical.

More than once, Pevsner attempted to argue that although the achievements of nineteenth- and twentieth-century engineering design looked very different from the great cathedrals, modern architectural forms and structures were not only 'functional' but also material embodiments of more abstract values. These values, however, he argued were anti-Gothic and anti-spiritual. Thus he ended *Pioneers* with this description of the Gropius and Meyer Model Factory:

> There is something sublime in this effortless mastery of material and weight. Never since the Sainte-Chapelle and the choir of Beauvais had the human art of building been so triumphant over matter. Yet the character of the new buildings is entirely un-Gothic.

Pevsner went on to say that, while in the thirteenth century all lines 'functional though they were' served the one artistic purpose of pointing heavenwards, to, as he puts it, 'a goal beyond this world', and walls were made translucent 'to carry the transcendental magic of saintly figures rendered in coloured glass', in the Gropius–Meyer factory, 'The glass walls are now clear and without mystery, the steel frame is hard, and its expression discourages all other-worldly speculation.' None the less, the building is, in Pevsner's view, symbolic of ideals and beliefs:

> It is the creative energy of this world in which we live and work and which we want to master, a world of science and technology, of speed and danger, of hard struggles and no personal security, that is glorified in Gropius's architecture, and as long as this is the world and these are its ambitions and problems, the style of Gropius and the other pioneers will be valid.

In other words, Pevsner recognized nothing specifically modern about 'functionalism': indeed, in his view, this was something modern buildings shared with their Gothic antecedents. It was the *values* expressed and affirmed through the changed, and yet still functional, forms of architectural modernism which distinguished it from the Gothic. It is clearly a nonsense to say that form follows function, since function itself is a derivative of values and beliefs.

Gothic architecture indeed began with structural change – but these changes were, as Pevsner implies, rooted in symbolization; the pointed arch and the vaulted roof expressed a jubilant desire to transcend material existence; inevitably, such structural transformations drew with them new conceptions of ornament. As Joan Evans has put it:

> No great art has so paradoxical a beauty as the Gothic cathedral, for nowhere else have pure architecture and pure naturalism been so perfectly allied. All its beauty is of antithesis; the vastness of scale and the smallness of detail; the purity of line and the confused glow of colour; the sense of transcendent greatness and the extraordinary minuteness of symbolism; the inclusion of all that is simple and human in a whole that is religious and divine. Unity was the aim of the Middle Ages; and in their religious art they achieved a synthesis that remains unequalled.

Modernism will only appear to be the *legitimate* and *inevitable* style of our century if we have entirely relinquished that sense of spiritual belonging and ultimate unity; if we can find nothing in ourselves which corresponds to what John Rothenstein once called the 'irrepressible delight in the multitudinous aspects of the world and human society, in its Creator, in the beauty of nature and of man, in the exciting spectacle of the surrounding stream of life', which is so manifest in the architecture of the past. Not everyone, of course, has lost this sense: as recently as 1980, Paul Johnson described Giles Gilbert Scott's Anglican Cathedral at Liverpool – perhaps the last significant Gothic Revival building to be erected in this country – as 'Britain's greatest twentieth-century building'. As the arrogance of Modernist claims becomes more widely understood, it is, I think, becoming quite generally recognized that, in this instance at least, Johnson's architectural judgement has as much to commend it as Pevsner's.

The point, however, is not to argue for a 'return' to the Christian values which inspired the structures and decorations of the Gothic world and the best examples of the Gothic Revival alike; it may be, rather, that the time has come to relinquish the ethic of 'Modernism'. In one sense, there is nothing original in this position: 'Postmodernism' has been generally declared. Even the Modernists are arguing that the age of the Machine has given way to the age of Information Processing, and that this necessitates a revolution in design aesthetics. What is now required is not a refusal of the values of modernity, but rather a profound scepticism concerning them, an attitude of mind well expressed by the Cambridge historian Maurice Cowling:

> For it is still the case, whether disguised by cosmetic or not, that modernity is the practice we have and the life we lead, and that we have all to accept it and live as it commands us, even when we despise it.

The point, according to Cowling, is 'avoiding the odium of responsibility for modernity'; and this conservative stance was, of course, that adopted by the great designers at the time of the first industrial revolution – those, like Morris, whom Pevsner wrongly designated as 'pioneers of modern design'. Today, many of us can no more contemplate a 'return' to the lost illusions of religious belief, than Morris could in the nineteenth century. Some such odium can none the less be avoided if we replace the desire for mastery and 'exploitation' with an ethic which resembles that of the 'Gothic' world in so far as it recognizes our place within nature and our duties towards it. We need to abandon the aesthetics of the machine and the market place, and to replace them with a new aesthetic derived from precisely those dimensions of labour which Loos and his Modernist successors sought to eliminate; in short, we must shift from an ethic of production towards an ethic of 'livelihood', which celebrates the unity in diversity of nature, and our place within it.

Modernism, in both its 'left' and 'right' variants, has always involved a contempt for the world of nature. The elements of passivity in our relationship to nature, and our ultimate dependence upon it, were disguised through a rhetoric of triumph and conquest. Indeed, Modernists have tended to regard nature more as a pastoral abstraction, 'a thing of the past', than as a present and concrete reality.

But all human needs are ultimately dependent upon nature, in which, and through which (in the absence of God) we have our being. We may choose to avert our eyes from it and, like an impetuous child, assert our omnipotent independence, but nature remains the *sine qua non* of our physical and spiritual existence. Our belief in a capacity for domination of nature, and denial of our passivity in relation to it, can lead only to the spoliation of it. This has been well expressed by the biologist O. Wilson:

> The world began to yield, first to the agriculturists and then to technicians, merchants and circumnavigators. Humanity accelerated toward the machine antipode, heedless of the natural desire of the mind to keep the opposite as well. Now we are near the end. The inner voice murmurs *You went too far*, and disturbed the world, and gave away too much for your control of Nature.

Wilson entertains the possibility that this will be the hell we earned for realizing truth too late; but he does not subscribe to any of the fashionable secular eschatologies. He rather suggests that the same knowledge that brought the dilemma to its climax contains the solution. He argues that 'the urge to affiliate with other forms of life' is innate within our species, and designates this urge as 'biophilia'. This urge has somehow been violated by the spreading of machines throughout the gardens of the world; equally, however, in re-asserting itself in the face of a crumbling modernism, 'biophilia' suggests an ethic which contains the seeds of a possible secular redemption.

But what sort of aesthetics might issue from such an ethic? Would they necessarily be 'nostalgic', a replay of the forms and structures of the earlier

Christian sense of spiritual unity with the world? I think not. It was Gregory Bateson, the anthropologist, who first pointed out that, if we do not believe (as I do not) that the world is the 'created' product of mind, we must none the less accept that mind is a creation of nature – that, as it were, mind is somehow immanent within the evolutionary process, and therefore objectively discernible outside ourselves. All this speculation, he said, becomes almost platitude when we realize that both grammar and biological structure are products of communicational and organizational process. He went on to argue that the anatomy of a plant is a complex transformation of genotypic instructions, and that the 'language' of the genes, like any other language, must of necessity have contextual structure. He added that in all communication there must be a relevance between the contextual structure of the message and some structuring of the recipient: 'The tissues of the plant could not "read" the genotypic instructions carried in the chromosomes of every cell unless cell and tissue exist, at that given moment, in a contextual structure.'

I believe that part of the problem for a new aesthetics based on an imaginative response to nature, on the recovery of biophilia, has been our inability to 'read' and make sense of these 'natural languages', or to find any affective symbolic equivalents for them. But it may be that it is just here that the higher mathematics, physics and new information processing procedures, associated with advances in computer technology, can help. Of course, a new aesthetic will spring out of new beliefs, not out of a new technology; but like Modernism itself, the postmodern structures and patterns will be informed and shaped by new technologies. I hope, however, they will be expressive of very different sorts of values, that is, of traditional and conservationist values, which emphasize our sense of belonging to and unity with the Nature of which we are a part.

Bateson has demonstrated that 'logic and quantity turn out to be inappropriate devices for describing organisms and their interactions and internal organization.' But he did not assume that intuitions alone were sufficient. He insisted upon the value of thinking about the problems of order and disorder in the 'natural' universe, and he emphasized 'a considerable supply of tools of thought' which had been insufficiently used in this terrain. One of these might be the work recently carried out by Benoit B. Mandelbrot, the Harvard mathematician, into what he calls *The Fractal Geometry of Nature*.

It is a well-known criticism of modernity that it suffers from a linear – or 'progressive' – teleology, and the constraints of a Euclidean geometry. Darwin, notoriously, found it hard to account for the infinite complexity of the patterns with which the natural world presented him; indeed, there is justification in the charge levelled against him by that relentlessly anti-modernist poet Alfred Noyes:

He only saw
This blaze of colour, the flash that lured the eye.
He did not see the exquisite pattern there,
The diamonded fans of the under-wing,
Inlaid with intricate harmonies of design;
The delicate little octagons of pearl,
The moons like infinitesimal fairy flowers,
The lozenges of gold, and grey and blue,
All ordered in an intellectual scheme,
Where form to form responded and faint lights
Echoed faint lights, and shadowy fringes ran
Like elfin curtains on a silvery thread.
Shadow replying to shadow through the whole.

Neither 'natural' nor 'sexual' selection can fully account for, say, the variations in the whorls on each individual's fingertips, or the infinite variety of the patterns on the fruit-fly. Noyes was describing what the critic Walter Jerrold has called 'a new kind of teleology' one which recognizes 'creative activity and design, not in the useful as Paley did, but in what appears to be useless, except as sheer beauty'. In other words, Noyes inverted the traditional argument from design. For him, the existence of a Creator was implied not so much by the perfect functioning of the mechanism of the watch, as by the richness, intricacy and apparent freedom from necessity of the ornamentation encrusting its case. But can we discuss these 'shadowy fringes' without resorting, once more, to an 'unseen Composer'? According to Mandelbrot, we can.

Mandelbrot's work begins with the assertion of a self-evident truth: that clouds are not spheres, mountains are not cones, and lightning does not travel in a straight line. This fact, he points out, was acknowledged in pre-scientific theories of creation: thus he makes much of the illustration which forms the frontispiece of a famous Bible Moralisée, compiled between 1220 and 1250, which is now in the Austrian National Library in Vienna. This reveals a familiar image of God as the Great Geometer, creating the world with his dividers; but, Mandelbrot stresses, the illustrator has emphasized three different kinds of form in this newly created world, 'circles, waves and "wiggles"'. He goes on to say that circles and waves have benefited from colossal investments of effort by man, and that they form the very foundation of science. 'In comparison,' he adds, '"wiggles" have been left almost totally untouched.' Mandelbrot claims to have conceived and developed an entirely new geometry of nature which is capable of describing many of the irregular and fragmented patterns around us; this geometry, he says, 'reveals a totally new world of plastic beauty' whose aesthetic implications appear boundless. The core of Mandelbrot's argument is the identification of a new family of shapes to which he has given the name 'fractals'. These involve chance, but, according to Mandelbrot, both their regularities and their irregularities are statistical. His argument is sometimes obscure, and can be hard for the non-mathematician to follow, but F. J. Dyson has provided a clarifying exposition. Dyson points out that classical mathematics had its roots in the regular geometric structures of Euclid and the continuously evolving dynamics of Newton. But, Dyson says, modern mathematics began with Cantor's set theory and Peano's space-filling curve. Historically, the revolution was forced by the discovery of mathematical structures that did not fit the patterns of Euclid and Newton. At first these new structures were regarded as 'pathologi-cal', or a 'gallery of monsters', akin, according to Dyson, 'to the cubist painting and atonal music that were upsetting established standards of taste in the arts at about the same time'. At first, the mathematicians who created these monsters regarded them as important in showing that the world of pure mathematics contained a richness of possibilities going far beyond the simple structures that they saw in Nature. And so modern mathematics came to maturity in the belief that it had transcended completely the limitations imposed by its natural origins. But, following Mandelbrot, Dyson says that Nature today seems to be playing a joke on mathematicians. 'The nineteenth-century mathematicians,' he writes, 'may have been lacking in imagination, but Nature was not. The same pathological structures that the mathematicians invented to break loose from nineteenth-century naturalism turn out to be inherent in familiar objects all around us.' Mandelbrot maintains that scientists will be 'surprised and delight-ed to find that not a few shapes they had to call *grainy, hydra-like, in between, pimply, pocky, ramified, seaweedy, strange, tangled, tortuous, wiggly, wispy, wrinkled*, and the like, can henceforth be approached in rigorous and vigorous quantitative fashion.' But this surprise and delight need not necessarily be confined to scientists. Here, as elsewhere, Mandelbrot strongly implies that his mathematical work carries profound implications for artists and designers – indeed for what I would designate as the development of a true 'post-modern' aesthetic. Mandelbrot has endeavoured to demonstrate that 'The property of scaling that characterizes fractals is not only present in Nature, but in some of Man's most carefully crafted creations.' But, he adds, a paradox emerges here:

> Modern mathematics, music, painting and architecture may seem to be related to one another. But this is a superficial impression, notably in the context of architecture: a Mies van der Rohe building is a scalebound throwback to Euclid, while a high period Beaux Arts building is rich in fractal aspects.

This, I think, may give us a clue both to the fallacy of modernity, and to an important characteristic of an emerging 'postmodern' style. Intriguingly, these higher reaches of modern mathematics take us back, as well as forward: they seem to conserve, even as they innovate. Mandelbrot feels that he has come close to identifying what might be described, even by an atheist such as myself, as 'the signature of God'. Now I do not possess the necessary higher mathematics to evaluate his 'discoveries'. But I can say that I have been deeply struck by the fact that the geometry he has developed seems very similar in its aesthetic implications to those elaborate arguments which John Ruskin presented to explain the similarities of form between leaf structures, estuaries, mountain ranges, Gothic ornament and roof vaults. He, too, was aware of a 'grammar' of nature, which he felt had been somehow intuitively expressed in the greatest artistic and architectural achievements. Mandelbrot himself recognizes the blow he has dealt to the pride of the modern mathematicians, and claims he has confirmed Pascal's observation that imagination tires before Nature:

> I show that behind [the mathematicians'] very wildest creations, and unknown to them and to several generations of followers, lie worlds of interest to all those who celebrate Nature by trying to imitate it.

Ruskin, too, ceaselessly taught the poverty of even the finest of man's creations in comparison to the richness and variety of natural form. He advised the young artist to 'go to Nature in all singleness of heart' and to 'walk with her laboriously and trustingly, having no other thoughts but how best to penetrate her meaning, and remember her instruction; rejecting nothing, selecting nothing, and scorning nothing; believing all things to be right and good, and rejoicing always in the truth.' Once these words seemed to signify the depths of aesthetic reaction; but research like that of Mandelbrot confirms the accuracy of Ruskin's intuition.

We cannot, of course, 'prescribe' the appearances of a new style merely from our knowledge of this work; but this much, at least, can be said with some certainty: it is in these sorts of directions that the pioneers of postmodern design should be encouraged to look, and to learn. For it is out of respect for, and responses to, the profusion, constancy and infinite varieties of natural form, that the true 'Cathedrals of the Twenty-first Century' (whatever their functions may be) will come to be built.

SOURCES

Anderson, Perry, 'Components of the National Culture', *New Left Review*, No. 50, July-August 1968

Bateson, Gregory, *Steps to an Ecology of Mind*, London, 1973

———, *Mind and Nature*, London, 1979

Cowling, Maurice, *Religion and Public Doctrine in Modern England*, Vol.1, Cambridge, 1980

Crawford, Alan, *C.R.Ashbee*, New Haven and London, 1985

Evans, Joan, *Pattern: A Study of Ornament in Western Europe from 1180 to 1900*, Vol.I, Oxford, 1931

Floud, Peter, 'The Influence of South Kensington in Dating Morris Patterns', *The Architectural Review*, July 1959

Jerrold, Walter, *Alfred Noyes*, London, 1931

Loos, Adolf, 'Ornament and Crime', in *The Architecture of Adolf Loos*, Arts Council Exhibition Catalogue, London, 1985

Mandelbrot, Benoit B., *The Fractal Geometry of Nature*, Cambridge,Mass., 1980

Noyes, Alfred, *The Torch-Bearers*, Vol.11, London, 1930

Pevsner, Nikolaus, *Pioneers of Modern Design*, Harmondsworth, 1968

Read, Herbert, *Art and Industry*, London, 1934

Rothenstein, John, *British Art Since 1900*, London, 1962

Ruskin, John, *The Works of John Ruskin*, ed. E.T. Cook and Alexander Wedderburn, 39 vols., London, 1903-12

Wiener, Martin J., *English Culture and the Decline of the Industrial Spirit*, London, 1983

Wilson, E.O., *Biophilia*, New York, 1985

—8—

The ideal world of Vermeer's little lacemaker

•

PETER DORMER

Introduction

In this century the world's industrialized areas – in particular Scandinavia, Western Europe, Britain and North America – have sustained numbers of people who call themselves craftsmen and craftswomen. The persistence of the breed in the light of their marginal relationship to mainstream manufacturing is of interest. The irrelevance of craft work has caused it to mutate from being the livelihood of working-class artisans into an activity of self-expression for middle-class aesthetes or quasi-artists.

The official contemporary crafts world of museums, galleries and magazines is not concerned with sheet metal workers or artisans in concrete, since they represent 'trade'. Their exclusion is understandable given that the interests of the museum/gallery world are aesthetic and, moreover, concerned not with teams of people who work and make together but with individuals who either set the design and prescribe its manufacture or design and make the product entirely by themselves.

On the other hand, former tradesmen and women such as basket makers, fence builders, thatchers and a few other 'rural' crafts workers are admitted into the modern crafts world because these activities are old-fashioned and need preserving. Being old-fashioned they are also safe. Basket makers *et al.* have left the trade category and become a part of the acceptable 'aesthetic-in-opposition'. A man making baskets is opposing the technological aesthetic of the (highly skilled) man shaping the lining of a nuclear reactor. The issue is more complicated than that, of course. The lining of a reactor may in fact be beautiful but its beauty is chilling: a basket may be beautiful and symbolizes a life in harmony with nature; a nuclear reactor suggests to some people too much tampering with nature: the craft aesthetic is anti-technology, anti-science and anti-progress.

This essay considers three aspects of the craft phenomenon: the attractions of being a craftsperson; the failure of the art–craft concept; and the role of craft as domestic decoration in contemporary western society.

Peter Dormer

Jan Vermeer's *The Lace Maker* Paris, Louvre, © Giraudon

The appeal of craft work

One of the most popular paintings in the Western world is *The Lacemaker* by Jan Vermeer, in the Musée du Louvre, Paris. This tiny painting (24cm × 21cm) of a young woman at work touches so many imaginations because it conveys that sense of perfect happiness which most people find when they too are, like the lacemaker, totally absorbed in an interesting activity.

As a student I took a job in a chocolate factory: it required the use of both hands to sweep stacks of chocolate bars from one conveyor belt on to another running at right angles to it. It was a boring job, but if I became inattentive the chocolate bars would tumble to the floor. The dissatisfaction of the work resulted from the effort required in maintaining the attention it demanded. Vermeer's lacemaker looks as though she has no need to make an effort to be attentive: the work engrosses her. Her complete engagement with her task is like a reverie and takes her out of the world, possibly out of herself. She has an expression of interested calm, untroubled by worries or queries.

The lacemaker is to be envied, and people argue that crafts workers are fortunate to have occupations in which they can 'lose themselves'. Other observers are more critical of crafts work. They believe that the craft life can cause complacency and that too much balm can close the mind down.

Formulae and repetition are at the heart of many craft processes, as Tom Stoppard suggests in his play *Artist Descending a Staircase*: 'Talent without imagination gives us many useful things such as wicker baskets, Imagination without talent gives us modern art.' The public does not look to the crafts or the craftspeople for speculation, scepticism, questioning of assumptions, too much innovation or challenge. Nor, it appears, do many of the practitioners themselves.

Most of us are not craftspeople although a surprising number of us do some kind of craft-related activity – cooking, gardening, painting a door or a wall, washing a floor, driving a car. In each activity we are careful about what we are doing, but careful in the sense of keeping an eye on ourselves – ensuring that we take the right steps and avoid the false ones. What we tend not to do in such activities is rethink the procedures.

However, these craft activities have to be done well – they cannot be skimped, and this is another part of their attraction. With a badly washed floor it is obvious how and why the work has failed. And with a poorly turned piece of wood or a poorly made piece of lace there are clear criteria about what constitutes success or failure. Clear criteria are comforting. A lot of basic craft activity banishes thought, it can be immensely therapeutic, and, no doubt because of this, becoming a craftsman is immensely attractive to those who find active engagement with the wider world too disquieting.

Craft and craft-related activities are pleasurable, and the pleasure derives from doing something well that you know well how to do. The criteria for doing the job well and judging whether the job has been well done are known in advance. The best craft jobs are those where the mind and the body are engaged entirely as one in the process. For example, here is a well-known American potter writing about the craft of throwing pots on a wheel: 'Not only is the material managed directly in the hands and guided from the formless to the formed but the process is fast . . . Thought need not intervene between the action of the fingers, the hands, the eyes, and the realization of the form. It is one of those rare areas of activity where intent and deed are as one.'

The absorption in the craft tasks, the losing of one's self in the activity and the temporary absence of other thought, amounts to a banishment of scepticism. The physical effort involved in some craft also helps to banish scepticism. The business of loading and unloading a kiln, or setting up a lathe, or preparing materials, quickly falls into a rhythm of routine and for many craftsmen and women becomes a part of the craft's aesthetic appeal. To lose oneself in ordering and re-ordering one's work postpones the questioning of purpose and the setting of goals; and it is, after all, the setting of purpose and the striving for goals, that makes men and women worldly.

There is nothing innately wrong with escaping into one's work. Scientists, mathematicians, doctors, lawyers, automobile mechanics, all escape into interesting work. And it is good for the rest of us that this is so. When a doctor attends to you, you hope that he or she will be thoroughly engaged in the job. And we expect the same of the mechanic, the lawyer and the person building our house.

Yet in the case of the jobs just mentioned there also exists an overriding concept of responsibility to the patient or client – a responsibility which not only maintains the worker's commitment to the task in hand but also provides a wider, more worldly framework for the work than his or her own fascination with it. The responsibility to the client also provides the reason for doing the work.

In the past an approach to the local artisan for crockery or furniture or cloth entailed the same expectations of responsibility and service that we expect from a garage mechanic. The potter, the carpenter and the weaver were making things for use and for service. Undoubtedly their success as potters, carpenters and weavers was in direct relation to how well they satisfied customers in terms of quality and value for money. Thus Vermeer's lacemaker, happy though she is in her work, is quite likely to be conscious of the demands of the real world – she has to perform to a suitable standard.

The idea of service is central to the relationship between an artisan and the customer or a professional and the client. There are responsibilities to be met and expectations to be fulfilled.

In a practice as complex as medicine the concept of service is also complex and good standards are fixed by a mixture of professional self-regulation, good science and, increasingly, the intervention of the law. In artisan potting or furniture-making the concept of service was relatively straightforward. The notion of service in contemporary craft practice has become less clear-cut because the customer is no longer sure of his expectations and the maker has no very definite responsibilites. In a situation where a steady stream of people visit your workshop because they need to buy your cups and plates to use, everyone is clear on what is needed; but in a situation where people turn up to see what you are doing and might or might not buy something depending on the luck of your work appealing to their fancy, then the some of the rules are lost.

This is what has happened in craft – 'taking their fancy' has replaced 'serving their needs' or, as many craftsmen would prefer it, aesthetic value has replaced utility as the goal. What remains, however, is the question of whose taste becomes predominant – the 'popular' taste of the consumer or the particular (and possibly recondite) taste of the individual maker. What occurred for a while in the revival of crafts after World War Two began to shape up into a new, if less rigorous, contract of service between craftspeople and consumers.

In the 1950s and 1960s the crafts were supported by ordinary householders, not by museums. In all kinds of ways both the image and the practice of contemporary craft in that period was affirmative. It was a practice which enabled the reintroduction of texture, colour, variety of form into homes at a period (1945-1970 and beyond) when the mores of contemporary design appeared to deny these ingredients or, worse, when manufacturing companies across the world palmed the consumer off with poor finishes and indifferent forms. The contemporary craftsperson was irrelevant as a producer of strictly functional wares, but became highly relevant when people wanted to add something to their homes that fed their eyes and their fingers. Fine art had long since failed in this because it had been taken into the temples of the high art galleries and was, in any case, either too expensive or too meaningless or both. People bought the new craft because they liked it and related to it. This gave what the craftspeople were doing a genuine point. It was an act of service.

The post-war craftsperson was also peddling an ideology. He or she declared a commitment to a way of life. Usually the lifestyle involved moving to the country and seeking to be as independent as possible. The ideal was to live from work that was one's own and done to the highest possible standard. It was a way of turning away from the structured routine of twentieth-century life. Craftspeople anticipated by a decade the hippies of the late 1960s. And there is an important caveat. A lot of the work that was peddled as craft was quite horrible – it was amateur, ugly, sentimental and kitsch and it was bought by the consumer out of ignorance as to what 'hand-made' could mean. In ceramics especially, people bought things simply because they looked old fashioned. For some reason lumpenness was taken as the *sine qua non* of the integrity of handicraft. Nevertheless, there was also good work and the essential point remains that there was an attempt to keep faith or serve the ordinary consumer even though the trade had been transformed into a 'luxury' market.

The basis of the 'alternative' wares economy is simple enough: the pots and other furnishings produced by a craftsman should look different from machine products. How they functioned, or even whether they functioned, was much less relevant. People buying craft have disposable and surplus income. Craft ware, though it had no functional role, kept the shape and form of functional objects and it was bought because it symbolized something special – a way of life that challenged contemporary norms. The craftsmen's wares were expressive of the hand, and implicit in every craft product was the idea of one human being producing for another, rather than the anonymity which is implicit in mass production. With a single piece of furniture made by a man or a woman in a craft studio in Pennsylvania there was the suggestion of a personal relationship between maker and user, but with a car mass-produced in Detroit there was not.

It is conceivable that if industrial design had concentrated on a lumpen, expressive aesthetic the craft movement would have produced a De Stijl look, or something similar. The modern craftsperson is forced by the dominant mass-manufacturing combines to be the author of the aesthetic-in-opposition. The crafts' commercial foundation consists in being different.

And the way in which crafts have been retailed has confirmed their role of 'aesthetic-in-opposition'. Craft is difficult to buy except through selected stores, and most buying, especially until the mid-1970s was done at craft fairs or by people driving from the towns to rural craft studios. Such difficulties added to the craft product's special identity.

Different craft specialities developed differently: craft pottery tended to eschew fine workmanship – the mark of the potter confirmed its specialness and you were not to mind paying a little bit more for the privilege. But not too much. Craft pottery is (or was) relatively cheap. Craft furniture has never been cheap. And so, since a piece of hand-made furniture is inherently expensive, it made marketing sense to make the furniture express its expensiveness. For a period there was a fashion in woodcraft circles in America (and to a lesser degree in Britain) for revealing the joints: this meant the craftsman lavished skill on turning a practical component into an ornament purely to emphasize the overall value of the product.

However, in the early 1970s, especially in the United States and Britain (and then later in north-west Europe) a new breed of craftsperson came into existence. This new craftsperson set up in opposition to his or her own craft. For example, in the mid-1970s textile works appeared which were entirely functionless and which were intended by their makers to question the nature of weaving and challenge all the conventions of the craft of weaving. The same held true in basket-making, pottery, glass and jewellery. In the USA it reached its apotheosis (or nadir) with a group of potters dunking their heads in pails of liquid clay and then sitting around until their heads dried: the event was filmed on video.

The economic structure for this quasi-art has been provided in Britain, Scandinavia, the Netherlands and the USA by art school teaching, state museums purchasing for collections, the development of applied arts maga-zines, state grants and, especially in America, the existence of rich people willing to be persuaded by dedicated dealers and gallery owners that to buy the new craft was to buy the new art. As far as the new breed of craftsperson is concerned there was a wide degree of licence to be enjoyed. As long as he or she produced work which more or less conformed to the new quasi-art establish-ment's expectations of what craft as art should look like, then he or she was free to make all kinds of useless objects.

For the ambitious craftsperson anxious for recognition challenging the tradition of your craft was a good wheeze because it quickly gave you an identity. You became known as the person who had made jewellery too big to wear, pots too wobbly to handle, textiles that were either very small, very large or very non-existent because you had decided they were conceptual. Something rather sad and predictable has since occurred: craftsmen and craftswomen whose egos became too large for the small world of art craft then tried to take their new 'broken-all-the-rules-in-my-Art-Craft' work and get it accepted as art by the real art world. They were rejected, although some are still trying.

None of the major fine art galleries in New York, Berlin, Dusseldorf, Paris or London will deal in the work and it is seldom, if ever, featured in major exhibitions in museums of the status of the Museum of Modern Art, New York. The rejection has baffled the makers concerned. But to be fair to the craftspeople, their rejection need have little to do with the quality of their work as such.

For however much craftspeople have twisted and turned – dunked their heads in clay, made their baskets sculptural and their pots subversive – their attempts to make it as artists have been damned by the very materials they use. Media such as clay, glass and textiles are seen as archetypal craft media and people who work in them are automatically regarded as non-intellectual. In the contemporary fine art world any work which has a craft pedigree does not stand a chance of being accepted. Craft does not have intellectual connotations. True enough, the craftsperson has a position, but it is perceived as rural, reactionary, hidebound, skill-orientated and rooted in the ethics of toil and conservatism. This may be unfair, and it is certainly arbitrary. But what is and what is not 'Art' is decided by the art world and so, without the acceptance of the art world, the concept of the artist-craftsperson will have no currency and has no currency beyond the pages of the crafts magazines.

Running to fat

The period of rule-breaking and head-dunking in the crafts ended by the early 1980s. The contemporary craftsperson has attempted to find a niche half-way between handicraft and art. Some have been trying to re-establish the concept of the decorative or applied artist. Unfortunately, few of them willingly use the term 'decorative' because they find it pejorative. They are surely wrong. It is surely an honourable title, and the role of decorator is an honourable profession and certainly more so than producing obscurantist art that none but the New York art world can understand?

The constraints and benefits of being a decorative artist are these: for the craftsperson it means that he or she is not expected to generate new insights into the world or to construct brilliant metaphors. Rather than lead the avant garde in art we expect craftspeople to use what art had discovered in order to embellish, for the pleasure of the rest of us, the home and civic and institutional buildings. It is a role which requires the craftsperson to use skill and be admired for it, but which also expects him or her to produce work that makes sense to the rest of us. This is a part of the pact between decorative crafts and the consumer. We, the consumers, want to be delighted, impressed, surprised and cajoled, but not mystified or subverted. Mystification and subversion we leave to artists and from them we demand insight and intelligence of a very rare order indeed. As part of the deal for decorative artists we are not expecting craftspeople to measure up to Picasso.

Unfortunately the role of craft as a decorative art has been corrupted by the rise of postmodernism. Whatever postmodernism is (or was?), it resists swift summary. As a philosophical condition postmodernism has affected all aspects of culture, political, economic and scientific as well as artistic. Suffice it to say that during the 1970s in the West there was a gradual loss of faith in several political ideologies (but especially Marxism). There was also a loss of faith in disciplines such as town planning and even economic planning. And there was greater caution about applying science to everyday life – whether it was chemical science applied to food production or social science applied directly to low income families. These losses of faith and feelings of caution became the *Zeitgeist* of the 1980s.

Whenever there is doubt, uncertainty or fear people ring home to mother and in a sense that is what the architects and some designers have done: they have gone back to history and dug out things that have proved successful. Postmodernist art, architecture and design is not ashamed to use nostalgia as its dominant emotion. Almost all variations of classicism, Art Nouveau, Art Deco and a mish-mash of the Greek, the Egyptian and the oriental have been applied to the exteriors and interiors of buildings and influenced the design of the furnishings. Some of the results have been pleasant, many have been peculiar.

When the craftspeople, especially the Americans, saw what was happening they leapt to it. In glass, textiles and most recently and dramatically in furniture, they copied the postmodernist architects such as Michael Graves and Robert Venturi and attempted to outdo them. The craftspeople's reaction was, looking back, predictable, because craft, decorative art, having no intellectual impulse of its own, depends on other people for its energies and ideas. For example, for the first twenty years of the post-World War Two revival, the craftspeople of Europe and the USA were heavily dependent upon craft models provided by Japan and Korea. In America they also borrowed from abstract expressionism, then when Pop Art came along they seized on that, and when postmodernism came through there was no stopping them.

A combination of postmodernist excess and an ambition to be seen as an artist has tempted many a contemporary craftsperson into some highly skilled work of exaggerated design, size and complexity and hugely inflated prices. This phenomenon is most widespread in America, where there are more rich men and women prepared to buy the work for their new craft-art collections. The collections are frequently appalling and are, in essence, handicraft gone to fat. Nothing in art or design or architecture or craft is more foolish than the sight of modest ideas ballooning and buffeting on the thermals of rich ignorance. A catalogue of this confusion is available from the American Crafts Museum in New York: it is called *The Poetry of the Physical* and it is the book which accompanied the exhibition of the same name that was staged in the autumn of 1986.

In Europe, especially West Germany, Britain and France, there is less rampant tutti-frutti postmodernism in craft furniture and more of a nihilistic postmodernism styled up into a post-Holocaust chic of deliberately crude workmanship in foul materials. This work, too, is often both shallow and inflated. The work is supported, less by rich collectors, and more by contemporary museum curators.

Among those with a vested interest in craft there has been too much reluctance to admit that the world of craft is a world of modest ideas with a straightforward, commonplace vocabulary of familiar and functional forms which can be used purely decoratively. No pot or chair or table or glass vase can stand translation into a monument. The inherent modesty of craft is its strength. It is linked historically to the domestic environment. Perhaps the word 'handicraft' should be resurrected. It is a word that serves to bring the craft ambition back to earth and allows us to reaffirm the link between craft and the home and not craft and the museum or the gallery. (If the contemporary craftsperson wants to learn from the art world, then let it look at painters such as Vermeer or Giorgio Morandi: painters who have observed the small change of the domestic world and shown us its grace, its beauty and its solicitude.)

The function of craft in this stage of the twentieth century ought not to be the silly caperings after exaggerated effects of quasi-art funded by the ignorance of the *nouveaux riches* anxious to become collectors. It should instead be the art of familiar forms and understandable decoration for the ordinary home. Craft does not need to seek out a new decorative order: its main vocabulary – the variety of domestic artefacts, comprehensible to all – already exists. Craftspeople should concentrate on the fundamentals that lie at the base of craft – service and truth to materials.

This does not mean, however, that the craftsperson is not to think about new design; on the contrary, without constant rethinking he or she will merely reproduce what already exists and the work will stagnate. Handicraft is not an intellectual activity, but it is an intelligent one; it does not preclude innovation, but what it does demand is a proper regard for the domestic, as opposed to the museum, constituency.

Handicraft and manufacturing industry

From time to time observers of the design and craft worlds are tempted (I am myself) to argue for a greater congruence between the craft aesthetic and the everyday one of mass-manufactured goods. We want to bring the craftsperson in from the outer margins of the opposition. In our more optimistic moments we new utopians see a marriage between crafts ideology, with its emphasis upon the expressive use of materials, and the manufacturing of everyday objects.

However, we seldom come clean as to what sort of objects we are talking about. There are, for example, a whole range of products, including electric kettles, irons, toasters, sandwich-makers, ovens, micro-wave ovens, dish-washers, washing machines, freezers, videos and television sets, where the craft aesthetic has no place. Technology has brought with it its own imagery and metaphors. There is an implicit decorative order in product design which is ill-suited to craft or art interference. From time to time manufacturers will try decorating a toaster or a kettle with a frieze of flowers or a rural scene and the result is ridiculous – the two kinds of imagery (product design and floral decoration) are hopelessly incompatible.

In Europe product design has veered ever further away from the craft aesthetic except in one respect. One of the tenets of modern crafts is a

Peter Dormer

preference for soft, organic shapes and such forms are also now present in late 1980s product design, where a variety of things from electric kettles to vacuum cleaners have become rounded and 'fat' in their appearance. But this imagery derives from such institutions as NASA. The new kettles, shavers and hair dryers, the new generation of cylinder vacuum cleaners and the matt black plastic clamped deep-fat fryers are all similar to the reassuring, mother-ship, high-tech accessories of space shuttle exploration. All are rounded and padded so that they cannot do you harm. They radiate both good sense and novelty. The new space age kettles are sensible: the handle is well away from the spout, the spout is at the top of the container and gives you maximum volume for water, and both filling and pouring are safer. Like all clever marketing-led design, these kettles are not only safe, they are an expression of safety.

The most modern objects in the world are in space; naturally these things provide the imagery for new design. Today technology is the avant garde, and it, not craft nostalgia or, indeed, visual art, provides the most vital source for new visual metaphors in product design. There is no role for the craftsperson in the design of such objects or in consultation about their production unless it can be argued that certain craftspeople (perhaps batch production potters) have a better grasp over what makes a texture desirable and what shapes are best to hold.

If not product design, then what about furniture and textiles? A combination of new technology and the craftsperson ought to make it possible for a rich variety of relatively reasonably priced furniture to be produced in small batches. However, to achieve this, the craftsperson would have to adjust his or her role and attitude, to spend creative effort in designing, not making. Secondly, he or she would need to abandon the workshop (except as a space for making prototypes) and do what the Italian furniture designers have done, which is to make use of a network of small but modern and well-equipped specialist businesses to make the various parts which are then assembled by someone else. The new craftsperson's role would be limited to overseeing the quality of the work. This approach is feasible but its disadvantages to craftspeople are that they lose the solace of a particular way of life in which pleasure is derived through the temporary loss of self in the all-engrossing act of making.

And so we always come back to the essential nature of handicraft activity: the pleasure of losing oneself in a practical activity offers a way of life which is different from that of the designer or designer-cum-overseer. The constituency of consumers necessary to support this way of life exists provided that the craftsperson does not default on the implicit contract of service that has evolved as craft has evolved in this century: the contract is to remain within the bounds of what is familiar and acceptable domestically. If these bounds are too restrictive, then the craftsperson can only seek fortune as a designer or as an artist – in worlds much tougher, more competitive and less tolerant of the gentle way of life depicted by Vermeer in his painting of the lacemaker.

— 9 —

Design and 'avant-postmodernism'

•

FRANÇOIS BURKHARDT

For ideological and economic reasons, there has as yet been no critical definition and description of what a postmodern design would be like – whereas architecture, by contrast, seems to have defined itself as postmodern for a good ten years now. One can, however, speak with some justice of a school of design attached to the Modern Movement. Indeed, design today is in difficulties and is facing a crisis just because of this attachment to the Modern Movement, and because there has been no ideological replacement for it. Modernist doctrines are hardly tenable these days; design appears ideologically out of step, tied to the past when functionalism was the order of the day. The profession as a whole still follows outmoded dogma; designers devote too little thought to the new aspirations of our own times.

Design, moreover, is deeply affected by the crisis now gripping every aspect of society, and is not ready to call in question its own fundamental principles, even though it now faces an unprecedentedly threatening situation.

Design suffers from a time-lag, as compared with architecture; it is still partly dependent on architecture, but is also gaining greater autonomy. In the modernist tradition, object and architecture are essentially linked, and design is a by-product of this conception; after all there was no such profession as 'designer' in the USA until the 1940s. The profession is a young one, derived partly from work on domestic architecture and partly from discussions about the relation between architecture and industry. The interdependence, then, is quite legitimate; there is no *fundamental* difference for modernists between designing a villa and designing a telephone. If we examine architectural history, moreover, we realize that the design of objects has always been conceived on the model of architecture: this was so in the Middle Ages, the Renaissance and the baroque period.

Objects are only subject to discrete attention when a special trade or profession is created and the profession of design – something that first took place in England, in the latter half of the nineteenth century, when everyone (architects, decorators, painters) was looking for greater specialization – illustrates this. Germany followed, and as a result the early history of design is to be found in the public and domestic architecture of these two countries. This is why we speak of an Anglo-Saxon tradition in design, a movement that went on to affect all the industrially developed countries, including France, the USA, Scandinavia, Italy and finally Japan.

The birth of design is bound up with the birth of functionalism. There was also a certain ethical aspect, a desire to restore to the object its 'truth' and 'honesty': this was a reaction against the dominance at the time of historicist ideas which saw objects as 'appearance' rather than 'reality'. The leading figures of this tendency, who represent functionalism's transcendence of earlier constraining doctrines, are such people as Webb, Lethaby, Voysey, Ashbee and Scott in England; Muthesius and Riemerschmid in Germany; Wagner and Loos in Austria; Sullivan in the USA. They understood that the relation between form, function and material must be interpreted in a cultural perspective, taking account of contemporary life-styles and aspirations. And if we analyse their work today, we can clearly see how closely they were linked to the leading artistic movements of the time: they had an aesthetic orientation, something that the design world finds difficult to acknowledge.

With the growth of specialization, the relation between design and architecture and domestic architecture grew more tenuous: design came to see itself as linked to systems of industrial production and to the growth of the economy, and it therefore took on a very pragmatic aspect. This is evident in the arguments about typology at the famous 1914 *Werkbund* congress. Industrial production came more and more to be seen as a tool for promoting economic expansion and the display of sovereign power. Design was drawn into this project and took on a key role in economic policy, in which the quality of what was produced was above all an instrument in the quest for market share and for the satisfaction of national ambition. In fact such goals were nothing new: since their origins soon after the 1851 Great Exhibition, professional associations aimed at promoting design have always brought together producers, salesmen and creative artists within a framework of industrial enterprise, and this remains the goal and the chief activity of 'design centres' today. The same mechanisms are used, state and private subsidies (from chambers of commerce and the like) being paid to set up overseas shows, which used to take the form of 'Universal Exhibitions' and which now consist of international exchanges and trade fairs.

Given all this, the logic of industrialism affects the world of design by introducing specialist subdivisions within it. What the French call *un graphiste* is called in England a 'graphic designer'; the Germans have a similar term, and there are also 'product designers' and so forth.

Before the war, certain creative workers such as Eileen Gray and René Herbst maintained quite close relations with industry. In retrospect, however, it is questionable whether we should call them 'designers'. Design implies a commitment to mass production, within an industrial logic; this makes it quite different from something like Art Deco, where the bias of research was towards formal and stylistic questions, not towards mass production. Design has always made every effort to follow developments in industrial technology, on which it is essentially dependent. This makes the designer different from the decorator, who does indeed have technical competence, but not of an industrial kind.

If we look at the forms of contemporary design, for instance the television set, they are all much the same, technically; they all correspond more or less to a single norm. But industrialists realize that if they made this internal structure the sole basis of their products, then they would all end up making the same machine. So design comes in as a way of differentiating products at the level of appearance. This is the main reason why we nowadays identify particular products with particular trade marks or brands. Design is concerned with the technique of *differentiation*, which implies a procedure with absolutely no rational basis in technology. However hard they struggle to take up a rational attitude, designers eventually reach the point where it can no longer be maintained: for marketing reasons, they have to style things, to round off the corners or smooth out the angles, to add trimmings and colours, and so on.

Despite this, designers generally remain resistant to those technical and aesthetic developments which open up alternative approaches. The illusions of rationalism die hard, even though the postmodernist phase should be encouraging designers to reflect and to ask themselves: 'What do I express, and on what does my expressiveness depend?'

If the profession is in a state of collapse, that is because designers are in no way ready to discuss such questions. They are very ill-placed to set themselves up as a pressure group able to produce real change, for they are no more than employees, working for companies within which they have little autonomy, at any rate in the Anglo-Saxon countries: they are too dependent on economic rationales. In order to make a real break, they would require greater institutional autonomy, as well as the necessary conceptual equipment.

It is true that there was an ecological and pacifist movement in the USA in the early 1960s, which rejected the idea of a highly industrialized society and pursued a policy of self-sufficiency, producing its own tools, dwellings and food. Ten years later, as a consequence of the energy crisis, this movement exerted an influence on certain designers in Europe, and especially in Scandinavia, the Netherlands, England and the German Federal Republic. These people advocated an ecological, naturalistic design. A whole series of experimental projects was set up, exploring alternative ways of producing, distributing and selling objects. The most interesting work of this period was done by the German *Des-In* group – as much in theory as in what they produced. A number of designers set out to examine the kinds of design that would be suitable for newly industrializing countries: Bonsiepe, who had to move his work to Brazil from Chile after the military coup, was one instance. The Italian situation is rather different, since the national design body, the ADI, has an openly critical approach. It is an autonomous grouping, and yet it is in dialogue with industrialists. In Italy there is still some respect for the idea of the artist, the creator, the work of art.

And this was what allowed various parallel movements to flourish alongside the mainstream tendencies. These parallel movements were forerunners of the upheaval we find ourselves in today. The 'counter-design' movement, centred on the work of Ettore Sottsass in Milan and on the Florentine Archizoom group, based itself on real, human concerns, on actuality and democracy; it took account of the violence of society, including the violence of production.

After 1960, this movement was in the forefront of the struggle against the functionalist approach, and played a key role in revitalizing the language of design. Even though its production process was only semi-industrial, being based on small batches, the movement brought international recognition for the researches of certain of its members. Opposed at first, it came to be accepted, and has at last been partially integrated into the design profession.

Its most significant recommendation was a renewed emphasis on the role of craftsmen in the design of industrial products; a highlighting of the 'poverty' of functionalism, and of the primacy of other, symbolically significant, forms of expression; an intention to arouse emotion through the use of a personal, variegated language; the use of irony to show up the absurdity of certain processes of production, so as to demonstrate their limitations; the deployment of utopian and fantastic themes as a way of demonstrating how certain expressive possibilities are blocked off by the objective conditions of production.

The movement found its first effective expression in the 'Global Tool' school which it brought into being, but which soon divided in two. One group was mainly concerned with critical research of an anti-industrialist kind and with exploring human behaviour; the other group believed that critical work could be really effective only if design was reintegrated with industrial production. This led to the creation of the Alchimia group, in 1978, by Ettore Sottsass, Andrea Branzi and Alessandro Mendini, and of Sottsass's Memphis Group in 1980. These two groups won very widespread renown, and the design profession felt the liberating force of their approach, which offered a way out of the constraints of functionalism. Their work was fundamental to the renewal which affected every country where the politics of industrial aesthetics were under discussion, and pioneered the search for a new iconography.

This renewal led to the re-emergence of various minority cultural tendencies, which had always existed alongside the mainstream – for instance, the aesthetic school derived from the Art Deco movement, which had traditionally been hostile to the large-scale industrial production of objects. In France, where interior decoration is so dominant and where it has been hard for design based on rationalist methods to make any headway, this renewal gave a new lease of life to the old traditional trade of the decorator, which played a very important role in domestic architecture. It gave fresh impetus to semi-industrial production in that sector, and has resulted in some interesting products. This has been a factor in the much higher international profile which France has enjoyed during the last few years. None the less, these are still minority tendencies. For instance, I visited a conference in Stuttgart, at which M. Lamy, a pen manufacturer, told us: 'Gentlemen, give us a rest from all this talk of aesthetics: our business has nothing to do with culture.' And this notion of an everyday culture, of culture as a means to emancipation, allowing people to distance themselves from the world and take a critical look at it – this barely exists at all in the Anglo-Saxon world, where designers are closely linked with industry, and where design associations occupy themselves not with critical discussion but merely with business problems.

Designers find themselves very bound up with the constraints of production and with its actual machinery, with the need to economize on time and raw materials, and with the demands of automation. What industry looks for is an aesthetic that will remain valid over time, which offers the prospect of a stable, long-term market position. Because it is often based on heavy, expensive infrastructures (with time always needed for the costs of new technical mass-production machinery to be written off), industry – as opposed to the clothing or fashion trade – can only move slowly when making changes of style linked to design changes or to the techniques and machines that it employs.

Dieter Rams, who has been in charge of Braun's 'line' or 'house style' for fifteen years, has constantly to defend the idea that there should be a separate design section within his firm, in the interests of design uniformity. Once you have a separate design section for hi-fis or for coffee grinders, then the whole idea of the Braun 'style' is finished. Rams struggles to convince his bosses that this style should be retained – something which they for their part conceive in terms of market logic, from the point of view of commercial profitability.

The furniture industry is one of the most relevant areas for analysis, and also one of the most striking. If we look at all the well-known 'historic' chairs, we soon see that not one of them has any real ergonomic qualities. The Russians, indeed, have produced a 'real' ergonomic chair, which has to be seen to be believed. For all that, there is a certain scientific-sounding language of ergonomics, in which some people place credence. What counts, though, is not ergonomics, but whether the chair is 'welcoming'. And a strong reaction is now setting in, in the Anglo-Saxon countries: people have had enough of all this rationalizing. For the moment, however, the reaction is not so much against the doctrine as against the logic of industrialism. It is being realized that consumers nowadays look for something playful, joyful, personal in the objects that they buy. As a result, objects have to develop 'sensual' qualities: as well as being understandable, they must be capable of being *felt*.

The matter might be put like this: 'good design' is perhaps the final intellectual stage in the way an object is apprehended. Someone sitting in a Mark Stamm chair today finds it beautiful in its most abstract quality – because Mark Stamm was part of the Bauhaus, and designed his chair in a particular doctrinal perspective and with a particular method. The chair consequently possesses considerable historical interest. But someone who knows nothing about that history can hardly be expected to find the object beautiful.

There is a similar difficulty in apprehending any and every object produced today: it is a question of accessibility and of understanding. A well designed object is one in which a critical approach is united with a sensual approach. It is along these lines that we must pursue the emancipation of objects and allow them to contribute to our everyday surroundings. But the disturbing thing today is that while a movement is indeed emerging that is critical of rationalism and of industrial logic, there are no longer, in a sense, any designers: they have no contact with the mass production aspect. Their role and status is very like that of the artist, but they often respect the needs neither of use nor of production. For instance, the developments associated with the French design group Néotu are really very interesting, full of promise, akin to painting or sculpture; but it is not really a matter of design any longer, since the question is never confronted of how this is to be made available to the masses.

At the time of the Bauhaus, people took a position which might be summed up like this: 'Put the minimum possible structure into the object, so that its user can put the maximum of affection into it.' That was the aim of someone like Breuer. There were two further beliefs; firstly, that the universe of forms could obliterate social differences (but this was totally mistaken! Boss and worker may sit in the same chair, but they remain boss and worker); and secondly, that the essential objective was to achieve the widest possible popular availability.

In connection with this there is a kind of popular vogue for pre-war objects, objects made by or derived from the Bauhaus and the Modern Movement. There are some Swedish firms, quite well known nowadays, whose work is based on certain by-products of rationalist doctrine: things must be pliable, you have to be able to set them up – kits and so on . . . not fixed so they take up space, but capable of being modified and adapted at will: this really does have roots in modernism. But I don't think that the kind of 'good design' that inspires the Habitat type of object could become universally popular. Imagine what a 'good design' society, a 'good design' neighbourhood, would be like: unbearable! In my view, the quality of a place and of its atmosphere depends on its *variousness*: one's eye is drawn first to one thing and then to another, and picks out the difference between one structure and the next. In architecture, as in other areas, the attraction comes from multiplicity.

Only about ten per cent of production is affected by 'good design'; but that is just as well. This may be no great shakes, after 150 years of systematic effort, but there is no doubt that it accurately reflects the existing need, which is felt by ten per cent of the population. One can defend the validity of this good design, in so far as it coexists with other tendencies. For my part, I also understand the point of view of the other ninety per cent of the population, and in a sense I think they are in the right.

Postmodernity involves an acknowledgement that there are many possibilities, whereas modernism put forward a model, together with the judgment implicit in it: this is good/bad, this is good design/kitsch. In our own time, we can hope for a diversity of schools, each corresponding to the aspirations of different social groups. We can hope that this characterizes our whole way of living: it is not a question simply of design (as Jean-François Lyotard makes clear in his writings). The point is not to oppose functionalism as such, but to combat its tendency to hegemony, especially in the field of thought. Any object can be an object of design, and their multiplicity of evocations should correspond to the multiple possibilities which our society offers of identification and identity. We can see that in marginal groups (punks, for instance), the search is for the maximum possible individualization, including an individualization of the self vis-à-vis the members of the group.

Design faces very varied tasks today. In large firms like Renault there is also a certain search for special production batches, for ways of variegating models. And this has a market. We are now moving away from the dominance of heavy industry into a perspective in which automation allows decentralization. New techniques allow work to take on a new 'soft' contour, whereas the past was dominated by the model of 'hardware' – the Cartesian pillar supporting the modernist edifice. The products resulting from this, which are very relevant for design, no longer have to follow machine-based styles.

How are the plastic arts responding to this shift? Post-modern art takes advantage of it by freeing itself of 'mechanical' forms and pursuing iconographies that evoke 'energy', which is a mark of dematerialization. 'Soft' art breaks out of fixed frames and spreads itself in space. It is produced and received by way of intermediate electronic equipment such as videos. Artists, too, are experimenting with the use of communications systems to mediate their work: dematerialization encourages them to mount performances and to give new value to insignificant and banal materials, recalling the old artists' cry for 'the death of modern art'.

We are also moving towards new distribution systems and manufacturing techniques. So far as design goes, one can very well imagine a form of production, for instance, that would combine craft skills with computers.

Young designers may move with this general tide, but only if they can find ways of establishing links with production systems: we can be sure that industrialization is not about to disappear, even if new technical developments are bound to change it considerably.

—10—
Invisible design
•
CLAUDIA DONÀ

Introduction: Athena's artificial limbs

Ever since mankind (through the agency of Prometheus) first acquired the use of fire so many centuries ago, objects have been created with a view to conservation and production of energy. And this is only one aspect of that creativity through which we have provided ourselves with an artificial world of human production alongside that of nature. The result is that we live in a world overflowing with our own productions, a world in which objects besiege us, suffocate us, and very often distance us from one another both physically and mentally. We are compelled, by the pervasive sameness of these objects, to respond to them with the same gestures: they make us forget how to feel, to touch, to think. Accustomed to living in a uniform light, we have grown oblivious of shadows and fearful of the dark. Locked away behind lightless windows, we have lost touch with the sun, the air, water and wind.

Yet although we can often enough find no use for the objects that entice us, we are incapable of living without them. Man loves challenge, and therefore cannot give up the dream of 'his' humanly created universe.

Rather than abandoning objects, then, we perhaps need to 'rethink' them. After centuries of building objects as projections of our bodies, we can now begin to consider them as projections of our minds. Innovations in technology and artificial intelligence allow us to conceive of new kinds of objects – objects that no longer function as mediations between ourselves and the external world, objects that are direct expressions of ourselves. Against the force exerted by the object, which is too often a 'relic' or 'totem' of something already dead, a new design can now reaffirm the power of the subject. Its aim must be to create objects that are intimate rather than alien.

Prometheus no longer needs to steal fire from the gods. His powers lie ready to hand, within his own grasp. In this victory of Athena, goddess of intelligence, over Prometheus lies the new challenge of our times. A very long cycle seems to have come to an end.

Those classical dichotomies to which we have traditionally had such ready recourse in interpreting reality are no longer adequate to sustain cultural development. What emerges in the post-industrial situation is not merely a formal approach to a new artificial landscape, but above all a new awareness of the possibility of living in a fusion of past, present and future. We have to devise new co-ordinates by which to grasp the different reality unfolding about us. We must bring a new design approach to the material and immaterial objects by which we are surrounded. The communicative qualities of objects cannot be captured by an aesthetic of 'good' and 'bad' taste. Nor is it any longer appropriate to apply the standard gender divisions between male and female roles: perhaps we need to explore a more androgynous perspective. Likewise, time and space, which have hitherto provided such dominant frameworks for our interpretation of acts and events, will need to be reconsidered, and we may look once more to mythology as a guide to our modern technological condition. Many old distinctions, in short, will have to be abandoned and supplanted by new ways of thinking if we are to respond to the different design needs of the new human reality now emerging.

Good taste and bad taste

'What's intoxicating about bad taste,' wrote Baudelaire, 'is the aristocratic pleasure of not pleasing.' By analogy, one might then hold that good taste is the pleasure – possibly less aristocratic, but certainly more reassuring – of pleasing. So we have good taste and bad taste: in human beings in their relations to one another, in the objects which surround them. Hence the problem of the historical dichotomization of pleasure, which, if it applies in regard to persons, does so all the more in regard to the world of objects, of 'things', to which the aesthetic principle of the 'beautiful' and the 'ugly' has always been applied. But is there any point in hanging on to these categories in a world where a certain refined bad taste is celebrated as kitsch – in a planet criss-crossed by live images and sounds and penetrated through and through by a communications culture that is of necessity skin-deep, high-speed, meteoric, poised for a leap into the next generation of things? Does 'taste' still have meaning as an objective value, or is 'taste' now a rediscovery of myth, a Baudelairean pleasure of 'nostalgia'? In today's fragmented and uncertain universe, the object is called upon to evoke a certain 'hyper-sensitivity', capable of taking root in our memories of the past and our intuitions of the future.

Past and future

It is characteristic of the new postmodern design that it maintains a balance, at once stable and precarious, between past and future; and this holds for its attitude to design itself. It is the attitude of a society which for historical reasons has introduced the necessity of continuously redesigning itself. The new design, then, avails itself of that formidable instrument, a changeable code: a natural process in which each 'new son' must kill his father as a means to his own self-renewal, and thus proceed, through an act at once sweet and bloody, to establish himself as a new, unique and always different being.

The technological revolution, which has undoubtedly brought us to the threshold of a major transformation, has proceeded along complex and subtle paths, exceptional not so much for the forms already made visible as for the endless catalogue of possibilities we are now enabled to conceive. Will the car of the future be like the one we know now, only 'intelligent' (endowed, that is, with an on-board computer)? Or will it be replaced by something altogether different, just as it once replaced the horse-carriage? We do not know, just as we do not know whether the trains of the future will run on cushions of air or on magnetic rails. If the only point of travel was to cover the maximum distance in the minimum time, we should obviously choose to go by air, but in fact the Orient Express is back in vogue, with its gold braid trim and Liberty lamps, its damask furnishings and lace napkins and pianos in the buffet where passengers sip iced vermouth. The development of new technologies is certainly altering our means of transport, but at the same time it is fostering a new hedonism of travel: today, one imagines the space-ships of the future as having an ambience redolent of the reign of Ludwig of Bavaria, quite unlike the rarefied atmosphere depicted in the science fiction films of twenty years ago. What, after all, could be more enticing than the prospect of an elaborate pendulum-clock or a veiled lady in an environment where gravity must be artificially maintained? The most sophisticated forms of contemporary technology seem destined to combine with the poetic forms of the past in a manner that allows us to envisage air flights as magical as the voyages of the original propeller planes, or solar-powered automobiles owing as much to the bizarreries of biogenetics as to the veteran styles of our forefathers. Or perhaps the whirligig of time will see us seated upon flying carpets, but investing that mode of travel with all the customary ceremony and ritual, bringing to it the old elegance and aestheticism, carrying along with us the little world of objects and memories and personal effects which we seem to need on even the shortest trip. And at the same time, we shall have the giddy sense of a new ubiquitousness.

To the extent that the claims of form and function are always held in a delicate balance, there is a tendency for one to prevail over the other at any point in time. Thus we currently see a decline in the modernist privileging of the ordered, the rational and the mathematical, in favour of an emphasis on colour and decoration that breaks with the former insistence on utility and brings fresh conceptions to the idea of the functional. This shift marks the beginning of a neo-modernist era. Its advent is necessary: it is of the nature of design that it continuously redefines, transcends and negates what has once been stated. It has come about through transformations that have brought to the fore a collection of unorthodox and ambiguous forms, which have furthered the inbuilt 'deconstructive' impulse of the design project.

These developments have brought us to the point of no return; we must heed the words of that poet of neo-design Alessandro Mendini, when he tells us that 'something else' is now required of design. It is no longer enough to deconstruct and dismantle what we have just built up: we have to look elsewhere, we have to take a sideways leap.

But where? There is talk of 'the sophisticated life', of 'the renaissance of subtlety', of 'soft' and 'hard' design, of 'fluid' objects whose new, 'suggestive' pleasures, associated with smells or sounds or lights, are supplanting the old values of aesthetic form or utility. There is talk of the object of the future as something evanescent, light, psychic; of immaterial objects akin to images or holograms. On the eve of the twenty-first century, we are seeing an era focused on the heightening of sensation – a development provoked in part by a more destructured use of language, but which will usher in a new harmonics. We no longer see space as something three-dimensional enclosed within an object or clinging to it; bodies are perceived in their transparency. The old material narrative is succumbing to a cosmic narrative – to the dance of atoms, molecules and galaxies.

Masculine and feminine design

Let us think about the words 'architecture' and 'design', and the activities where they come together: building and furnishing. These are essentially affirmative acts, by means of which man has from the first structured his environment: the city, the building, the house in which he lives, the objects he makes use of.

Let us now consider how all this has always been done, at any rate in 'classical' architecture and design. Changing and developing technologies and materials have been combined to create structures which man has endowed with forms and functions. Within this overall system, to which we may give the name 'design', he has arrived at aesthetic sub-systems and defined certain dimensions of taste and style. Against a background of birth and death, of bloody struggles, victories and defeats, he has impressed on history his rigid and deterministic models, as if in a quest for a kind of genetic code by which to perpetuate himself forever.

New post-industrial society, however, is open to much more varied desires. It can offer objects of greater personal intimacy, and stands ready to respond to the silence of the computer with a more primitive and primordial language. It allows for flexibility of design even when it comes to the very materials of which objects are composed. This is why I believe that there are now pressing reasons, generated by design's current crisis of direction, to speak of a 'feminine' design.

The fragility of life, the chaos of everyday existence, the eruption of new technologies, the great pain of living with an outmoded concept of design while intuitively responding to the call of something new – it is in and through all this that the creative process renews itself. In just the same way, we now see objects and interiors created and enriched by the senses, so long lost in oblivion. That same technology which has been geared until now to the production of infinite numbers of identical objects, an endless multiplication of replicas (children, we might say, of a mere handful of fathers), now puts within our grasp a much more individual and particular consumption, whose attraction is essentially intimate and personal. Such goods will entice us partly because of the way they stimulate our sense of touch and hearing, and cosset our whole sensuality; but, above all, their appeal will rely on design qualities requiring a lingering period of gestation, which while it fosters and heightens the original impetus also injects it with a potent cosmic energy. This is why I see the new design as 'feminine' – or perhaps ultimately androgynous.

Art and design

The historical division between art and design, between precious and useful objects, now threatens to plunge us into an irreversible crisis. With the shattering of the myth of mass communication, the idea of the universal message addressed to each and all, we now confront a fascinating Babel of primitive, tribal, violent and elemental languages. The violence is liberating: the urban desert is being transformed into a vibrant jungle, in which all are free to discover a new autonomy and licence in the communicative use of bodily gestures, objects and desires.

The content and motive of the communication are not important: what matters is this new awareness of the possibility of communicating. This novel primitivism of signs and colours, of improvised and uncodified technique, signals the beginning of an epoch that promises to be fabulously rich in fantasy and creative potential. The new tribal art – post-punk, post-graffiti – weaves a tapestry of designs which matches and mirrors the mood of the times. This is as far from being 'committed art' as it is from being hieroglyphics. It celebrates the delights of choosing and acting for oneself, in a world where no one looks to anyone for assistance, and everyone dips at will into the haphazard of the cultural bazaar, and comes up with something casual, something uncontrived – not with the aim of making some anti-industrial statement, nor for love of kitsch, but just for the sake of overthrowing, transforming, expanding existing horizons, so as to make room for fresh methods, objects and materials. Design, here, is a way of getting a taste of reality.

Perched somewhere between figurative art and the design of objects, and inevitably bearing the marks of the present and the recent past, these artists/designers of the new wave represent neither an end nor a beginning, but both at once. They simply stand at a nodal point of the present, at the heart of the widely heralded confusion – at the point where the unified, homologous and unidirectional message is suddenly revealed in all its dumbness.

This new tribe of designers behaves in ways which draw its members into a different communicative orbit, whose signs perhaps mark the advent of a new culture and a new historical, existential, linguistic and behavioural terrain. It is of course true that the relations between art and design and qualitative leaps in

technology have always produced the appearance of fundamental reorienta-
tions of language. Technology – or rather, its more specialist refinements – has
always operated on two fronts: on the one hand, it gives a 'final' seal of
endorsement to existing representative processes, while on the other it operates
as the 'initial' stimulus for new and so to speak 'primitive' values and languages.

The global village is now wired up. Communication is undergoing a crisis of
content that calls in question its very purpose and functioning, which depends
on the privileging of particular linguistic systems and the reproduction of
certain sets of signifiers. This is why we can expect the eventual triumph of a
more tribal, anarchic, expressivist strategy, which scavenges what it can from
all previous cultures in order to free itself at last from the influence of any.

Time and space

The modern age, which has brought the demise of the linear conception of
historical time, now ushers in a co-presence of past, present and future, viewed
as the outcome of a 'single time' within which various signs are emitted.

The other aspect of this is an indefinite multiplication of temporal unity: the
technical possibility of measuring time to the millionth of a second induces a
kind of temporal 'syncopation'. The awareness that minutes and seconds are no
longer the smallest units of measurement invites the attempt to hold time back,
to seize on it with a spasm of energy, to saturate it. This minimal unity of
perceptual time, the basis of the cinematic image, underlies the advent of a new
'cinematic hypertrophy': lights, messages, scenes and actions, darkness and
immobility, silence and uproar, are nothing but the fixation of a greed without
end or purpose. Greed and obesity, transferred from food to time, mark out a
new aesthetic frontier. The city itself, acme of cosmopolitanism, stands on the
verge of a new fragmentation into atoms of time: what counts now is not the
function of a place or an object, but its role as temporal metaphor, its capacity
to stand in artificially for another time or place. A day's journey through the
city today no longer involves simply the movement from one zone of activities
to another (from home, to office, to restaurant), but rather an immersion in a
many-dimensioned temporal environment which offers, in design terms, an
identity within a chronological difference: a thirties nightclub, a fifties bar, a
futuristic discotheque.

All this calls in question those concepts of space and time which have
traditionally grounded every linguistic abstraction. Conventional clock time is
in process of becoming a single, unitary time. The prevailing conception of
space, which views it in terms of distance and of the relation between journey
times and the means of transport employed, will be annulled in the immediacy
of contact with virtual images at once highly realistic and quite removed from
sensory experience. The holographic images of the future will be devoid of
smell and scent. The image will thus be obliged to enrich itself with attributes
of the visible, the acoustic, the dynamic, so compensating for what it cannot

provide in the way of other sensory gratifications. Moreover, despite this possibility of reproducing an infinity of events, there will be no blunting of the appetite for high-speed instantaneous images, whose perceptual time will become ever shorter and more synthetic. Just as today we commit ourselves not to a material product but to five-tenths of a second of a television image, so we shall come to 'know' a multitude of people, places and ideas, but solely as momentary flashes, with the transience of an apparition.

Technology and myth, the telematic nomad

After a long phase of history during which the artificial has always been presented either as an imitation of the natural or as its antithesis, we are now entering a new era in which the highly artificial overlaps the natural, in an imitation not so much of its results as of its processes.

The fruits of the latest technology have returned us, as it were, to our original point of departure: our intelligence. Miniaturized, powerful, pared down, the objects it now has to offer refer us once more to the body and bear witness to the close resemblance between the artificial and the natural.

The low voltage current flowing in a printed circuit functions in a manner akin to the bodily cell. The traces of an electronic circuit are taking on organic forms. Artificial memories are now tending to dispense with their mechanical supports and to establish themselves as solid concentrations of information; and with the elimination of the interface, the user's relationship to the microprocessor has also taken on a 'natural' quality.

This hyper-artificiality, through which design is enabled to approach more nearly to the natural, is a condition at once super-technological and poetic, a condition of whose potential we are still too little aware. Endowed with quasi-divine powers – speed, omniscience, ubiquity – we have become Telematic Nomads, whose attributes approximate ever more closely to those of the ancient gods of mythology.

As Telematic Nomads, we have been freed from the constraints of a historical and 'unique' coincidence between 'place' and 'time', and can realize in its stead the power of being everywhere while remaining in one place: a power, then, of continuous movement within one and the same location. The Telematic Nomad is equipped for ubiquity.

The revolution in telecommunications and information technology is now radically transforming the very notion of dwelling and habitation. In the home, some vestiges of identity may still be conferred by the memory of the dweller and the 'presence' of human occupants; but the office, now a mere link in the information chain, has lost its identity, while the city is no longer present to us as architecture, but as a scenery of objects.

Still immersed in the novelty of these profound changes, we are as yet unable to grasp and appreciate the new situation they create. Like the ancients, we look to dream and myth, to some narrative able to explain the complexity of an elusive reality.

It is thanks to the dream of Icarus that we are able to fly today. And when the dream becomes collective, and thus takes on the status of a myth, it acquires the power to shape the growth of technology.

—11—

Culture as commodity: style wars, punk and pageant
•
PETER YORK

Just what is it that makes British design so different, so appealing to the waiting world outside? Well, it certainly isn't the design qualities in most of our mass-manufactures in all the critical areas of the world trade in *things* . . . our cars, aircraft, shipbuilding, computers and consumer electronics. I'm hardly revealing family secrets to say our shares in all those businesses have gone on slumping since the war, and before; our average income dropped below even the Italians recently. What exactly *is* our unique contribution to the wonderful world of design? What do the Americans, the Japanese, the French, even the Italians, want from us?

What they want, I would suggest, is *anti-design*. Call it culture, lifestyle, the past, the future, Britain as a theme park, a 'Fantasy Island' of new primitives – anything in fact that doesn't suggest it was conceived by a rational being called a designer, or still worse a design team working at a drawing board in an air-conditioned office with pure Stuttgart windows, Dieter Rams-type fittings, grey carpets, those French nylon door handles, Tizio lamps, or any of that stuff.

The world doesn't want *designer* design from Britain, it wants magic; the designer stuff it can buy elsewhere. This is not to suggest we don't manage to sell some technical excellence under the counter when no one's looking – Rolls-Royce aero-engines for instance – but that isn't our big line, it isn't what the world knows us for.

In a brilliant parody of George Orwell's *1984*, America's native genius Tom Wolfe imagined Britain in AD 2020 when the country has been taken over, *as a theme park*, by Walt Disney Enterprises to service viddie American tourists who all walk about with video cameras stuck to their heads, enjoying the eighteenth- and nineteenth-century Aristocratic or nineteenth-century Cosy Holiday Lifestyle Packages.

Millions of Englishmen become viddie-humpers – they put on costume as permanent extras dressed as Pickwicks, Brummells, bobbies, pram-pushing nannies, beadles, lamp-lighters, coachmen, stable boys, blacksmiths, Carnaby Streeters, eighties debs, and colonial officers in solaro cloth. At every major intersection are twenty-foot-high miniatures of Big Ben – designed in Britain but made in Japan. London has been re-made architecturally by revivalist architects in all the great styles of the past – it's absolutely caked with columns, pilasters, quoins, groins, arches, spires, cupolas, clock towers, cornices and pediments.

Wolfe is not often wrong.

Britain's principal export specialities are punk and pageant, the future and the past. The past you know, it's obvious, it's 'Queen and Country'. You can't write it off as *just* tourism; you can't say it isn't relevant to a discussion of design futures. Because that stuff, the class stuff, the archaic stuff, the great dressing-up box of the past, is massively important in selling things and ideas from Britain; and never more than now.

The English look that a certain kind of American, French, Italian and Japanese consumer likes is 'atmospheric', it's mouldered-down and *patinated*. It's kind of *organic*, this look. They're on about selling it as an art that defies art. The makers of English glazed chintz, like the celebrated decorating firm of Colefax and Fowler, would be ruined if they ever admitted that anyone called a designer, anyone who looked, thought, talked or wrote like one, went anywhere near those floral patterns. Those rosy bowers just *grew* there. And those eighteenth-century country houses just grew out of the ground, and eighteenth-century furniture grew on trees. As that English sherry ad says: 'One instinctively knows when something is right.'

From pilgrim daughters like Consuelo Vanderbilt (who married the Duke of Marlborough and topped up the Churchill money) through the thirties decorator Lady Colefax, another American, to a kind of *us* magazine typically called *Colonial Homes*, the romance of waspy style based on the English eighteenth century has meant a lot in America. The truth is, there aren't really enough Duncan Phyffe chairs or Maryland highboys to go round; an awful lot of them were found or faked in England. 'Colonial' is British. You only have to consider what Lisa Birnbach's wonderfully accurate *Preppy Handbook* (sales pushing 4 million and still going strong, so it's mainstream) says about the magic of Shetland sweaters and English shoes. And Mr Ralph Lauren, a great American romantic of our day, with a wonderfully Gatsby vision of the world, has a similar feeling about Jermyn Street menswear styles.

The English past sells: it sells whisky; mackintoshes (Burberry) (why else is there a mackintosh called London Fog – made in the USA); Laura Ashley (the most successful and influential English designer of her time); tea; jam; shoes (Church's); Rolls-Royces; interior design; spread-collar, striped shirts from makers who sound like classy law firms – Harvie & Hudson.

And, of course, we're world leaders in the Royalty market. No one comes close: all the other Royalty market contenders have severe design and 'positioning' (as marketing men say) faults: the Dutch are too bourgeois by half (they ride bikes); the Monegasque are pure show business; the Spanish – I ask you, re-appointed by the Government; the Scands – who's ever heard of them? I could put the entire Royal Families of Europe, apart from ours, on a platform and you wouldn't recognize any of them except for Princess Caroline of Monaco, and Princess Stephanie, who models swim-suits and cut a disco record. You wouldn't catch the Queen doing that, the woman of whom Bette Midler said 'She's so white, she makes me feel like a Third World person'. We're actually increasing our Royal dominance with exciting new models – this is one business that's *not* winding down. The Sloane Ranger juniors like Princess Diana and her generation of *good-looking* young Royal people are just made for TV. I recently had one of my books published in Japan – it's about Sloane Rangers. In the original, Princess Diana featured, but modestly. In the Japanese edition, she *dominates*, like Queen Kong – huge pictures of her on the cover and all over the inside. The Japanese publishers know what their market wants.

The Royalty business is crucial to the apparent *anti-design* tradition. It's typically English and paradoxical that the Duke of Edinburgh used to present his yearly prize for elegant design for the Design Council – he's its patron – talking in precisely *that* kind of English voice and wearing *that* kind of English suit that hasn't changed since the 1930s. The Duke of Edinburgh does not wear 'designer' clothes – he wears *tailored* clothes. His style is the antithesis of design as the design professional knows it; so are his houses. But that voice, and those suits, are *truly* influential now while those prizes he gave are mostly forgotten.

So the point about all these things, these Queen-and-Country romantic exports, is that they are antipathetic to the good bourgeois *profession* of designer as we know it. The impression one gets is that they were produced by craftsmen in workshops or servants in kitchens, or that they were *suggested* by aristocrats who'd been keen on a Grand Tour. They just *grew*.

I should stress that this phenomenon does not just apply to exports. In times of trouble or triumph there is a national Styliste resource, a nineteenth-century and Edwardian view of the eighteenth century, so splendid, so comforting, so *commercial* that it works at every level. It's a style that suits new money with a Conservative cast of mind. Curiously enough at this moment it also appeals to the real avant garde which, as ever, isn't composed of the kind of designers who draw everything in squares, nor of architectural critics who invent such things as Decorated Sheds.

But good design types will be able to share in the Anglo romance. When they've made enough money they can put the graph paper behind them, forget they've ever seen Beaubourg or Bauhaus. Their aspirations to Anglo style show in their taste – half-Fabian, half-Brideshead – for stout English brown shoes that shout leather, for thick cords in moley green, Oxford shirts and bright yellow V-neck cashmere sweaters. Go to Margaret Howell in St Christopher's Place and you'll see the versions of Anglo style the proprietors of large design practices are settling for.

Ask anyone in America, Japan or Italy – a *real* person, that is, not a designer – what they think of first when they think of England and of *course*, they'll say

Royalty, Diana, upper-class and old, old, old first. But running a very close second will be something apparently quite different; one or other of our roll-call of juvenile delinquent pop-stars or alternative comedians. Ask them to name a British car (apart from Rolls-Royce or Jaguar), a British electronics product or a British designer, and you'll draw a blank.

If the past is half our business, the other big English design export is the *future* – not the designer world's fair 'we-are-standing-on-the-brink-of-a-new-adventure-for-mankind'–type future, but an 'oh-my-God-I'd-never-wear-it' future. The future is called 'your-punks-are-wonderful'. It's called: MTV; New Wave; New Romantics. No one seems to be quite sure *what* to call it, but the nearest is *video style*, because that original British art, the promo video that sells a record, bundles up all the key factors in one go: pop music; clothes designers; young film directors (usually trained in TV commercials); set designers; graphic designers. Any time you see the following motifs in a film, TV music packaging or graphics, remember where they come from: spiky hair; white faces (Jackson Pollock's paint splash??); very red lips; girlish boys; boyish girls: cross-dressing; period clothes; rocking horses (think of Robert Palmer's 'Addicted to Love' where those girls' lips vibrate like a volcano designed and shot by a British photographer). All these clichés of popular, modern design – the *video style* – started in British design of the late seventies in music and fashion and graphics. They had never been seen on American soil outside SoHo in New York, which, as we know, contains un-American activity. English promo videos are postmodernism come to life

Anyone who's even wondered what postmodernism could really mean apart from Mr Venturi's decorated sheds will find it in an English pop promo. They're all about dressing up and making-up and playing around. They call on the past and the future in a fantastical, ironic way. They're about dreams, they're like dreams, full of ambiguities and gender-confusion – another British triumph – and of course jokes.

When I think of the English promo video I think of Adam Ant's 'Stand and Deliver' in 1982 at the height of the New Romantic style. It featured Adam as a 'Dandy Highwayman' in eighteenth-century kit, Trucome hat, brilliant make-up and Walkman, swinging through post-modern English period settings to music stolen from African Burundi drummers at the suggestion of Malcolm McLaren.

Ordinary Americans – *real* Americans – call this style 'wacky', they think it's kinda weird, but they also think it's kinda cute. Duran-Duran mean something very different from Bruce Springsteen. American design types say, 'It's fun but it's really nothing. London's so *boring* now' – then they copy it and run with the ball.

This British future style is a dandy one – it's software rather than hardware. What they're setting up is the cellar club of the future rather than the next shuttle station. They're working on the great look, rather than the five-year plan.

Now there's no doubt that this kind of British style involves *designers* – of a kind – in fact it's knee deep in them: clothes designers; make-up designers; set designers: graphic designers. And they've – mostly – been to art schools. But the kinds of designers who pitch in to this peculiarly British enterprise aren't like design *professionals* either – they're as far away from the masters of modern design as Princess Diana is. We're talking about a generation of designers who took their first cues from Malcolm McLaren and the Sex Pistols. And what they want to do hasn't got the word 'design solution' anywhere in it.

These promo designers don't want a line in monogrammed towels in Bloomingdales; they don't want to run the design department in RCA Victor; they're doing something quite different: they're in show business; they're in media; they're not in crafts; or in mass-production *things*. For better or worse they don't want to build a better mousetrap. They want to create some fun or some mischief and then get on to something else.

The software theory

British design, the kind the world's interested in, has two key characteristics: it conceals its *intent*, its design origins; it seems accidental, even wayward; this is a mark of sophistication and confidence. And second, it operates in very different areas from other national design skills, areas that aren't always 'recognized' so you don't always know it's design and you don't always know it's British because it's about *influence* as much as things. In other words, 'British design' is actually a Trojan horse for a much bigger dose of cultural imperialism called British *style*, which shows up most strongly in a whole range of skills and approaches that developed in the 1960s and after, in some very particular places. For instance:

The music business. The music business in England is a *look* business; presentation, hair, make-up, clothes, the video, the album graphics are all crucial to the British music industry. And British design skills in these areas operate as a kind of cheap out-of-house R & D department for American record companies. After the American one, our music business is the only one that counts in world markets; it's one that's grown since the sixties. In design terms, it counts for more: the clothes, presentation, direction of American videos is now based on English models, and often using British designers and directors.

Media. British designers go into television. TV graphics in Britain, using the most sophisticated kinds of computer animation, are a big field. Design goes into sets and, above all, into costume drama. Just think of all these British shows that are bought for *Masterpiece Theatre* in the USA – those British designers in their element. And we're in style publishing with design-led young magazines like *Face* and *ID* which every art director in New York and Tokyo has to have, now.

Advertising. British design goes into advertising: when Saatchi and Saatchi take over Ted Bates to become the world's largest advertising agency, I think you'll concede there's probably something in the boast that British advertising is the best in the world.

Advertising in Britain has been a training ground for movie-makers and promo-directors and every other kind of electronic design type. 'Creativity' – to use a word that makes an Englishman cringe – even more than 'originality', is important in English advertising. It doesn't use formula hard-sell approaches that have been Burke-tested to minimum risk potential. It isn't mechanistic. It takes chances with the viewer – and with the client. And the interesting thing is that this kind of British advertising has become more important, not less, as a new breed of British advertising agency takes a larger share of billings. We know this kind of design talent is attractive to America because American agencies are forever offering to buy this kind of British company, knowing they simply can't grow it themselves.

Above all, British advertising is full of humour. Someone, David Ogilvy I think, said people don't buy from clowns. They're wrong. In British culture there are enough shared assumptions to take a few risks in the family. Advertising humour is realistic, ironic, often a bit archaic. The kind of new British humour represented by 'Spitting Image' has been taken up by British advertising with a vengeance.

I don't think Lenny Bruce got to do too many 'Twinkies' commercials. *Packaging and Presentation* is another post-war British art. If you look at what designers in Britain actually *do*, you'll find far more of them in these 'secondary' areas than in the design of *things*. They may not design the objects but they certainly design the bottles or the cardboard boxes they come in; presentational graphics are something the British understand.

Fashion. The British actually export a lot of clothes, more than shipbuilding and aerospace combined. Our problem has been that our traditional, undesign-ed clothes have been the ones that sell best – the Burberrys and Church's shoes, the cashmere sweaters and Argyle socks. This has put a brake on the development of a serious modern fashion industry. Historically, the British have tended to marginalize themselves with clothes so idiosyncratic that they can't be universal i.e. exportable. And manufacturers haven't put enough money behind designers to make a business like Calvin Klein, Ralph Lauren or Esprit. For years, British art students have learned fashion at art schools like the Royal College of Art and St Martins, but there they've tended to make *events* rather than sales. Young British fashion shows involve more music, dancing, props and ideas generally than occur in any other national fashion industry. So they designed for pop-stars, and had a good time – and other people have taken the ideas and done well with them: Vivienne Westwood has inspired more sales from careful French and Italian adapters than she's ever actually sold herself.

The great expansion of British design during the early and mid-eighties has been in retailing and environments generally where big design businesses have had massive patronage from huge retailers to re-design national chains with shops in every High Street in every town. It's as if MacDonald's and Burger King, Safeway and A & P had suddenly gone crazy for modern design. Something like seventy per cent of British multiple retailers had their shops completely redesigned during this period. It was one of the most skilful and mature achievements of British design – a combination of tough logistics, understanding consumer expectations and retail systems, and making things happen in a hundred sites at a time and following very demanding design briefs. After all, a shop has to work, and express something for at least three years.

These strengths prove, I think, that Britain is really in software, rather than traditional hardware. The British do not make video recorders; they make what goes into the tape. Theirs are post-industrial design skills used in value-added inspiration. Sometimes we don't get enough of the value we add, but that's our problem.

Visitors often ask why British kids are so wonderful – why do they come up with a style that changes everything in popular design every ten years or so – even though they don't reap the rewards long term? I always say, it's all about deprivation. It's what they don't have that makes them like that. What don't they have? You name it: sun, street life, sport, good food, education, interesting things to do. That means *style* is all you have. And you can see it: it's the 'he's the greatest dancer', Halston, Gucci, Fiorucci, good threads syndrome of any US big town ghetto. Deprivation throws you in on yourself, on clothes, hair, music and dancing, local clubs, and *developing taste* in a few things to an obsessive degree.

This pale little underclass is very style-conscious. Who buys the Giorgio Armani sweaters at £75 each? – kids in housing schemes, who are the best dressed people in Britain, and football hooligans. Real style sensitivity in Britain is often bottom up.

Increasingly since the sixties people who've made it in the new design areas we're talking about have often come from a bit *outside* in class terms. If not as vividly proletarian as they like to present themselves, they're still outside the great design agenda: the role of the craft tradition, and the masters of the modern movement. Those things just aren't issues to them; postmodernism and post-industrialism aren't theories and games – they're a real condition which they've grown up with. Their influences aren't craft, Cotswolds, common sense, or even Queen and Country. They're not bothered by the modern movement. Their key influences have been music hall (or vaudeville), media, pop music culture, but, above all, America. And it's been going a long time. A few examples: David Hockney, and his LA swimming-pool dream, and his early decision to follow Clairol and live life as a blonde. Or think of those artists and sixties musicians who say the unofficial USA – particularly Black America – is very heaven. In *Absolute Beginners*, a British movie about the late 1950s roots of British teenage-ism and the new post-war world – music, photography, advertising, fashion – David Bowie played an early English advertising man who affects a *very* shaky transatlantic accent. Then, America-worship was at its height; we were producing weedy cover versions of American records, buildings and cars, and every British B movie had to have a Grade Z Hollywood reject actor in it to guarantee modernity.

We've worked through all that now, but the *experience* has been important in shaping young British designers. In the mid- and late seventies America couldn't have been more discredited in style terms for young people; the music was for hippies only, and the clothes were laughable: young America still wore long hair and *flares*, for God's sake. We were literally working on two different time-tracks, because a real revolution in the look of things had started in Britain, and there was just no response in America. No one in America actually bought our punk rockers in the seventies.

We started to link up again during the great disco boom of the late seventies. Travolta's clothes were absurd, and he couldn't really dance, but *Saturday Night Fever* was on the right lines. And we started to produce a 'look' that did catch the American imagination – a fantasy old/new 'look' called *New Romance*.

No one appreciates unofficial low-life America like a certain kind of British designer type. No one in the world collects sixties soul music like a certain type of British fan. And yet it's done in a completely different, *realistic* way: we clearly pick. The British design type often feels as if he's a protection society for what's good in America. It's not slavish; all that influence gets changed and reworked in British conditions to make something completely different and utterly, characteristically, post-war British.

The design boom

The world's television viewers have seen a raft of specials on the 'British problem' – de-industrialization, unemployment etc. – familiar, painful stories to smoke-stack America and other western countries. So let me tell you instead about one of our sunrise industries one where there's: money, prestige, glamour on toast – and where there are new millionaires every day. It is one where Government and business are pumping money in as fast as they can. What is this 1980s Silicon Valley? It's Design.

Britain gained a crop of design millionaires during the eighties – Messrs Conran, Fitch, Michael Peters; and Pentagram don't do too badly. Terence Conran developed a designer-led business into retailing and now controls a significant chunk of the high street. There's nothing like a few millionaires around to give design serious social standing – it beats years of special pleading. In Britain, design business consultancies are beginning to win what I call 'the battle for the Chairman's ear', over other business services like even advertising. Rightly or wrongly British businesses are beginning to think design will save them.

And Government support is quite clearly sincere. The Prime Minister spends more time on it than she needs – there aren't many votes in design. And they've put their money where their mouth is with increasingly huge consultancy funding.

Whether it will work is one thing. The effect on perceptions of design in Britain is undeniable, however, and that's an important start. Because traditionally in Britain a lot of the proselytizers for design have given the lie to their message by coming on so nannyish, and looking so frightful, because they haven't really been visual men and women at all.

So the reason the world doesn't always recognize Britain's new design is that so many designers are working in areas that aren't called design; many, indeed, have been despised by many design professionals, because some are working on purely domestic things, and others have let foreign adapters take their ideas.

But the newest, youngest breed of British design professional is a different animal, a more realistic commercial animal, with a much better grasp of the real issues. One symptom of this is their willingness to do research, and respond to users' real needs. Architects and designers of the older school feel very threatened by market research – they've bad-mouthed it as stifling creativity, as over-slick. The new breed, in contrast, do research quite naturally; they're pragmatically interested in the social context.

Why Britain now? What can the world possibly learn from us? I've tried to spell out some of the ways British design is singular – and therefore often under-appreciated. A friend of mine in London called Robert Elms has made his living for the last four years by talking up English youth style. He says we're twenty years behind and ten years ahead (or maybe it's a hundred years behind and twenty years ahead).

Anyway, what he says is that we've dummy-run the future in many ways: first to industrialize and de-industrialize; first to develop a successful non-American commercial youth culture; first to re-work our traditions – we've been doing it since the mid-nineteenth century. The key British design exports are *culture*, and culture is, as we know, after electronics, after bio-technology. It is the industry of the future. Walt Disney knows it; the Japanese Trade Ministry MITI knows it. That's why it's working so hard on developing new habits of mind for the 1990s – why it's putting so much effort into style and fashion.

British design recognizes some of the truths of the modern world: it's inter-disciplinary (things change); resources are finite (we've always gone for cheap thrills and re-cycling); there has to be a social responsibility dimension to design (or it'll come back and hit you in the face); realism – you don't live forever.

TECHNOLOGY
•
SOFTWARE
•
PROCESS

—12—

The system of objects

•

JEAN BAUDRILLARD

Models and series

The pre-industrial object and the industrial model
The status of the modern object is dominated by the opposition of the unique object to the mass-produced object — of the 'model' to the 'series'. To a certain extent, this has always been the case. A privileged social minority has always provided patrons to a set of successive styles, the solutions, methods and tricks of which are then emulated by local craftsmen. We cannot, however, really speak of models and series before the industrial era. For one thing, because their method of production was always by hand, because they were less specialized in their function, and because the cultural spread of their forms was less extensive (I am not referring to earlier or non-western cultures), there was a greater homogeneity among the objects of pre-industrial society. On the other hand, the separation between a set of objects which could take advantage of 'style', and local production which had only a strict use-value, was greater. Today farmhouse tables have cultural value — only thirty years ago they were only worth the service they could provide. In the eighteenth century there was no relationship between a Louis XV table and a peasant table: the two types of object were separated by a chasm which also divided the two social classes that they represented. No cultural system integrated them. Nor can we say which table was the model for the countless mass-produced tables and seats which subsequently imitated it. There was a controlled dissemination of craft techniques but not of the values contained in the objects: the model remained absolute. No mass-produced objects flowed from it in the modern sense of the concept. The social order assigned status: people were either noble or not, the nobleman was not the end of a social set, nobility was a quality which distinguished him absolutely. The equivalent for objects of this concept of transcendence was what we call 'style'.

The distinction between objects of 'style', whether pre-industrial or today's models, is important. It alone allows one to be precise about the real relationships between the model and the series in our contemporary system, beyond their mere formal differences.

In fact, observing that a large sector of society lives with mass-produced objects which, both formally and psychologically, refer to the models of a social minority, the temptation to simplify the problem by opposing one set to another, in order, therefore, to transfer the quality of reality exclusively from one pole to the other, is great. In other words, to separate the model from the series in order to assign one or the other to the real or to the imaginary. But the ubiquitousness of serial objects does not make them unreal, in relation to a world of models which represents true values, nor is the world of models imaginary simply because it arises from a tiny minority and seems, as a result, to escape from social reality. Today, through information and mass communication which disseminates models, a circulation — not only of objects but a 'psychological' circulation, which radically differentiates between the industrial era and the pre-industrial era where the transcendent concept of 'style' is concerned — has been established. Anyone who has bought a walnut bedroom set from Dubonbois or some mass-produced pieces of electrical household equipment, and in so doing has realized a dream, a kind of social promotion, knows, through the press, the cinema and the television, that superior 'harmonious', 'functional' interiors exist in the market-place. He experiences the latter as a world of luxury and prestige from which he is totally separated by lack of money, but from which he is no longer separated today by any legal class status, any rightful social transcendence. This is psychologically necessary, for in spite of the frustration, the material impossibility of entering that world, the use of a serial object never exists without an implicit or explicit postulation of models.

In turn, models are no longer entrenched in a caste system but, through inserting themselves into industrial production, make themselves available for mass dissemination. They present themselves, also, as 'functional' (which a 'style' table could never have done) and rightfully accessible to everybody. And everybody, through the most humble object, participates rightfully in the model. There are, moreover, fewer and fewer pure models or series. The transitions from one to the other disappear as they differentiate themselves from each other in infinity. The object passes through all the colours of the social prism in the image of production. And these transitions are experienced daily, on the level of the possible or on that of frustration: the model is interiorized by he who participates in the series — the series is pointed out, denied, overtaken and experienced on a level of contradiction by he who participates in the model. This uninterrupted dynamic, which goes through the whole of society, carrying the series towards the model and continually making the model move into the series, is the real ideology of our society.

The 'Personalized' Object

We can observe that the distribution system of models and series does not apply equally to all categories of objects. It is clear where clothes are concerned: in the contrast between a dress from Fath and a ready-to-wear item, or, in the case of an automobile, between a Facel-Vega and a 2CV. It becomes less obvious when we turn to categories of object which have a more specific function: the differences between a Frigidaire from General Motors and a Frigeco, between one television set and another, are blurred. On the level of small appliances, such as coffee grinders, the idea of the model tends to be confused with that of the 'type', the function of the object absorbing, to a great extent, the status differences which end up by disappearing into the distinction between the luxury model and the mass-production model (this opposition making the notion of models the point of least resistance). If we move on, in contrast, to non-consumer objects, such as industrial machinery, we see that there are no longer any luxury examples of a pure machine: even if a set of rolling mills is the only one of its kind in the world, it is, from the moment it appears, a mass-produced object. Although one machine can be more 'modern' than another, it does not become, through that fact, a model providing a prototype for other, less perfect, mass-produced versions of it. To obtain the same performance, you would have to make other machines of the same type, that is to say, create a pure series from the first example. There is no room here for a range of calculated differences on which a psychological dynamic could be based. On the level of pure function, because there is no combination of variables, there are no models either.

The psychological dynamic of the model and of the series does not operate on the level of the primary function of the object, but on the level of a secondary function, i.e. that of the 'personalized' object. That is to say, it is based at the same time on individual needs and on a system of differences which is properly the cultural system.

Choice
No object is offered for consumption as a unique type. You may be denied the material means of buying it but what you are given, a priori, in an industrial society, as a kind of communal grace and a marker of formal freedom, is choice. Through this individualization is made possible. To the extent to which a whole range is offered to him, the purchaser moves past the strict necessity of the purchase and engages himself personally beyond that point. Moreover, we no longer have the possibility of avoiding the act of selection, of buying an object simply on the basis of its function — today no object presents itself this way, at the 'degree zero' condition of the purchase. Either from taste or from necessity, our freedom to choose forces us to enter into a cultural system. This choice is illusory, but if we experience it as a kind of freedom we are less inclined to feel that it is in fact imposed on us, and that through it the global society imposes itself on us. To choose one car rather than another individualizes us perhaps, but above all the action of making a choice links us to the whole structure of the economic order. 'The sole fact of choosing such or such

an object to distinguish yourself from others is in itself a social act' (John Stuart Mill). In multiplying objects, society focuses on the faculty of choice and thereby neutralizes the danger that this personal need constitutes for it. It is clear that the notion of 'personalization' is more than a publicity stunt: it is a fundamental, ideological concept of a society which, through 'personalizing' its objects and beliefs, aims to integrate individuals better.

The Marginal Difference

The corollary of the fact that every object is obtained by an act of choice is the fact that no object presents itself as a mass-produced object but rather as a model. Every object distinguishes itself from others through a difference, whether of colour, accessory or detail. This difference is presented as a specific quality, for example, 'This pedal bin is absolutely original. Gilac Decor has put flowers on it for you'; 'This refrigerator is revolutionary: it has a new freezing compartment and a heater for the butter'; 'This electric razor is highly progressive. It is hexagonal and anti-magnetic'.

This kind of difference is a marginal difference (to use Riesman's term), or rather an inessential difference. In fact, where the industrial object and its technological coherence are concerned, the need for personalization can only be satisfied by inessential details. To personalize cars, the manufacturer need only take a mass-produced chassis, plus a mass-produced engine and modify some exterior characteristics or add some accessories. As an essential technological object the car has no need to be personalized, only its inessential features need be.

Naturally, the more the object must respond to the requirements of the personalization, the more its essential characteristics are burdened with exterior extras. The coachwork is weighed down with accessories, the forms contradict the technological norms of fluidity and mobility which are fundamental requirements of a car. The 'marginal' difference is, therefore, not only marginal, it approaches the essence of the technological being. The function of personalization is not only an added value, it is a parasitic value. It is not possible to conceive, in an industrial system, of a personalized object which does not lose some of its best technological qualities in the process. But the heaviest responsibility is carried by the system of production which plays unreservedly with the inessential in order to promote consumption.

Thus forty-two combinations of colours, in monotone or twin tones, allow you to choose your Ariane, and even the extra-special beautifier is for sale at the dealers at the same time as the car. Of course, all these 'specific' differences are taken up again in turn and serialized in mass production. The second level of serialization constitutes fashion. In the end everything is a model and there are no more models. But at the roots of successive series there is a move towards ever more limited series founded on increasingly tinier and more specific differences. There are no more absolute models to which the devalued, mass-produced objects are categorically opposed. For there will no longer be a psychological basis to choice, consequently a cultural system is no longer possible. Or at least no cultural system suited to integrate modern industrial society into its structure.

The Ideal of the Model

How does this system of personalization and integration operate? Through the fact that within the 'specific' difference, the serial reality of the object is continually denied and subordinated to the advantage of the model. Objectively, as we have seen, this difference is not linked to the essential qualities of the object: often it conceals a technical defect. It is in fact a difference by default. But it is always experienced as a distinction, an exponent of value, a difference by excess. It is not necessary, therefore, that actual models exist for every category of objects, some have none: the tiny differences which are always experienced positively, are enough to suggest the series in advance, to create the aspiration towards the model which can only be illusory. The marginal differences are the driving force of the series and they feed the mechanism of integration.

It is not necessary to think of the series and the model as two terms in a systematic opposition: the model is a kind of 'essential' quality which, divided and multiplied by the concept of mass-production, ends up in the series. It is like a more concrete, more solid, condition of the object which sees itself, subsequently, diffused into a series in its image. The model/series opposition often evokes a kind of entropic process, similar to that of the more noble forms of energy towards heat. This deductive understanding of the series developing from the model conceals the live reality, the process of which is exactly the reverse, i.e. that of a continued induction of the model developing from the series, not of a graduation (which would be utterly intolerable) but of an aspiration.

In fact we see that the model is always present in the series. The slightest 'specific' difference distinguishes one object from another. We see the same process in the collection, each aspect of which brings with it a relative difference which turns it, for a brief instant, into a privileged term – a model – all these relative differences referring to each other and coming together in the absolute difference; but, in the end, only the model operates on the level of absolute difference. It either exists or does not exist. The Facel-Vega certainly exists, but all the colour variations or numbers of cylinders finally relate only to the idea of the Facel-Vega. *It is essential that the model should only exist as the idea of the model.* That is what allows it to be present everywhere in each relative difference and, in that way, to integrate the whole series. The effective presence of the Facel-Vega radically challenges the satisfaction of individualism in every other car. But its idealized base serves, on the contrary, as an alibi, as an effective springboard to individualization in everything which is not the Facel-Vega. The model is neither poor nor rich: it is a generic image, made up of the imaginary assumption of all the relative differences, and its fascination

Jean Baudrillard

derives from the process which allows the series to deny differentiation – the formal idealization of transcendence. This is the evolving process of the series which is integrated and invested in the model.

Moreover, only the fact that the model is only an idea makes the very process of individualization possible. It is absurd to think that consciousness knows how to individualize itself in an object; it is individualized by difference because, in referring to an idea of absolute singularity (the model), only difference is able to refer simultaneously to what is really signified, i.e. the absolute singularity of the user, the purchaser, or the collector. Paradoxically, it is through this vague aspiration to singularity, satisfied by the proliferation of superficial adjustments to the series, that the imaginary consensus, the idea of the model, is reactivated. Personalization and integration go strictly together. It is the miracle of the system.

From the model to the series

The technical loss

Having analysed the formal structure of differences through which the series defines itself and sees itself as a model, it is now necessary to analyse the *real* differences which distinguish the model from the series. For the ascending system of differential valuation which refers to the ideal model clearly marks the opposite reality to that of deconstruction and to that of the huge disqualification of the mass-produced object in relation to the real model.

Of all the limitations which affect the mass-produced object, the most obvious is the one which concerns its life-span and its technical quality. The imperatives of industrialization, combined with those of production, result in a proliferation of accessories at the expense of the strict use value of the object. All the innovations and tactics of fashion make the object more fragile and more ephemeral: this phenomenon is underlined by Packard: 'One can voluntarily limit the life-span of an object or render it useless by acting on: its function – it is outclassed by a technologically superior alternative (but this is a form of progress); its quality – it is broken or worn out at the end of a given time which is usually quite short; its presentation – it is made deliberately unfashionable, it ceases to please, while it retains its functional quality.'

The last two aspects of this system are linked. The increased renewal of models alone has an influence on the quality of objects – the basic examples will be offered in all colours, but they will be of the lowest quality (or the technological research will have been economized on in order to finance a publicity campaign). But if the controlled fluctuations of fashion are not enough to renew demand, recourse will be made to an artificial sub-functionality: the 'vice of voluntary construction' (Brook Stevens). 'Everyone knows that we deliberately cut short the life-span of the things that come out of our factories and that this political position lies at the very base of our economy' (Packard). It is not absurd to talk continually, like Olivier Wendell, of 'this

—176—

marvellous cabriolet, so rationally conceived that it falls to pieces with a single blow on a day which has been decided in advance'. Thus certain American cars are made to last not longer than sixty thousand kilometres. Most mass-produced objects could be, as the manufacturers themselves quietly acknow-ledge, much superior in quality for the same production cost: flimsy items cost as much as normal items. *But the object must not escape ephemerality and fashion.* This is the fundamental characteristic of mass production: the object is controlled by an organized flimsiness. In a world of relative plenty flimsiness follows rarity as a dimension of loss. The series is forcibly sustained in a brief synchrony, a perishable universe. *The object must not escape death.* The strategy of production which is used to maintain this is opposed to the normal process of technological progress, which tends to absorb the object's mortality. People speak, in this context, of a 'strategy of desire' (Dichter); they could also speak of a strategy of frustration, each complementing the other in order to guarantee that production has exclusive rights not only over the life, but over the death, of objects.

The model is allowed to have a longer life (relatively speaking, that is, as it also is engaged in the accelerated cycle of objects). It has a right to solidity and to 'loyalty'. Paradoxically, today, this takes it into an area which seems traditionally reserved for the series: use value. This pre-eminence adds techni-cal qualities to those of fashionable form in order to create the superior 'functionality' of the model.

The loss of style

In parallel, when we move from the model to the series, the qualities which appeal to the senses fade away with the technical qualities. Take fabric for example: the armchair which in Airborne is made of steel and hide will, at Dubonbois be made of aluminium and artificial leather. The translucent glass cupboard in the model interior is, in the mass-produced interior, made of plastic. The item of furniture made of solid wood will come in veneered whitewood. The dress of top quality wool or wild silk will be mass-produced in mixed wool or rayon. With fabric, the disappearance, in varying propor-tions, of its weight, resistance, texture and warmth marks the difference. These tactile values come near to the fundamental qualities which distinguish the model – the visual values of colour and form tend to be transposed into mass production more easily because they lend themselves better to the tactic of marginal differentiation.

But certainly, neither form nor colour are transferred more intact into mass-production. The final product lacks something – invention: even when they are faithfully transposed, forms are subtly deprived of their originality. What faults mass-production is not therefore so much the use of a certain fabric as a certain coherence of the fabric and of the forms which determine the special character of the model. This coherence, or totality of necessary relationships, is destroy-ed by the strategy of the differentiation of forms, colours or accessories. Style is replaced by a mere combination of elements. The loss that we have observed on the technical level takes on here the appearance of a form of deconstruction. In the model-object, there are no details, nor any pretences of details: this object is outside mass-production, outside the game – it is with the 'personalized' object that the game expands in relation to the character of mass production (we find in fact fifteen or twenty different variations in the same brand) – until we get back to pure utility, or when the game no longer exists (for a very long time 2CVs all came in unpainted grey metal). The model has a harmony, a unity, a homogeneity, a spatial, formal, substantial, functional coherence – a syntax. The mass-produced object is only a juxtaposition, a fortuitous combination, an inarticulate discourse. Deconstructed, it is only a sum of details which mechanically characterize a parallel series. A particular armchair is unique through the conjunction of its fawn leather, its black iron, its general line and the space which surrounds it. The corresponding mass-produced item sees its leather turn into plastic, the fawn shade fade away, the metal become flimsier or galvanized, the volumes change, the lines break and the space narrow: in fact the whole object is deconstructed and its substance vanishes to join the series of objects in simulated leather, its fawn colour turned into a brown that is shared by thousands of others, its feet confused with all the tubular seats, and so on. The object is now merely a combination of details, the common ground of several series. Another example: this luxury car comes in unique red: 'unique' means not only that this red is not found anywhere else, but that it harmonizes with the other qualities of the car; it is not an extraneous addition. But the fact that the red of a more 'commercial' model is no longer the same means that it is suddenly the red of thousands of other cars – and thus this colour red becomes a mere detail, an accessory: the car is red as an afterthought, as it could have been green or black.

Class difference

This helps us to be precise about the shift between the model and the series. The model is distinguished by nuances even more than by its coherence. Today we can observe a process of stylization in mass-production interiors, in an attempt to 'promote taste to the level of the masses'. As a general rule this ends up in the use of a single colour or a single style: 'Have a baroque living-room, or a blue kitchen' etc. What is described as style is, in essence, only a stereotype, a generalization without variation of detail or of particular aspects. The question of nuance (within unity) is linked to the model, while difference (within uniformity) is linked with mass-production. Nuances are infinite, they are an inflexion, renewed continually by invention within a free syntax. Differences are finite in number and result from the systematic bending of a paradigm. We must not make a mistake here: if the nuance seems rare and the marginal difference unquantifiable, because it benefits from being diffused widely, structurally it is still only the nuance which is inexhaustible. (In this way the model is linked to the work of art.) The serial difference returns into a finite combination, into a system which changes continually according to fashion but which, for each synchronic moment in which it is considered, is limited and narrowly restricted by the dictates of production.

When all is said and done, a limited range of objects is offered to the vast majority through the series, while a tiny minority is presented with an infinite variation of models. The first social group is offered a repertoire (however vast) of fixed elements, while the latter is given a multiplicity of opportunities (the former is given an indexed code of values, the latter a continually new invention). The question of class is therefore fundamental to this whole business. Through the redundance of its secondary characteristics, the serial object makes up for the loss of its fundamental qualities. The colours, the contrasts, the 'modern' lines are given extra significance; the idea of modernity, at the moment when the models detach themselves from it, is accentuated. While the model retains a life of its own, a kind of discretion, a 'naturalness' which represents a high point of culture, the serial object is limited by its need for singularity – it is part of a restricted culture, an optimism of bad taste, a primary humanism. It has its own class language, its own rhetoric, just as the model has its own version, made up of discretion, hidden functionality, perfection and eclecticism.

There is another aspect to this redundancy: the question of accumulation. And if there are too many objects, it is because there is too little space. Rarity brings with it a reaction of promiscuity, of saturation. And quantity makes up for the loss of quality in objects. The model has its space: not too near, not too far. The model interior is made up of these relative distances and tends towards the opposite of redundancy, connotation through emptiness.

The privilege of the present

Another distinction between the model and the series is one of time. We have seen that the mass-produced object has not been made to last. As, in underdeveloped societies, generations of men die quickly so that others can replace them, in the consumer society the generations of objects behave in the same way, and if abundance grows it is always within the limits of a calculated rarity. But it is not the problem of the technological life-span of the object which concerns us at the moment. Another factor is the question of its lived moment within fashion.

A brief sociology of historical objects shows us that the market, in this context, is ruled by the same laws, and is organized, basically, according to the same model/series system as that of 'industrial' objects. In that *olla podrida* of furniture, for example, covering a range of styles from the Medicis to the baroque to Chippendale, moving on through the Modern Style to reproduction rustic, we can see that leisure and culture have encouraged us to go in search of continually higher goals within the range of 'class' values. There is status value in the use of the past, and according to its rules one can choose between an authentic Greek vase, or a reproduction one, a Roman jar or a Spanish jug. The

Jean Baudrillard

past and the exotic contain, in the context of objects, a social dimension as well as cultural and economic implications. From the leisured class which furnishes its interiors with pieces from the Middle Ages, the High Period or the Regency, supplied by the antique dealer, to the educated middle-class consumer who goes in search, in the second-hand shop or the flea market, for the cultural decor of the bourgeoisie mixed with 'authentic' peasantry, to the 'rustic' furniture made for the tertiary sector (in this case the highly bourgeois peasant decor of the previous generation, the 'provincial' styles, in fact an undated pot-pourri of stylistic nostalgia), each class has its personal museum of second-hand objects. Only the worker and the peasant do not like the past. This is because they have neither the leisure nor the money to be able to indulge in it, but also because they do not participate in the process of 'acquiring culture' which influences the other classes (they do not consciously reject it, they simply side-step it). However, they do not like the 'experimental' modern, the avant-garde,. either. Their museum is made up of humble hardware combined with a complete folklore of porcelain and terracotta animals, trinkets, cups, framed souvenirs and so on, a complete imagery of Epinal which sits alongside the latest model of electrical domestic appliance. This detracts nothing, however, from the need for individualization, which is the same for everybody. Everyone simply takes from the past what he can. This is the difference, in a cultured form, which turns into value and pays for itself. Within cultural nostalgia there is still, therefore, as in the moment of fashion, a system of models and series.

If we observe what, in this range, qualifies as full value, we can see that it is either the extreme avant-garde or, indeed, an aristocratic dimension of the past; it is the glass and aluminium villa with elliptical lines or the eighteenth-century castle, the ideal future or the *ancien régime*. In contrast, the pure series is not found exactly in the present, which is, with the future, the time of the avant-garde and of the model, nor in a transcendent past, which is the privilege of leisure and of acquired culture, but in an 'immediate' past, an undefined past which is just behind the present, an intermediate temporality into which yesterday's models have fallen. Replacement is most rapid in the area of fashion clothing: today's employees wear dresses copied from last season's *haute couture*. In furnishing the most widely sold item is one which was fashionable a few years ago, or a generation earlier: thus the majority of people live, where furniture is concerned, in a time which is not their own but which belongs to generality, to insignificance, which is neither modern nor antique, and will undoubtedly never become so, and which corresponds, in time, to the impersonal concept of the suburb, in space. Deep down the series, in contrast to the model, represents not only the loss of singularity, of style, of nuance, of authenticity, it also represents the loss of the real dimension of time – it belongs to a kind of empty area of daily life, a negative dimension, nourished mechanically by worn-out models. For only models change: series simply follow one another behind a model which is always ahead of them. Their true unreality depends on this fact.

The misadventure of the individual

'The product that is in most demand today,' claims Riesman 'is no longer a primary material, nor a machine, but a personality.' This is, in fact, a real restriction to personal achievement which haunts today's consumer in the context of the forced mobility which the model/series system instigates (and which is only an aspect of a much wider structure of mobility and social aspiration). In our case this constraint is also a paradox: in the personalized act of consumption, it is clear that the subject, in his actual need to be a subject, ends up as an object of economic demand. His aim, filtered through and broken up by the socio-economic system, is disappointed by the very process which aims to accomplish it. As the 'specific differences' are produced industrially, the choice that he can make is frozen in advance: only the illusion of personal distinction remains. In an attempt to add something that will individualize it, consciousness is reified in the detail. This is the paradox of alienation: living choice is incarnated in dead differences, and in experiencing this the aspiration denies itself and despairs.

This is the ideological function of the system: only formal promotion is achieved by it, as all the differences are integrated in advance. The deception which underpins the structure is integrated in the system.

Can we speak about alienation? The system of controlled individualization is experienced as freedom by the vast majority of consumers. Only to the critical eye can this freedom appear as formalized, and personalization as the deception of the individual. Even when advertising just manages to get one's motivation operating (through the use of competing brands for the same product, illusory differences, varieties of presentation etc.) we have to admit that even the superficial differences are real, from the moment when they are valued as such. How can we challenge the satisfaction of someone who buys a pedal bin covered with flowers or an anti-magnetic razor? No theory of needs allows us to give priority to one experience of satisfaction over another. If the need for personal value is so deep that, in default of anything else, it is incarnated in a 'personalized' object, how can we challenge this process, and in the name of which 'authentic' essential quality?

The ideology of models

This system is upheld by a democratic ideology; it takes on the dimension of a social progression, i.e. the possibility of everyone gradually gaining access to models. This continuous sociological ascent brings all levels of society, one by one, in contact with increasingly luxurious materials and, from mere difference to 'personalized' difference, nearer to the absolute model. But,

1   We are, in our consumer society, further and further away from equality in the face of the object. For the idea of the model takes refuge within ever more subtle and definitive differences. A certain length of skirt, a certain shade of red, a certain stereophonic perfection, the few weeks which separate *haute couture* from its availability in the Prisunic stores – all these are ephemeral

things which cost a great deal. An impression of equality has been established through the fact that all objects obey the same 'functional imperative'. But this formal democratization of cultural status hides, as we have seen, other inequalities whch are more serious, since they affect the actuality of the object, its technical quality, its substance and its life-span. The model's privileges have ceased to be institutional ones, in other than an interiorized way, but they are none the less tenacious. There is no more likelihood of consumers achieving equality in the face of the object after the industrial revolution than there is of all classes obtaining political responsibility after the bourgeois 'revolution.'

2   The idea that the model is an ideal point which the series will be able to reach is a trap. Possessed objects do not free us except as possessors, giving us the unlimited freedom to possess other objects: the only possibility remains a progression on the ladder of objects, but this is a fruitless ascent because it feeds the inaccessible abstraction of the model. Because the model is, in essence, only an idea, that is to say, an 'interior transcendence of the system', it can continually flee as we advance. As a system this is inescapable. There is no possibility of the model's moving into a series without being replaced simultaneously by another model. The whole system moves forward in one block, but the models provide substitutes for one another without being overtaken, and without the series, which follow one another, being able to overtake their precursors either. Models move faster than series, they are of the moment, whereas series float somewhere between the past and the present, trying hard to catch up. This aspiration and this permanent deception, dynamically orchestrated by production, constitute the central dimension of the hunt for the object.

This all takes place in a predestined manner. From the moment when an entire society organizes itself and converges on the model, when production uses its skills systematically to break down models into series and series into marginal differences in varied combinations – to the point when objects take on a status which is as ephemeral as words or images – when by the systematic bending of series the entire structure becomes paradigmatic but in an irreversible order – the ladder of status being fixed and the rules of the statutory game the same for everybody – in this controlled convergence, in this organized fragility, in this continually destroyed synchrony, there is no longer any possible means of resistance. No more open contradiction, no more changes of structure, no more social dialectic. For the process which seems, according to the graph of technical progress, to animate the whole system is still fixed and stable in itself. Everything dies, everything changes to the view, everything is transformed and yet nothing changes. Thrown into technological progress, our society has accomplished all the possible revolutions but they are all internal revolutions. Its accumulation of productivity encourages no fundamental structural change.

—13—

From Socrates to Intel: the chaos of micro-aesthetics

•

THIERRY CHAPUT

Alvin Toffler used to be accused of sensationalism because he foresaw major changes linked to the 'monstrous' rise of information technology. However, these accusations have proved rather hasty: Toffler's vision fell far short of the reality of the late 1980s.

He rightly sensed and forewarned us of an imminent and decisive technological breakthrough, but he did not envisage the uncertainty and anxiety which now surround the whole question of the role and status of human beings, electronic machines, and their contradictory interrelationship.

As the power of micro-processors begins to grow at an exponential rather than a merely linear rate, we find ourselves in uncharted conceptual territory.

In this untried context, and within the world of micro-electronic research, issues are now joined as decisive and fundamental as those which, in the field of biology, culminated in the discovery of the genetic code. Moreover, since micro-electronics explores such an especial area (memory, thought, intelligence), it takes on a particular status as the integrating focus of a quasi-religious quest for being and unity.

Fragmentation

Manufactured products, and craft objects before them, have developed, in their forms as well as in their uses and functioning, in line with developments in tools and production techniques. Form, whatever elements of style it may contain, is the result of certain constraints and expresses a certain state of technique.

A direct and primary linkage binds together materials, operators and forms (messages); and this linkage becomes an element in how the development of science and technical expertise is communicated.

Innovations in technique and the advent of miniaturization and electronics have considerably blurred this formerly clear-out causal picture. Objects can no longer be apprehended as aesthetic and technical wholes; they have been fragmented.

It is no longer possible to master the composition of an object through the old semantic procedure – component parts, structure, system, product. Instead, we find superimposed on one another a multitude of mutually unintelligible codes. Each field of knowledge has its own code, and the synthesis necessary for the apprehension of any particular object could be reached only by the common labour of a group of specialists, putting their various grids at one another's disposal in the hope of resisting for a few moments longer the continental drift that is reshaping the world of science.

In the absence of this impossible synthesis, everyone is left to develop or grasp whatever his competence allows – to deal with one element of the system, one more or less secret and deep-lying layer.

As we move in from the outer strata, from the shell towards the kernel, we are faced with one reading after another, in a discontinuous and dizzying series that rushes us in as a zoom lens does, until we reach the structural core.

It is vain, here, to pursue the chimera of encyclopaedic knowledge, unless we restrict ourselves to the anonymous realm of data banks and the like.

The loss of mastery is all the more important in that we must rely on a considerable degree of magnification, which itself causes partial blindness.

Function creates formlessness

Since the technical object is now made up of elements each requiring its own specialized, detailed and indispensable knowledge, the aesthetic and expressive realm has also been brutally invaded by mutually impenetrable techniques.

Just as we can no longer find our way into the giddy depths of technical objects, so also the path is blocked which leads from the world of advanced electronic technology to the world of forms.

The aesthetic continuum of technique has been broken. Micro-processors are based on a secret aesthetic of their own, and those who can perceive it (those endowed with the necessary *magnifying vision*) are alone in possessing the rules of a game which is never visible on the object's *skin*.

If for instance there have been changes in the design, the aesthetics, of radio sets, this has nothing to do with the introduction of integrated circuits and micro-processors, which has simply led to a reduction in the size of the finished product and to an improvement in quality of service. Such a course of development is quite unlike the development of automobile styles under the influence of metallurgical innovation.

Now, in the depths of fragmented technique, in the minutest minutiae of electronics, is there not an opening for an autonomous, unique aesthetics, whose 'hard' material aspect would be the indissociable support of its 'soft' and immaterial operative qualities?

The design and conceptualization of micro-processors is the formalization of thought, of concepts; as such, we can think of it as both a product of traditional culture and an avant-garde project.

It is a matter of putting logical concepts into operation through the medium of high technology and mass-production systems deploying a micrological analytic vision: from Socrates to Intel (Intel is the brand name of a micro-processor producer).

This involves a double competence, at once technical and historical, scientific and logical, technologically competent and culturally literate (albeit in mathematical 'culture'). Endowed with this double skill, the designer working on micro-processors abolishes previously instituted structures to replace them with new ones of his own.

And we have in fact to decipher the 'truth' of this micro-electronic 'work', just as we do with great works of art (cf. Adorno).

The secret of its content is transcendence.

The micro-processor, already invisible, has about it a quality which eludes appearance – a quality, Kant might perhaps have said, of *formlessness*. And also of the *sublime* (cf. J.-F. Lyotard)?

Black boxes, beautiful networks

Micro-processors represent a kind of town-planning of communication. They are manufactured networks which transport energy and support bits of information.

In the imagery of the schoolroom or lecture theatre, they are moreover represented as grid-like webs, among which pieces of information travel at very high speeds until they take up residence in little apartments, having visited and rejected several others en route. (Images of this kind are found both in Walt Disney's film *Tron* and in a film made on behalf of Renault by the Sogitec firm, specialists in computer graphics.)

Micro-processors put us in mind of a town like Los Angeles, a town without façade or image, reduced to its technical functionality. Micro-processors are spaces in which things are stored and transferred, and their aesthetics is a matter of complexity, of the endless proliferation of their networks and the extent of their combinatories.

This derealization of the real thus gives birth to an aesthetics of integration whose criteria (like those of the mathematical formula which is 'beautiful', not because it is a result, but because it meets a need) are to do with 'purity', 'power' and even 'poetry'.

Aesthetics and prosthetics

The micro-processor is a formless representation of the real, and is beginning to determine the real, to *be the real*, through its capacity to establish its own basis. Its techno-logical ('pre-pensive'?) activity makes it, as has been said, the site of artificial intelligence.

Indeed, its status as an android grown autonomous of the original artefact (and this is especially the case if we consider 'self-programming') endows the micro with an unstable character: half-materiality and half-spirit, half-hard, and half-soft, it evokes and incarnates mythologies and perhaps ecstasies of all kinds.

A host of bits of information which express nothing but what they are, and which depend on a formally indifferent basis, it will link anywhere with anywhere and can carry whatever connotation you wish. Henceforce, our projects find a home in empty space.

'Bugs' and identities

Once loaded up (if we can still use such a 'metaphysics') with the software that operates its combinatories, the micro becomes an *individual*. Only up to the moment when information and operating instructions are applied to them are micros identical, multiple.

Even if the communication taking place within its circuits is of the rawest kind, without interruptions or hiatuses and at the highest ratio of signal to noise; even if the machine (*machine?*) is operating with no losses, its energy dissipating without waste, and if it has vis-à-vis itself neither interpretative licence nor freedom of response – still, fluctuations and deviations will appear that cannot be controlled.

Such unforeseen events can be caused only by bugs ('parasites', the French call them) or by the noise of the material itself. This noise of impertinent and rebellious matter reminds us that what we agree to call 'artificial intelligence' lies somewhere between mind and mathematics: in so far as it is a prosthesis, an artificial organ, it partakes of humanity and subjectivity.

Only in their 'pre-prosthetic' life are micro-processors identical. They become unique as disorder grows more dense within them. This *density of disorder* is a measure of the density of impurity, or in other words of singularity.

By way of a provisional conclusion

Electronic integration opens up a new aesthetics. Free of artifice in its presentation, knowing nothing of decorative impulses and liberated from the tyranny of the image over thought, this aesthetics cannot take beauty as its criterion. As new generations of electronic artifice succeed one another, a process now acquiring its own momentum, each new generation displaces its predecessor. At every stage there is a burst of joy as new rules of play come into force, and an accompanying shadow of anxiety as we approach nearer to the point at which this artificial extension of ourselves will become autonomous. And all this strikes a blow against the pride we take in our uniqueness and in our poses of mastery.

As, with each successive stage, *computing* grows more complex and more farreaching, so it becomes clear how urgently we need to meditate on this aesthetics, so as to make of it the spirit or genius of the *computational*.

—14—

The demise of classical rationality

•

PHILIPPE LEMOINE

Only in form can potential energy find expression. The forces of technology are not just held in check by social relations; they are hampered above all by the absence of a creative vision capable of unleashing their latent possibilities.

It may well be that this second phase of crisis which we are now living through derives from the contradiction between the world-encircling scope of our intellectual and informational tools, and the absence, in the sphere of form, of the revolutionary changes which might allow their energies to be tapped.

Art, which has for over a century taken on an avant-garde role, finds itself discredited along with the very notion of the avant-garde. Is it none the less capable of breaking new ground?

Everything is unstable, fragile, disrupted. But the shock-waves running through out society mark a revolution that has nothing to do with any self-proclaimed avant-garde.

Communication, thought, expression, creation: all are at issue, and in reflecting on them we are more than ever obliged to consider the question of form. Economic thought, reluctant to grasp what lies ahead, clings to distinctions which technological change is rendering inappropriate – distinctions between the material and the immaterial, between the content and what contains it, between innovative products and innovative processes. Misconceived like this, the future becomes opaque. Investments are made, but – as the dole queues testify – no outlet is found for the product.

We need to take our bearings from some landmark capable of signalling towards the future. Design, we believe, offers good prospects for such an orientation: since its inception, it has been concerned with the interplay between technology, aesthetics, language and democratization, and it necessarily raises certain pressing questions. These include: the role and status of the act of conception, of design as conceptualization; the 'theatricality' of forms, and their future development; the working out of a contemporary theory of consumption.

This paper proceeds by way of these three questions. Its aim is to explore the gap between new technological problems and certain aesthetic positions which some still pretend to regard as modern – and to summon others to the quest, at once iconoclastic, destructive and healthy, for a new approach.

The role of design as conception

Design has always been influenced by the development of production technique. The first object to be sold by the million was the Thonet chair. Its rounded form – the famous 'bistro chair' – resulted directly from new techniques for bending and moulding wood invented in the mid-nineteenth century at the Thonet factory at Koritschen in Moravia.

Today, design is faced with information-based technologies of conception and conceptualization. What consequences does this have for the content and nature of creative activity?

The most important effects, contrary to the intuitive idea we may have of this, are not those directly related to style and form. For the new computer-assisted design technologies have grown rapidly to maturity, and the rigid lines derived from machine-based systems have swiftly grown blurred. In the past, the aim was to increase the productivity of designers and inventors involved in all those activities based on the drawing up of numerous plans, in spheres such as aeronautics, automobile manufacture, shipbuilding and architecture. There was thus a risk of sacrificing inventiveness and skill to the demands of productivity, in that the repertory of forms had to be limited so as to keep them within the range of the computer's memory and capacities.

However, none of this applies now that technological development and the new computerized design systems have brought with them a previously unheard-of flexibility. Objects and the transmutations to which they are subject can now be simulated by altering just one variable; their volume can be represented as revolving in three-dimensional space; different instructions for their fabrication can be automatically programmed. The miniaturization of computers has brought information technology into the world of consumer goods – into the textile industry, footwear, packaging, the design of logos and trademarks, the interior layout of shops, the planning of product lines. It is the rapidity of design and conception that constitutes the crucial advantage, allowing swift adaptation to changing markets: not just the fashion market, but the market in bids and tenders, and also in consumer goods such as cars where it is important to speed up the rate of replacement and thus the rate at which new models come out.

This speeding up, and its unavoidable consequences, immediately changes the role of conceptualization and design in one important respect: these activities no longer enjoy their own autonomous phase. The strict separation of conception from execution was indeed a fundamental step in the scientific organization of industrial labour, but there is no longer space or time for the cumbersome procedures involved (separate documents and portfolios pertaining to products, their industrial manufacture and the organization and method that this required). Informatics now allows conception and design to be rapid, which is to say adaptive and interactive.

In the clothing and footwear industries, one task of the new computer-assisted design systems is to set out the different variants in which a given model is to be produced, and in particular to ensure the optimum cutting-out process given the particular dimensions, qualities and shortcomings of the cloth or leather to be used. The design and conceptualization phase thus takes account of flows of information from the factory floor as well as from the point of sale. In seeking the best range of product lines, stores develop programmes based on the acquisition of exact information about the rate of sale of different products, using computerized cash-registers and point-of-sale terminals.

The rhythm of design is thus linked to the other rhythms of economic life. However, the most important transformation, and the one which indirectly affects the styles and theories which have been regarded as the prerogative of design, is the change in the *situation*, the *positioning*, of design. Once designing becomes interactive, once it is based on powerful miniaturized information tools, once it is in the hands of less professionally qualified users, what is to stop consumers themselves from designing what they consume? Some manufacturers are already making commercial capital of the range of options that they offer their customers. Quite simple computerized design systems, based on image-banks stored on video discs, allow the consumer to get a visual picture of 'her' car or 'her' fitted kitchen.

Of greater significance are those increasingly frequent cases in which the consumer is involved in the design and conceptualization of the product because he or she figures as the only 'expert' able to lay down its specifications. These include, first of all, all those types of service offered under variable conditions of time and place, which have to meet particular choices made from a range of suggested alternatives and specified options. In this extensive field – including tourism, legal and financial services, insurance, consumer credit – a specialized computer-assisted service is developing: the design of what is offered draws on systems/experts accessible to those in immediate contact with the consumer. As telematics develops, the users themselves will be put in direct contact with these services, acquiring the capacity to do their own designing.

Micro-informatics is itself structuring in advance this redistribution of design capacity. Computers are universal tools, whose use value is given only in their programming. Those who buy their own micro must first of all define exactly what use they wish to make of it in such personal fields as education, health programmes, the management of financial assets, personalized access to forms of artistic expression and so forth.

There is a whole range of standard software to help the individual user, but as a rule these packages are simply tools designed to compress the range of possible objectives sufficiently for the user to feel that his freedom of expression is coming up against logical constraints, and thus to establish the autonomy of his own requirements.

It is not that this more dispersed computerized design technology signals the demise of the professional, central conceptualizer/designer. The status of design is changing, rather, in that we now have a conceptual chain: the centre provides adaptable tools and those at the periphery specify the manner in which they are to be used. But in looking for a new balance in design and conceptualization, we must have recourse to the right models. In the realm of interactive information technology, it is particularly inappropriate to refer to some abstract representation of needs, or even to some expression of needs and demands that are as yet unconscious. The dynamics of consumption can only be mastered in terms of prefigurative images, made attractive and intelligible because they have been incarnated in a particular form.

But what matrices will allow us to draw up these forms? If one thing is henceforth outside the designer's control, it is the determination of function and functionality. In the new condition of conceptualization and design, form can no longer take function as its guide.

This is why the terms in which the Bauhaus prompted us to think about the relations between aesthetics, technology and industrial production have been so radically and irrevocably altered.

The theatricality and future development of forms

The iconography of computer graphics (for instance, Bill Atkinson's Mac Paint programme for Macintosh) has a secret link with Ricardo Bofill's architecture: both have rediscovered an aesthetic which is theatrical, superficial, literally 'flashy'.

This rediscovery of the theatrical, and the break with functionalist doctrines that it implies, has been seen by some philosophers and theorists as proof that 'postmodernism' has arrived. For our part, we simply suggest that we find here the first stages in the quest for a style in keeping with the new patterns of information-based design.

Software packages are characterized by the fact that they are organized in layers. The programme, a complex transmission mechanism allowing man and machine to communicate with one another, operates like a stratified stack of languages: the lower levels are modelled on the mute logics of electronic wiring, the upper levels strive to mirror directly the human mind, its workings and its imagination. Educational programmes derived from artificial intelligence, such as Logo, are aimed less at giving the child access to preconstituted knowledge than at presenting it with a reflection, a material image, of its own logical operations. Such programmes (or, rather, the interactive situations which their use creates) are based on a play of symbols which intervene between child and machine, and which seduce and captivate, provoke reflection and transformation, and so permit, stimulate and develop the revelation of the self to the self.

Such a patchwork or veneer of symbols, such a surface, is only effective if it is appropriate. We have all been irritated, some time or another, when in using telematic equipment we have found ourselves assailed by a tiresome and irrelevant barrage of graphics, which merely illustrates the aesthetic sensibilities of some institution. Software designers are aware of this: to dress up packages is their new specialist skill, and they know that a package must be striking, concise, firm. There has consequently been a renewal of interest in various mental techniques used down the ages, which can be a guide to designing packages more concisely and targeting them more accurately. The classical works on the art of memory fall into this category, as do Cicero's suggestions on how to memorize lists of objects and how to organize one's mind as an ordered and coloured space within which the orator will readily locate the detailed references useful when making a speech.

The art of memory was transformed into an occult science at the time of the Renaissance, becoming a vehicle for the communication of secret knowledge just at the time when printing was opening up new public spaces. Today, it is a treasury of forms for those who design educational software. One form that seems especially effective is that of a vast dwelling, a palace whose echoing halls are decorated with columns that break space down into recurrent rhythmic interludes — an image that catches the essence of memory and memorization. The pupil is encouraged to enter into this scene, to wander there, and to take on a role which leads him to seek out the different messages hidden behind each column.

This theatrical decor, simulating the past even as it teaches a new identity, is the exact counterpart of the towns built by Ricardo Bofill. Is this a coincidence? Maybe so, when we remember the infinite repertoire of symbols, drawn from every culture, which computer simulation will soon make available to us: video discs, ROM CDs, and other accessible stores and banks of imagery are bringing the imaginary museum closer to realization every day. What is surely not a coincidence, however, is that the symbols used have some resonance of theatre scenery, which of all the plastic arts is most at the service of language and communication.

This represents an important shift from the notions of classical design: but is this shift total? Here, we must draw a distinction between the European and functionalist origins of industrial aesthetics, and the way it developed in the USA around the theme of aerodynamics. The basic Bauhaus principle was to use the power of industrial mass production in the service of beauty – but a beauty which, since it must find an entry into the great mass-consumption market, must be free of all extraneity, given over to its role as universal message.

To see things like that involved the development of a rigorously ascetic doctrine, allowing space neither for the imitation of art already acknowledged by the elite nor for the creator's subjective inspiration. In this doctrine, design was adapted to the rationalization of production and organized around the product's structure and function. The object achieved beauty in so far as it was the judge and master of its own aesthetic and its expression.

American industry later made intensive use of design, but in a different social and cultural context. It was no longer so important to distance oneself from the charms of Art Deco, and, since the pace of innovation was already speeding up, markets grew more quickly into mass markets: the relation between elite consumption and popular consumption was changing. Thus American design, during its birth in the mid-thirties and during the exotic post-war period, was centred on an image which was more and more a veneer, something applied to the surface of an object whose function it in no way reflected: the image of speed, of aerodynamics. These forms could to some extent be employed in the design of a Studebaker, a Ford or a Chrysler without breaking with the teachings of functionalism. But when more and more refrigerators, radio sets and toasters began to look like racing cars, it was clear that design was no longer in any way derived from the object's technical and structural properties.

American design, in endowing the inanimate world with an effect of ceaseless movement, was certainly inspired by the consequences of a technology. But the technology in question, the cinema, had nothing to do with production. It was the cinema which gave meaning to the instability of earthly things, their speediness, their promise of a new destiny – adventurous, competitive, 'progressive' – for humanity. The American way of life is a streamlined motorway where designated/designed objects follow and overtake one another: a long journey on which we can all be the heroic traveller. The rationally democratic project which left its mark on German design has been set aside, and projection has come into its own: the projection of the cinema on to life, of forms on to objects, of models on to identities.

The postmodernist current thus represents a rupture, but a rupture within a certain continuity; for it, too, responds to the question of identity by recourse to a language of projected, veneer-like forms. Information technology, how-ever, transforms the meaning precisely of this question. Where the imagination of earlier generations was organized around great collective models, our contemporaries aspire to become actors on the worldwide interactive scene constituted by the interlinked realms of objects, services and media.

Objects speak, communicate, interact. The most rigid tools find themselves swathed in electronic instructions that tie them in to the universe of signs. Form now sets out to solve this problem: how to celebrate the wedding of the imagination with reality, to the glory of the sensitive and fine-nerved man? Cinema no longer provides the point of reference: theatre now lays claim to the role of educating the individual in life's aesthetics.

Some big Japanese shops, of the kind that call themselves, 'creative life stores', seem to prefigure some theatrical scene in which a moment of artistic inspiration has merged the roles of designer and consumer. The goods on display are not especially technical, but technology directs the scene and everything that takes place within it.

Whoever comes in here is recognized as at once actor and individual, master both of his looks and of his identity. Nothing is offered en masse, and the humblest items – a dress, a pair of shoes – are badly set out, exposed and isolated, lit up by spotlights like museum pieces.

The value put upon the goods and upon their particular qualities will depend on the individual's self-image. Meanwhile authentic works of art, placed amidst the objects for sale, stimulate his perceptions and his sensibility. Scope for choice is provided by data- and image-banks, which at the same time allow the scene to remain uncluttered. Computer-assisted design systems devoted to clothes and furnishings add to the feeling that everything is growing flexible, everything is adapted to one's representation of oneself.

The art of make-up, itself so theatrical, is given a new lease of life by interactive technology. Computer-controlled programmes capture the appearance of a face, transforming its image in real time to show the effect of this or that cosmetic.

These technologies of information and communication by no means create a clinical atmosphere: rather, they invoke the world of the baroque, of the theatre. However, their underlying aesthetic has no stable basis as yet. The risk today is that we will be overwhelmed by a flood of symbolic decors, such is our need to find identity, authenticity and clarity, and to make signs and signals.

As the manufacture of the simplest goods is automated, they are plunged deeper into the information world (a world, that is to say, where they can be reproduced at almost no cost). The various manufacturers are increasingly impelled to protect their products by 'copyright'-type insignia requiring the selection of a special iconography. Graphic design enters the consciousness of everyone at the very moment when it is becoming impossible for the plastic arts any longer to guarantee the identity of objects.

Objects, at once hardware and software, are entering the double and divided world of language, bursting apart into a number of different entities.

A contemporary theory of consumption?

During a certain period, design played a part in reinforcing the notion of a unity comprising the object, its structure, its functioning, its aesthetic qualities and the need it met. It was thus a useful counterpoise to the positivistic theories of consumption which attempted to throw light on the phenomenon of twentieth-century economic growth.

In the inter-war years, the slogan according to which 'beauty boosts sales' was like a banner summoning to some new combat. It would be an overstatement to claim that modern capitalism has followed straight in the paths of the expansionary incomes policy now known as Fordism. It is certainly important that workers' incomes should be sufficient to allow them to buy what they produce, but the consumer society developed only gradually, and did not rely simply on altered patterns of money circulation.

In Germany, especially, the ideas of the Bauhaus movement formed part of a wider project of democratization, which might be called the theory of popular consumption. Since the beginning of the century, industrialists and manufacturers had joined together in such bodies as the Deutscher Werkbund to discuss the relationship between aesthetics, industrial production and social quality. Was this simply a latter-day version of Bismarckian reformism? Interest in these ideas was felt in the most various quarters, and they took on widely varied connotations in the vast chaos of German ideology.

The growth of big business during the 1920s gave it a stake in society, and industrialists sought to play a part, through the democratization of the marketplace, in the anxious quest for a firmer social framework. Could consumption provide the cement which would ward off social division and violence? The idea of the popular store was the brainchild of German retailers at the end of the twenties, and these themes paradoxically survived in some efforts of Nazi economic planning (as, for instance, in that well-known symbol the Volkswagen – the people's car).

In France (unlike the Scandinavian and Anglo-Saxon countries), this social and egalitarian dimension of the design debate went altogether unacknowledged. French interest focused on the aesthetic revival as such, and Le Corbusier saw the high value that German designers set on technical mastery as a token of modernist neutrality and political indifference. French society was indeed keen to keep its privileged role as a centre for artistic expression, but when it came to goods and commodities no one saw any reason to abandon the styles that suited the elite, which mass production was content to imitate.

France, moreover, was not especially well placed to register the impact of the positivistic theories of consumption which developed alongside the establishment of modern design. After the financial crisis of 1930, sociological discussion of consumption tended in any case to give way everywhere to Keynesian economic theory with its emphasis on investment. It seems, however, that the original positivist impulse has sufficed to protect the semantic bundle of notions called 'consumption' from any exposure to deeper questioning.

Today, as object and design alike split up into fragments, we are forced to reconsider the very meaning of consumption. Rapid technological progress might be thought to herald a massive expansion of markets, but the identity crisis suffered by the notion of the product has stopped this from happening. That is why we urgently need to formulate a contemporary theory of consumption that takes account of the nature of the new productive forces.

If we reflect on the development of forms, we can state precisely which questions now have to be answered:

What, first of all, should we make of the idea that information technology may herald a situation in which 'information goods' take their place alongside existing industrial goods? The vicissitudes of design show that *all* objects are now escaping from their sheath of plasticity, and submitting to a play of interactivity in which their information aspect is revealed.

It would be mistaken to believe that the universe of signs penetrated the world of industry thanks to the voluntarism of the Bauhaus movement. At the most, the latter may have engendered a temporary and illusory belief in the unity of the object.

From the start, the industrial project has felt the pull of signs, of communication. As McLuhan has pointed out, mass production was based on the model of the printing press. In the eighteenth and early nineteenth centuries, the industrial revolution was a textile revolution: a revolution in seductive appearances. Is it nothing more than a play on words to suggest that textiles have something in common with texts?

At any event, the wider industrial changes wrought by the textile industry derived from the development not just of mechanical looms, but also of printing methods, of encoding and programming devices (the forerunners of the punch-card) such as are used in the Jacquard loom, of formulas aimed at obtaining brighter colours – and, through this manufacture of colourants, of the new-born chemical industry itself.

The history of design might suggest that forms are imposed upon the power of industry. But the contrary is true: industry is born out of the boundless attraction men feel towards signs.

If everything is a sign and everything is a symbol, what then becomes of functionalist accounts of consumption? This is a second fundamental question, since so much research still seeks to explain market exchange by way of theories of need. In this perspective, the basic functions, derived from agricultural and artisanal production, have to do with food and clothing. Industrialization then gives rise to secondary functions, to do with the dwelling and its furnishing and with personal mobility. Finally, there arise tertiary functions, supposedly linked with the development of information technologies, in the spheres of health, culture, form and communication.

There seems little hope of illuminating the future by such means as this, for function itself is now losing any stable and predictable identity. Design has more and more to do with ephemeral processes, and less and less to do with products and functions. But in this, design designates and reveals nothing. Interactive technologies oblige us to see our society as it is, and to move from theories ruled by the notion of supply towards a perspective that pays attention to demand, to styles of life.

The new textile town at Osaka is the site of a Japanese telecommunications project which is interesting in this regard. Designers in the various firms there have access not just to cables linking them with computer-assisted design systems, but also to channels that make available video-discs about fashion. These image banks contain, alongside footage of the top couturiers' collections, films showing what people have actually been wearing in the street: here, classified by year, can be seen the silhouettes of those who walk in the fashionable districts of the four corners of the earth: Tokyo, St. Germain-des-Prés, Fifth Avenue, Central Park ...

Philippe Lemoine

This body-watching surely gives a better foretaste of the future than could be acquired from any amount of statistical material?

These various levels of interaction leave us with the sense of a society in motion, in transition. But the vicissitudes of consumption also impel us to ask: what is being constructed? This last question, above all, must be posed in new terms.

Economically, consumption is first of all destructive. We have left behind the positivist theories of consumption prevalent in the first half of this century, we have been through the phase of critical theory that can be traced back to the Frankfurt School and which found an echo in the 1960s critique of the consumer society, and we can now start from the above definition.

But what is destroyed, in consumption? And, faced with the multifarious patchwork of postmodern design, what is it important to destroy: the need, its material embodiment, the aesthetic, the language, or that material incarnation of inequality inherent in the ownership of certain goods? Information looms larger and larger, creating an ever more reproducible universe. Icons, signs and symbols accumulate, proliferate and grow suffocatingly dense.

A revolution of forms should surely have as its goal the heightening of our faculties – our perceptiveness, our charm, our cruelty – in this confrontation with what must most urgently be destroyed in a world already overburdened with communication.

—15—

From Brunelleschi to CAD-CAM

•

MIKE COOLEY

Around the sixteenth century, there emerged in most of the European languages the term 'design' or its equivalent. The emergence of the word coincided with the need to describe the occupation of designing. That is not to suggest that designing was a new activity, rather that it was being separated out from wider productive activity and recognized as a function in its own right. This recognition can be said to constitute a separation of hand and brain, of manual and intellectual work; and the separation of the conceptual part of work from the labour process. Above all, the term indicated that *designing* was to be separated from *doing*.

It is clearly difficult to locate a precise historical turning point at which this separation occurred; rather, we will view it as a historical tendency. Up to the stage in question, a great structure such as a church would be 'built' by a master builder. We may generalize, and say that the conceptual part of the work would be integral to that labour process. Thereafter, however, there began to be the concept of 'designing the church' – an activity undertaken by architects – and 'building the church' – undertaken by builders. It is in no way suggested that this represented a sudden historical discontinuity, but rather it was the beginning of a discernible historical tendency which has still not worked its way through many of the craft skills even today. As recently as the last century, Fairbairn was able to say of the millwright:

> Generally, he was a fair mathematician, knew something of geometry, levelling and mensuration, and in some cases possessed a very competent knowledge of practical mathematics. He could calculate the velocity, strength and power of machines, could draw in plan and section, could construct bridges, conduits and water courses in all forms and under all conditions required in his professional practice. He could build bridges, cut canals and perform a variety of work now done by civil engineers.[1]

To this day, there are many jobs in which the conceptual part of work is still integrated with the craft basis. The significant feature of the stage in question is, however, that by separating manual work from intellectual work, it provided the basis for further sub-divisions in the field of intellectual work itself, or as

Braverman put it, 'Mental labour is first separated from the manual labour and then itself is subdivided rigorously according to the same rules.'[2]

Dreyfus locates the root of the problem in the Greek use of logic and geometry, and the notion that all reasoning can be reduced to some kind of calculation. He suggests that the start of artificial intelligence was probably around the year 450 BC, with Socrates and his concern to establish a moral standard. He asserts that Plato generalized this demand into an epistemological demand, where one might hold that all knowledge could be stated in explicit definitions which anybody could apply. If 'know-how' could not be stated in terms of such explicit instructions, then that know-how was not knowledge at all, but mere *belief*. He suggests a Platonic tradition in which 'Cooks, for example, who proceed by taste and intuition, and poets who work from inspiration, have no knowledge. What they do does not involve understanding and cannot be understood. More generally, what cannot be stated explicitly in precise instructions – all areas of human thought that require skill, intuition or sense of tradition – are relegated to some kind of arbitrary fumbling.'[3]

Gradually, there was evolved a view which put the objective above the subjective, the quantitative above the qualitative. That the two should and can interact was not accepted, in spite of a systematic effort and intellectual struggle to assert that they could do so.

One important example of the attempt was the work of Albrecht Dürer (1471-1528), who was not only a 'master of the arts' but also a brilliant mathematician who reached the highest academic levels in Nuremberg. Dürer sought to use his abilities to develop mathematical forms which would succeed in preserving the unity of hand and brain. Cantor[4] recounts the significance of his ability to relate complex mathematical techniques to practical uses, whilst Olschki[5] compares his mathematical achievements with those of the leading mathematicians at that time, in Italy and elsewhere. Indeed, some ninety years after Dürer's death Kepler was still discussing his geometric construction techniques. Alfred Sohn-Rethel points out of Dürer: 'Instead, however, of using this knowledge in a scholarly form, he endeavoured to put it to the advantage of the craftsman. His work was dedicated "to the young workers and all those with no one to instruct them truthfully" and what is novel in his method is that he seeks to combine the workman's practice with Euclidian geometry.' Further, 'What Dürer had in mind is plain to see. The builders, metalworkers etc., should, on the one hand be enabled to master the tasks of military and civil technology and architecture which far exceeded their traditional training. On the other hand, the required mathematics should serve them as a means so to speak of preserving the unity of head and hand. They should benefit by the indispensable advantages of mathematics without becoming mathematics or brainworkers themselves. They should practice socialized thinking yet remain individual producers, and so he offered them an artisan schooling in draughtsmanship permeated through and through with mathematics – not to be confused in any way with applied mathematics.'[6]

It was said that on one occasion Dürer proclaimed it would be possible to develop forms of mathematics which would be as amenable to the human spirit as natural language. Thereby one could integrate into the use of instruments of labour the conceptual parts of work, building on the tradition in which complex shapes were defined and constructed with devices such as 'Sine-Bars'.

Thus theory, itself a generalization of practice, could have been reintegrated into practice to extend the richness of that practice and its application while retaining the integration of hand and brain. The richness of that practical tradition may be found in the sketchbook of Villard de Honnecourt in which he introduced himself thus

> Villard de Honnecourt greets you and begs all who will use the devices found in this book, to pray for his soul and remember him. For in this book will be found advice on the virtues of masonry and the uses of carpentry. You will also find strong help in drawing figures according to the lessons taught by the art of geometry.[7]

This extraordinary document by a true thirteenth-century cathedral builder contains subjects which might be categorized as follows:
1   Mechanics
2   Practical Geometry and Trigonometry
3   Carpentry
4   Architectural Design
5   Ornamental Design
6   Figure Design
7   Furniture Design
8   'Subjects foreign to the special knowledge of Architects and Designers'
The astonishing breadth and holistic nature of the skills and knowledge are in the manuscripts for all to see.

There are those who, while admitting to the extraordinary range of capabilities of craftspeople of this time, tend to hold that it was a 'static' form of knowledge which tended to be handed on unaltered from master to apprentice. In reality, there were embodied in these crafts, and in their transmission, dynamic processes for extending their base and adding new knowledge all the time. Some of the German manuscripts describe the *Wanderjahre*, in which craftspeople travelled from city to city to acquire new knowledge, anticipating by some six hundred years the sabbatical of modern academics. Villard de Honnecourt travelled extensively, and thanks to his sketchbook we can trace his progress through France, Switzerland, Germany and Hungary. He was also passionately interested in mechanical devices, and one system he invented was subsequently adapted to keep mariners' compasses horizontally level and barometers vertical. He devised a variety of clock mechanisms from which we learn 'how to make the Angel keep pointing his finger towards the sun', and he displayed extraordinary engineering skills in devising a range of lifting and other equipment to provide significant mechanical advantage. Thus he invented a screw combined with a lever with appropriate instructions: 'How to make the most powerful engine for lifting weights.' In all of this, we see brilliantly portrayed the integration of design with doing – a tradition which was still discernible when Fairbairn described his millwright.[8]

Villard was likewise concerned with 'automation', but in a form which freed the human being from backbreaking physical effort while retaining the skilled base of work – in the case of woodworking, a means of replacing the strenuous activity of sawing by a system in which he described 'How to make a saw operate itself'.

He was profoundly interested in geometry as applied to drawings: 'Here begins the method of drawing as taught by the art of geometry – but to understand them one must be careful to learn the particular use of each. All these devices are extracted from geometry'; and he proceeds to describe 'How to measure the height of a tower', 'How to measure the width of a water course without crossing it', 'How to make two vessels so that one holds twice as much as the other'. Many modern researchers have testified to Villard's significant grasp of geometry, but side by side with this 'theory' we find practical advice to stonecutters on the dimensions of building elements: 'How to cut an oblique voussoir', 'How to cut the springing stone of an arch', 'How to make regular pendants'. All of this latter, drawn from his own practical experience and skill, is a vivid portrayal of the integration of hand and brain.

Another thirteenth-century manuscript, written in the same dialect as Villard's is still preserved and can be consulted in the Bibliothèque St Geneviève in Paris. Its author likewise concerned himself with mathematical problems: 'If you want to find the area of an equilateral triangle', 'If you want to know the area of an octagon', 'If you want to find the number of houses in a circular city'. Throughout this period the intellectual and the manual, the theory and the practice, were integral to the craft or profession. Indeed, so naturally did the two coexist that we find practical builders (architects) with the university title Doctor Lathomorum. The epitaph of Pierre de Montreuil, the architect who reconstructed the nave and transepts of Saint Denis, runs: 'Here lies Pierre de Montreuil, a perfect flower of good manners, in this life a Doctor of Stones'.

I have cited these sketchbooks and quoted from these manuscripts in order to demonstrate that the craft at that time embodied powerful elements of theory, scientific method and the conceptual or design base of the activity. In doing so, I am myself guilty of a serious error. I accept that a matter can only be scientific or theoretical when it is written down. I did not provide an illustration of a great church or complex structure and state that the building of such a structure must itself embody a sound theoretical basis, otherwise the structure could not have been built in the first instance. We can also detect in the written form the basic elements of that which we regard as scientific – namely, a process must display the three predominant characteristics of what subsequently became known as Western scientific methodology, that is,

predictability, repeatability and mathematical quantifiability. These, by definition, tend to preclude *intuition, subjective judgment* and *tacit knowledge*.
Furthermore, we begin to regard design as that which reduces or eliminates
uncertainty; and since human judgment, as distinct from calculation, is itself
held to constitute an uncertainty, it follows from some kind of Jesuitical logic
that good design is about eliminating human judgment and intuition. Furthermore, by rendering explicit the 'secrets' of craft, we prepare the basis for a
'rule-based system'.

In the two centuries that succeeded there followed systematic attempts to
describe, and thereby render visible, the rules underlying various craft skills.
This applied right across the spectrum of skills of the artist/architects/
engineers, from the theory of building construction through to painting and
drawing in the Giotto tradition. Giotto's method was not precisely optical. The
receding beams of his ceilings converge to a reasonably convincing focus, but it
is only approximate and does not coincide with the horizontal line as it should,
according to the rules of linear perspective. 'This method is however, systematic and based on rational factors which no doubt provided a powerful stimulus
for the more fully scientific rule seekers of the subsequent centuries. Priority
amongst those who preceded Leonardo in searching for precise optical laws in
picture making must go to the great architect and erstwhile sculptor Filippo
Brunelleschi.'[9]

According to Manetti, at some time before 1413 Brunelleschi constructed
two drawings which showed how buildings could be represented 'in what
painters today call perspective, for it is part of that science which is in effect set
down well and with reason the diminutions and enlargements which appear to
the eyes of man from things far away and close at hand.' One of the paintings
showed the octagonal baptistery (S. Giovanni) as seen from the door of the
Cathedral. The optical 'truth' was verified by drilling a small hole in the
baptistery panel. The spectator was intended to pick up the panel and press his
eye to the hole on the unpainted side. With the other hand he was then required
to hold the mirror in such a way that the painted surface was visible in
reflection through the hole. By these means, Brunelleschi established precisely
the perpendicular axis along which his representation should be viewed. By use
of a mirror, there was a precise matching of the visual experience and the
painted representation, and this was to become Leonardo's theory of art and
indeed his whole theory of knowledge.[10]

The same scientific methods were to be applied to architectural and other
designs. One interpretation of these events is that they represented a significant
turning-point in the history of design and design methodology. Thereafter,
there is to be seen a growing separation of theory and practice, growing
emphasis upon the written 'theoretical forms of knowledge' and, in my view, a
growing confusion in Western society between linguistic ability and intelligence. There has been a denigration of what (after Polanyi) I call 'tacit
knowledge', in which there are 'things we know but cannot tell'.[11] In this

regard we may cite that most illustrious embodiment of theory and practice, Leonardo da Vinci:

> They will say that, not having learning I will not properly speak of that which I wish to elucidate. But do they not know that my subjects are to be better illustrated from experience than by yet more words? Experience, which has been the mistress of all those who wrote well and thus as mistress I will cite her in all cases.[12]

In spite of such assertions, the tendency to produce generalized, written down, scientific or rule-based design systems thereafter continued space. In 1486 the German architect Mathias Roriczer published in Regensburg his 'On the Ordination of Pinnacles'. In this, he set out the method of designing pinnacles from plan drawings, and in fact produced a generalized method of design for pinnacles and other parts of a cathedral. These tendencies had already elicited bitter resistance from the craftsmen/designers whose work was thereby being deskilled. For example, in 1459 master masons from such cities as Strasburg, Vienna and Salzburg met at Regensburg in order to codify their Lodge Statutes. Among the various decisions, they decided that nothing was to be revealed concerning the art of making an elevation from a plan drawing to those who were not in the Guild: 'therefore, no worker, no master no "wage earner" or no journeyman will divulge to anyone who is not of our Guild and who has never worked as a Mason, how to make the elevation from the plan.' Of particular note is the exclusion of those who had never *worked* as Masons.

There is, as our German colleagues would put it, a *Doppelnatur* to this craft reaction. On the one hand there is the negative elitist attempt to retain privileges of the profession (rather as the medical profession seeks to do to this day). On the other hand there is the highly positive aspect of seeking to retain the qualitative and the quantitative elements of work, the subjective and the objective, the creative and the non-creative, the manual and the intellectual, and the work of hand and brain embodied in the one craft. The pressures on them were twofold. Not only was the conceptual part of the work to be taken away from them, but those who still embodied the intellectual and design skills were being rejected by those who sought to show that theory was above and separate from practice. In this context, the growing academic elite resented the fact that carpenters and builders were known as Masters, e.g. Magister Cementarius or Magister Lathomus. The academics sought to ensure that 'Magister' would be reserved for those who had completed the study of the liberal arts. Indeed, as early as the thirteenth century, doctors of law had been moved to protest formally at these academic titles for practical people.

It is both fascinating and illuminating to trace these tendencies through the five intervening centuries which take us up to the information society of Computer Aided Design and Expert Systems. Suffice it to say that a number of researchers, drawing on historical perspective, and viewing the implications of these information-based systems, conclude that we may now be at another historical turning-point in which we are about to repeat in the field of design and other forms of intellectual work, many of the mistakes made in the field of craftsmanship in the period under review.[13].

Part of the skill of a draughtsman or a designer was the ability to look at a drawing and conceptualize what the product would look like in practice. That conceptualization process is now also being eliminated by computers. I have, in my lectures, illustrated systems which are capable of tracing round the profile of the conventional type of drawing which includes plan and elevation views, and producing an accurate three-dimensional representation of the object on the screen before it actually exists in practice. The computer will rotate it through any angle for you when given instructions. This can be extended further in the field of architecture. Normally, a plan of a proposed municipal building is available for inspection in the town hall, but for most people this means very little. It is intelligible only to an elite group. A visual display such as the one described could be made of any proposed municipal building, and local people *could* be involved in deciding whether they approved of its design and its location.

In the case of architectural design, each building and object is defined in its own three-dimensional co-ordinate system. These are then presented as a hierarchical structure of co-ordinate data. This means that all the existing buildings can be input as data structure and the new building to be designed is shown within the context of the existing architectural arrangements. That is to say, we can experience in the equivalent of 'real time' walking towards a building that still does not exist in practice. We can have the sensation of going inside the proposed building and looking out at the existing buildings. We can take windows out, move them about, enlarge the whole thing and take it right away from the proposed site. The aim is to assess the total effect of the new building on the whole environment before constructing it. There are already grounds for believing, however, that images of reality as presented in that form are still very different from the actuality. When the building is erected, a sort of ghetto-like prison atmosphere can result which is not apparent when the relationship between the object and the real world is severed.

A discernible feature about modern equipment of any kind is the rate of change that is now driving us along at an unprecedented speed. Over the last century alone the speed of communication has increased by 10^7, of travel by 10^2, of data handling by 10^6. Over the same period energy resources have increased by 10^3 and weapon power by 10^6. We are being drawn along in this tremendous technological mill-race, with the result that the knowledge we have, and the basis upon which we judge the world about us is becoming obsolete at an ever increasing rate, just as the equipment is. It is now the case in many fields of endeavour that simply to stand still, specialists must spend 15 per cent of their time updating their knowledge. It has been said that if you could divide knowledge into quartiles of out-datedness, all those over the age of forty would be in the same quartile as Pythagoras and Archimedes. This alone shows the incredible rate of change; the stress it places upon design staff, particularly the older ones, should not be underestimated.

Where computerized systems are installed, the operators are subjected to work which is alienating, fragmented and of an ever increasing tempo. As the human being tries to keep pace with the rate at which the computer can handle the quantitative data in order to be able to make the qualitative value judgements, the resulting stress is enormous. Some systems we have looked at increase the decision making rate by 1800 per cent, and work done by Bernholz in Canada has shown that getting a designer to interact in this way will mean that the designer's creativity, or ability to deal with new problems, is reduced by 30 per cent in the first hour, by 80 per cent in the second hour, and thereafter the designer is shattered. The crude introduction of computers into the design activity in keeping with the Western ethic of 'the faster the better' may well result in a plummeting of the quality of design.

It is a fact that the highly constrained and organized intellectual environment of a computerized office is remarkably at variance with the circumstances and attributes which appear to have contributed to creativity in the arts and sciences. I have heard it said that if only Beethoven had had a computer available to him for generating musical combinations, the Ninth Symphony would have been even more beautiful. But creativity is a much more subtle process. If you look historically at creative people, they have always had an open-ended child-like curiosity. They have been highly motivated, and with a sense of excitement in the work they were doing. Above all, they possessed the ability to bring an original approach to problems. They had, in other words, very fertile imaginations. It is our ability to use our imagination that distinguishes us from animals. As Karl Marx wrote:

> A bee puts to shame many an architect in the construction of its cells; but what distinguishes the worst of architects from the best of bees is namely this. The architect will construct in his imagination that which he will ultimately erect in reality. At the end of every labour process, we get that which existed in the consciousness of the labourer at its commencement.[14]

If we continue to design systems in the manner described earlier, we will be reducing ourselves to bee-like behaviour.

It is significant that Weizenbaum, himself a professor of computer science at MIT, in his seminal work *Computer Power and Human Reason*[15] uses the subtitle 'From Judgement to Calculation' and highlights the dangers which will surround an uncritical acceptance of these computerized techniques. The spectrum of problems associated with them are already becoming manifest, including the spectacular separation of theory and practice whereby some of those who have been weaned on CAD are unable to recognize the object that they have 'designed'.

Epitomizing this was the designer of an after-burner igniter who, on the CAD screen, calculated, and then set out, the dimensions with the decimal point one place to the right (which in an abstraction is very much like one place to the left), and then generated the numerical control tapes with which deskilled manual workers succeeded in producing an igniter ten times larger than it should have been.[16] Perhaps the most alarming aspect of this extraordinary state of affairs was that when confronted with the resultant monstrosity, he did not even recognize that it was ten times larger than it should have been.

Less spectacular, but in the long term of growing significance, is the design rigidity which *menu-driven* systems tend to produce. In the field of architecture there are systems in which there are optimized windows, doors, rooms, and architects are being reduced to behaving like a child with a Lego set: they can make a pleasing pattern of predetermined architectural elements but cannot change those elements. Rosenbrock has cautioned that our existing forms of CAD systems design are permanently closing off options in a manner which reflects 'a loss of nerve, a loss of belief in human abilities, and a further unthinking application of the doctrine of the division of labour'.[17]

Given the scale and nature of these problems and the exponential rate of technological change within which they are located, it behoves all of us to seek to demonstrate, as Dürer did, that alternatives exist which reject neither human judgment, tacit knowledge, intuition and imagination, nor the scientific or rule-based method, and that we should unite them in a symbiotic totality.

Rosenbrock has charged that the present techniques fail to exploit the opportunity which interactive computing can offer. The computer and the human mind have quite different but complementary abilities. The computer excels in analysis and numerical computation, the human mind in pattern recognition, the assessment of complicated situations and the intuitive leap to new solutions. If these different abilities can be combined, they amount to something much more powerful and effective than anything we have had before. Such systems already exist in narrow specific areas, as Rosenbrock has demonstrated with the computer aided design of complex control systems, where the performance is displayed as an inverse Nyquist array on the screen.[18]

Likewise, the present writer has described the potential for human-centred systems in both skilled manual work and the design activity.[19] Furthermore, we worked in the technology division of the Greater London Enterprise Board (through our technology networks) on the development of expert medical systems which provide an interaction between the 'facts of the domain' and the fuzzy reasoning, tacit knowledge, imagination and heuristics of the expert. No attempt is made to reduce all these aspects to a rule-based system; rather, the system is seen as that which aids rather than replaces the expert.

An important breakthrough for these human-centred systems has been the recent decision by the EEC's ESPRIT programme, to fund jointly a project to build the world's first Human Centred Computer Integrated Manufacturing System. The ten-partner project, with teams in Denmark, Germany and the United Kingdom, was initiated by the Greater London Enterprise Board. The Danes are dealing with the CAD end of the system, the German partners are handling the computer aided production and the United Kingdom is designing the CAM system; GLEB is acting as overall programme co-ordinator. At each of the levels, from design through production planning to manufacturing, the system builds on human skill rather than marginalizes it. Thus the human being handles the qualitative subjective judgement and the machine merely the quantitative elements. The human being dominates the machine rather than the other way round. Professor Rauner and his colleagues at the University of Bremen are developing an educational program which will go with the system, since we are concerned, not merely with production but with the reproduction of knowledge.

The education will differ dramatically from the 'Mickey Mouse' training schemes now so prevalent in Britain, frequently run by those who seem to believe that if you have trained a labrador to retrieve, you can train a highly qualified engineering designer. It is, after all, just 'training'. Apprenticeships in the historical sense were not just the transmission of narrow technical skills, they were the transmission of a culture. Technology is itself part of culture, and just as culture produces different language, different literature and different music why should it also not produce different forms of science and technology? The objective in the Human Centred System is to build in a set of values which embody such concerns as self-motivation, dignity, sense of quality and motivation, and commitment to work which links hand and brain in a meaningful and satisfying productive process. The new technologies will force upon us dramatic restructuring. That restructuring can either take the form of narrow, Tayloristic, mechanistic and deskilled forms of production in the fields of both manual and intellectual work, or it can be constructed to build upon the greatest asset society has, which is the skill, ingenuity and the creativity of its people. We appear to be at another historical turning point and the options are still open.

It may be regarded as romantic or succumbing to mysticism to emphasize the importance of imagination and of working in a non-linear way. It is usually accepted that this type of creative approach is required in music, literature and art. It is less well recognized that this is equally important in the fields of science, technology and design, and in the so-called harder sciences like mathematics and physics. Those who were creative recognized this themselves. Isaac Newton said, 'I seem to have been only like a boy playing on the sea shore and diverting myself in now and then finding a smoother pebble or a prettier shell than ordinary, while the great ocean of truth lay all undiscovered before me.'

REFERENCES

1 Fairbairn, William, *Treatise on Mills and Millwork*, preface to 1st edn, London 1861.
2 Braverman, Henry, *Labor and Monopoly Capital: the degradation of work in the twentieth-century*, New York 1974.
3 Dreyfus, Hubert *What Computers Can't Do*, Rev. Ed. New York/London 1979.
4 Cantor, Moritz, *Vorlesungen über die Geschichte der Mathematik*, vol.2, Leipzig, 1892.
5 Olschki, Leo Samuel, *Geschichte der neusprachlichen wissenschaftlichen Literatur*, Leipzig, 1919.
6 Sohn-Rethel, Alfred, *Intellectual and Manual Labour – A Critique of Epistemology*, London, 1978.
7 Bowie, T., *The Sketchbook of Villard de Honnecourt*, Indiana, 1959.
8 Fairbairn, op. cit.
9 Kemp, M., *Leonardo da Vinci: The Marvellous Works of Nature and Man*, London, 1981, p.26.
10 ibid.
11 Polanyi, Michael, 'Tacit Knowing: its bearing on problems of philosophy', *Review of Modern Physics*, vol.34, 1962.
12 Kemp, op. cit., p.102.
13 Cooley, M., *Architect or Bee?*, Slough, 1981; 'Computerisation – Taylor's Latest Disguise', *Economic and Industrial Democracy*, vol.1, London, 1981.
14 Cooley, M., *Architect or Bee?*' op. cit.
15 Weizenbaum, J., *Computer Power and Human Reason*, San Francisco, 1976.
16 Aspinal, Cooley, et al., *New Technology and Employment* London, 1981.
17 Rosenbrock, H.H., 'The Future of Control', *Automatica*, vol.13, 1977, pp.389–92; 'The Redirection of Technology', IFAC Conference, Bari, 1979.
18 Cooley, M., *Computer Aided Design – its nature and implications*, Richmond, 1973.
19 Cooley, M., 'Trade Union, Technology and Human Need' (50-page report), Geneva, 1984.

—16—

The product as illusion
•
TOM MITCHELL

Traditional methods of product design have proved unsuitable in application to new information technology design tasks such as the making of computer software. A number of high technology industries in Japan and the United States have been compelled to abandon traditional design methods, which were developed for the mechanistic design of the industrial era, and develop new, post-mechanical design methods.

The transition from mechanistic to post-mechanical design methods closely parallels the changes which have taken place in science itself. The mechanistic science which provided the impetus for the industrial revolution has been seriously challenged throughout this century by new scientific concepts such as quantum mechanics, relativity and, most recently, non-equilibrium thermodynamics. Each of these theoretical developments abandons the static, objective world view of classical science and stresses instead the importance of dynamic processes in which the observer's presence is an inseparable element of the scientific effect itself.

The assumptions behind classical science are articulated by Ilya Prigogine, winer of the 1977 Nobel Prize for chemistry, who says, 'The classical ... view of science was to regard the world as an "object", to try and describe the physical world as if it were being seen from the outside as an object of analysis to which we do not belong'.[1] In contrast to the static, deterministic view of classical science, the new concepts in science are dynamic and evolutionary. The founding principles of classical science – order, simplicity and stability – have been abandoned in the new world view of science in favour of new organizing principles – disorder, complexity and change. The transition in the world view of science is described by Prigogine, who says, 'The deterministic laws of physics, which were at one point the only acceptable laws, today seem like gross simplifications, nearly a caricature of evolution . . . Even in physics, as in sociology, only various possible "scenarios" can be predicted. But is is for this very reason that we are participating in a fascinating adventure in which, in the words of Niels Bohr, we are "both spectators and actors".'[2]

The disparity between classical science and the new, process-oriented, observer-dependent approaches is analogous to the difference between traditional, mechanistically derived design methods and the developing post-mechanical design methods. In design, as in science, the static 'object' or 'product' approach must be abandoned for new process-oriented and observer/user-dependent design tasks such as the design of computer software.

The shifting focus in designing, away from machines and objects to processes and people, has been called the 'Human Age' by several major Japanese high technology companies. The phrase is used by Japanese industries to describe the growing importance of people's needs over technological innovations in determining the course of the product planning process. The development of the 'Human Age' concept in Japanese industry is traced by Bill Evans in an article in *Design Studies*. 'Without fail', Evans says, 'the major (Japanese) companies are developing a sophisticated analysis of the future which is becoming increasingly user conscious; they are looking to a period where advances in electronics are consolidating rather than rapidly advancing. As Ricoh puts it: We have moved from the "Hardware Age" (1965–75) through the "Software Age" (1975–85) towards the "Human Age". By this they mean that the users' requirements will take over as the major dictator of a product's capability: "we have the technology". So the companies are now concentrating on the input of consumer lifestyle into the product, making the technology more intelligent, more flexible for users of different cultural backgrounds and generally considering the social context of their products.'[3]

Evans says further, 'Many companies employ social scientists to work along with their product designers in the product planning centres. These are not necessarily taken on to practise their specialization, but to let their education make a contribution to the complex and iterative product design process. At Sony's "PP Centre" they have a cultural anthropologist helping to brief the software engineers for their range of personal computers ... As Sony say, "You have to know people first before making any product."'[4]

The changing design strategy of Japanese high technology industry toward a more interdisciplinary approach is echoed in the computer industry in the United States. In an article in *The Times*, Kevan Pearson reports that a survey of American data processing managers indicates that they are 'increasingly looking for "generalists" rather than technicians ... they prefer arts, social science or business studies graduates, to those who have studied specialist subjects like computer science'.[5] As in the Japanese high technology industries, people with non-technical educational backgrounds are not employed to practise the subject they studied, but rather because the data processing managers, 'want people who can approach problems with an open mind, rather than from a technical, computer science orientation'.[6]

Visually oriented product design has a relatively brief history. The idea of 'The Product' as an object considered in isolation from its context of use did not exist before the advent of industrialization, nor did design professionals who planned, but did not construct, products. Before industrialization objects were made using craft processes in which the planning and the making of objects were inseparable aspects of the same process. Using hands-on, trial-and-error techniques, craftwork was evolved directly within the context in which it would be used to suit each client's specific requirements. The production methods of pre-industrial craftwork are described by George Sturt, a nineteenth-century craftsman, in his book *The Wheelwright's Shop*. Sturt says 'We got curiously intimate with the peculiar needs of the neighbourhood. In farm-wagon or dung-cart, barley-roller, plough, waterbarrel, or what not, the dimensions we chose, the curves we followed (and almost every piece of timber was curved) were imposed upon us by the nature of the soil in this or that farm, the gradient of this or that hill, the temper of this or that customer or his choice perhaps in horseflesh.'[7] The direct experience of materials, patterns of use and clients described by Sturt is in sharp contrast to the isolation of product designers from the manufacture, use and users of their designs.

The methods of craft evolution and visually oriented product design are contrasted by John Chris Jones in his book *Design Methods*, and in his contribution which follows this one. According to Jones the principal difference between product design and the process of pre-industrial craft evolution is, 'that trial-and-error is separated from production by using a scale drawing in place of the product as the medium for experiment and change'.[8] Rather than interacting directly with the object being made, as in craftwork, experimentation in product design is largely confined to the manipulation of two-dimensional scale drawings. The use of drawings as a model of reality, though permitting larger projects to be attempted than are possible by an individual craftsman working alone and making increased rates of production possible, often leads to results which less satisfactorily respond to people's individual requirements than those attained using the craft process. Unlike pre-industrial craftwork, in which thinking and making were both integral parts of the same process, all product design since industrialization has been characterized by a strict division of thinking from making.

The separation of planning from making, and the consequent isolation of designing from using which is engendered by the use of drawings as a design tool, has led to two separate criteria for evaluating design – those of designers and those of design users. Designers use static, visual criteria which result from their use of drawings to evaluate design, while the people affected by designing base their judgments upon how successfully their requirements are satisfied during their dynamic, multisensory interactions with design. The disparate aspirations of designers and design users has led to some well publicized anomalies.

The discontinuity between the wishes of designers and the people affected by design is epitomized by the failures of many of the tower blocks constructed in the 1960s. Though now perhaps a clichéd example, the Pruitt-Igoe housing project in St Louis, Missouri, illustrates how strikingly these different criteria for evaluating design can conflict.

Upon completion, the Pruitt-Igoe housing project was given design awards by the American Institute of Architects which considered the project to be an exemplar for future low-cost housing projects. By contrast, it was experienced as a complete failure by those who lived there. The project's highrise design proved unsuitable for the lifestyles of the people who inhabited it; parents on upper floors had difficulty supervising their children playing outside; inadequate public toilet facilities were provided, which led to the halls and lifts becoming *de facto* lavatories; and the dehumanized scale of the project led to a breakdown of the residents' traditional social relationships, enabling crime and vandalism to flourish on the estate. Sixteen years after completion large sections of the project were, at the inhabitants' request, destroyed.

Pruitt-Igoe illustrates how members of the architecture profession evaluated the project *before any of the buildings had been occupied* – according to static, visual criteria – and judged it to be a success. Pruitt-Igoe inhabitants formed *their* opinions upon their experience of living in the building, rather than by looking at it. When the residents were finally asked at a public meeting what they thought of the project they chanted, 'Tear it down!'

The incongruity of the designer's models of reality – drawings – and the reality within which design is used highlights the problem created by the separation of planning from making. Craft-derived approaches have many advantages over their mechanically-derived predecessors. By actually making, rather than simply planning products, designers are able directly to experience how well their products work. The emphasis in making computer software, as with traditional craftwork, is upon the processes of using the product, its ease of operation, its suitability for the task and its adaptability to the user's specific requirements. With all computer software, the user's experience, rather than the physicality of the product, becomes the focus; the traditional concept is extended from physical objects to intangible processes.

The contrast between traditional product design and the new craft-derived approach of many software makers is analogous to the conflicting purposes of traditional and avant-garde modern art. Just as the transition from traditional art to modern art entailed not so much a change of style, but rather a complete change of attitude, approach and method, so the traditional product design approach and the emerging notion of designing as a process represent fundamentally different conceptions of design. The work of the artists of the avant garde provides a useful insight into how the transition from work with physical outcomes to purely conceptual work can be realized.

The composer John Cage has written extensively on the philosophy of the avant garde; in an essay on the artist Robert Rauschenberg, Cage contrasts the approach of modern art to that of the art which preceded it. He says, 'Modern art has no need for technique. (We are in the glory of not knowing what we're doing.) So technique, not having to do with painting, has to do with who's looking and who painted. People. Technique is: how are the people?'[9]

Several artists have forsaken their product, the art object, for an art based upon process. Cage, for example, often restricts his compositions to the definition of a process, specifying methods and systems within which chance is permitted to determine the piece's outcome. Having initiated the composition process, Cage becomes a listener, just like any other, hearing each of 'his' pieces anew at each performance. The intention of Cage's use of chance and indeterminacy is described by another composer, David Cope, who says, 'Indeterminacy implies art as process. No beginning, no middle, no end; that is, no longer will "objects" of music exist in that sense, but each new performance, each new circumstance will create a continually variable process of ideas.'[10] Harold Rosenberg calls the trend away from a product oriented art to a more conceptual art of process, 'De-aestheticization . . . the total repudiation of the art object and its replacement with an idea.'[11]

Two art works which embody the philosophy of a conceptual art as process are Rauschenberg's *White Paintings* and Cage's *4'33"*. *White Paintings* consist of seven canvases uniformly covered with white house-paint. Initially the paintings look 'empty', but they come to reflect the character, colour and shadows of the room in which they hang. Similarly, *4'33"*, a piece in three movements for any instrument (or instruments) none of which are played, focuses the audience's attention on the sounds naturally occurring in the room they are occupying. Cage describes the philosophy behind contextual works such as *4'3"*: 'Where it is realized that sounds occur whether intended or not, one turns in the direction of those he does not intend. This turning is psychological and seems at first to be a giving up of everything that belongs to humanity – for a musician, the giving up of music. This psychological turning leads to the word of nature where, gradually or suddenly, one sees that humanity and nature, not separate, are in this world together; that nothing was lost when everything was given away. In fact, everything is gained.'[12] Both Rauschenberg's *White Paintings* and Cage's *4'33"* reflect the giving up by their initiators of their traditional roles as artists or musicians and the turning, instead, to a more passive approach initiating processes which assume that there is a unity in the world which will be created anew by each viewer or listener each time the works are experienced.

The work of Rauschenberg and Cage, with its preoccupation with process, provides a precedent for understanding designing as a continous process. Just as John Cage, a musician, had to give up music in order to realize his experiments with composition as process, so designers must dismantle their traditional roles as arbiters of taste and dictators of physical forms in order to participate in the more conceptually oriented understanding of designing as a continuous process.

Within the avant-garde many artists have modified their role in the design of processes or physical systems by allowing chance to influence, and in some cases determine, the outcome. Indeterminacy enables them to relinquish total control over the outcome of their art; describing Cage's philosophy, David Cope says, 'Indeterminacy philosophy must lie in a concept of disassociating man's significance as a creator, emphasizing the possibilities of man as a creative performer/listener; understanding being something pedagogical and within the realm of language, not aesthetics.'[13]

The passive approach advocated by Cage and present in software making is echoed through different methods in the work of the composer/videomaker Brian Eno. Describing the philosophy behind the *Discreet Music* album, Eno says, 'I have always preferred making plans to executing them, I have gravitated towards situations and systems that, once set into operation, could create music with little or no intervention on my part. This is to say I tend toward the roles of planner and programmer, and then become an audience to the results.'[14] Eno uses systems to avoid directly affecting the music he produces. Describing the process he followed in making the piece he says, 'If there is any score for the piece it must be the operational diagram of the particular apparatus I used for its production . . . it is a point of discipline to accept this passive role, and, for once, to ignore the tendency to play the artist by dabbling and interfering.'[15] By his adoption of a passive role in relation to his work, Eno has been able to develop his compositions based upon the processes of making sounds, rather than concerning himself directly with the sounds produced by his systems. He largely completes his task of composition when he has specified the way in which sound will be made, establishing a framework within which chance can determine the actual outcome. Through his use of systems which incorporate chance, Eno, like Cage, assumes a passive role towards his work and becomes, with his audience, a listener rather than a creator.

A corollary of the passive approach assumed by Eno and Cage is that *everyone may participate in the creative process*. No longer do artists produce an art object to be appreciated or judged; rather, they provide a system, a stimulus, which can be variously interpreted by each person who experiences it, including the artist. The experience and interpretation of art by the observer becomes the true creative act and is the focus of the artist's work, rather than an attempt at an ideal physical expression.

My own work on 'perceptually based design' is an attempt to evaluate environments by varying spatial scale and music tempo, and to see how these changes affect people psychologically/perceptually. This approach differs markedly from the current self-referential geometric/architectural approach to environmental design. Eventually it is hoped that these results will be used to design environments which will specifically enhance certain perceptual qualities.

Designers already intuitively use this approach, which is why discos are different from churches, and banks look different from schools. The work will make certain perceptual qualities of an environment explicit.

Developing a formal understanding of the perceptual effect of the environment is particularly important in relation to new media and new concepts of environments such as environmental/ambient music, video, light intensity, colour and image complexity – as well as the combinations of these factors for which there is, as yet, no intuitive knowledge. It is hoped through the present research into the effect of spatial scale on time perception to develop a perceptual metric, or scale, into which future studies into these media may be fitted.

By creating systems which focus upon people's experience of using their product, rather than upon the physicality of the product itself, software makers have created new roles for themselves. Like the avant-garde artists, software makers assume the passive role of providing systems in which everyone may participate. Unlike traditional product design, which is intended solely as a means of producing physical objects, post-industrial designing, as typified by software making, is a continuous and non-instrumental thought process participated in equally by software makers and users.

For new, post-mechanical design tasks, such as the making of computer software, current product design methods are completely inapplicable. 'The Product' as a solely physical entity is an illusion of the mechanistic era which can no longer be sustained in an age preoccupied with information. In place of the concept of design as simply a means of producing objects, develops an understanding of designing as a continuous and non-instrumental thought process, a creative act in which everyone, designers and non-designers alike, may participate equally. The designer's role in the post-mechanical era is to make the design process equally accessible to everyone. In order to realize this programme, design, like the avant garde of art before it, must abandon aesthetics and become instead a socially oriented process in which, like the new scientists, we are all both spectators and actors.

REFERENCES

1 Prigogine, Ilya, *From Being to Becoming: time and complexity in the physical sciences*. San Francisco, 1980, p. xv.
2 Ibid., p. xvii.
3 Evans, Bill, 'Japanese-style management, product design and corporate strategy', *Design Studies*, vol. 6, no. 1, (1985), pp. 25–33.
4 Ibid.
5 Pearson, Kevan, 'In a renaissance world, IT skills may not be enough', *The Times*, 6 November 1984.
6 Ibid.
7 Quoted in John Chris Jones, *Design Methods*. New York, 1980. p. 17.
8 Ibid., p. 20.
9 Cage, John, *Silence*, Middletown, Connecticut, 1961, p. 101.
10 Cope, David, *New Directions in Music,* 2nd edn, Dubuque, Iowa, 1976, p. 169.
11 Rosenberg, Harold, 'De-Aestheticization', in Gregory Battcock (ed.), *The New Art*, rev. edn, New York, 1973, p. 180.
12 Cage, John, op. cit., p. 8.
13 Cope, David, op. cit., p. 169.
14 Eno, Brian, sleeve notes on *Discreet Music*, London, 1975.
15 Ibid.

—17—

Softecnica

•

JOHN CHRIS JONES

...book, clock, phone, TV, computer, credit card, game, and process–
Softecnica, the soft technologies, or some of them. Not that the names of the
products, the objects, gives the feel of them. That is more evident in the verbs,
the processes: printing, publishing, reading, 'what time is it?', phoning,
watching TV, computing, programming, credit-rating, cash-dispensing, playing space invaders, designing the process. What is it that these have in
common? Most obviously, I'd say, it is that they are non-mechanical, depending not on wheels, gears, pistons, rivets, or heat engines, but on electric power,
low currents, complex circuits, minute components, invisible processes, relati-
vities (in place of absolute standards), and on finding external analogues and
processes fast and delicate enough to be matched to the operations of the eye,
the ear, the brain or any other organ of the body.

I type these words, on a machine, half electric, half mechanical, through an
antiquated 'qwerty' keyboard that makes typing far more difficult than it need
be, to be read in a different typeface and page format, perhaps in another
language. Whoever reads these words will not be experiencing directly my
present thoughts, but firstly deciphering the black marks on paper and then
inferring, consciously or unconsciously, a pattern of meanings and assumptions
that may well differ somewhat from what I am thinking now.

In writing, if not yet in all those other technologies, it is possible, permitted,
to think aloud, to share the moment. Through these little marks. And through
the conventions. What would it be like if not only writing, and telephoning,
but all technologies were opened up to the personal, to you and me? . . .
Perhaps that is what is happening? Is that the meaning of the post-modern; the
shift, in so many fields of life, from the planned and predictable, the multiplied
ideal, the impersonal, to the empiric, the memory, the present thought? To the
product not as means but as presence, as thing-in-itself?

Software. The word, like others coming from computing and the new
technologies, implies a far more than accidental change from the rigid to the
gentle, the mechanical to the automatic, the imposed to the adaptive. But can we
rise to it? Are we, by our inheritance and experience of the harsher technologies
of coal, and steam, and iron, by our acceptance of specialization as norm, so far
adapted to all those things and practices that we have lost the original basis of

organic adaptiveness that enabled us to put up with them? Is it possible to undo all that, to recover mind, and the freely adaptive body of the child, the pre-industrial, in reacting to the so unexpected flexibilities that now appear?

Clock

'Punctuality is the first pillar in the Hall of Success.' The punishment for arriving late at school was to write that out a hundred times. And when I worked in a factory we had precisely 42 minutes for lunch and lost 15 minutes pay if we clocked in one minute late, 30 minutes pay if we clocked in 16 minutes late, and so on . . . There were card-punching clocks even in the most human of factories, that of Adriano Olivetti at Ivrea where I went in the fifties (to try to learn the secret of good design) and found it to be quite a paradise compared to other factories I knew. But there, as everywhere, was the unquestioned obedience to the clock, and to the constant rhythm of the presses, the never-ceasing appetite of the assembly-lines demanding another and another and another identical action from every worker. And nobody seemed to mind. Though to a bystander, like myself, all this seemed, and seems, nothing but a living death, an intolerable, or even laughable, distortion of the very basis of life, both bodily and mental. Yet there, at the Olivetti Fabbrica, I was shown what seemed to be the reason for it all: cost reduction, the rapid creation of wealth and of material benefits at prices many can afford, even those tied to those repetitious jobs. They showed me a hand-built prototype of a new typewriter soon to be manufactured at a price of, I think, £80. I asked how much it cost to make the prototype. They said £5,000, or was it £15,000? In any case, of the order of 100 times as much. That is the miracle, the underlying reason why, and how, modern life is so astonishing, so unlike anything before, so fast, so unnatural, and so attractive. The dreams of gold and magic carpets made real, not through magic, not through art, but through the oldest rationality there ever was. The tick of the clock, the turn of the wheel, and the willingness of everyone to live and work in precise obedience to time-tables, shifts, rush-hours, appointments, and the ceaseless pace of jobs planned to the second for every hour of the working day.

According to Immanuel Kant, whom I believe, 'time is nothing else than the form of internal sense' and 'in itself, independently of the mind or subject, it is nothing. '[1] It does not originate in objects but in ourselves, in how we experience being alive. No wonder, then, that the clock, the external and artificial time scales of hours, minutes, seconds, constructed as one would a toy, or a piece of music, but then believed and imposed as fact or law, with penalties for disbelief or disobedience, is felt to be so wrong. A false model of what is inmost to us masquerading as that which is outside, as if it were space, as if it were 'objective'.

But why, then, it this illusion so necessary, so essential to modern life as we have known it so far? And *is* there a possibility (in the post-mechanical, in the softening and enlivening of technology, in our walking away from that narrow path in which we were taught to believe) that this primary fact or error can be corrected?

The necessity for clocktime, as governor of industrial action, comes, I imagine, from the simplicity of mechanical machines. The only way in which they can be harnessed to human wishes is for those wishes to be fixed in advance, in the form of objective goals, which can then be broken down into stages or operations, backwards in 'time' which can then be endlessly 'replayed', as process, as production line, to create the magic speed, or wealth, which we have come to depend upon and also to obey ... And can all this be undone, while retaining the speed, the low cost, the choice, the enlargement of life for everyone? I think it can. It can if we can change as much as the machines have changed. The new machines tend not to have a goal, they are becoming free processes that will play as fast, or as well, without a preset plan, without forcing us to unify the times and differences that make us each distinct.

The clock itself has never had a goal. It has always been pure process, music, quite sublime. And the new ones are silent.

Computer

Automation, robots, artificial intelligence, expert systems . . . and now personal computers and intelligent cars, cookers, typewriters, phones, videos, weapons, toys. The coming of live objects, a new presence in the world.

This is being composed in Osborne, my first computer, and it will be printed by Praxis, an electric typewriter on which mistakes can be corrected at the touch of a key. There is quite a fundamental difference between them. The computer is a new category of machine, being designed for no specific purpose but able to do various things if programmed to do them. This seems to make it difficult to use and is I suppose the source of the widespread feeling that 'computers are not for me'. The typewriter-with-memory, a familiar but now intelligent object, is a more friendly idea.

Computer-assisted design, computer-assisted writing, computer-assisted life . . . what do these imply? As I try out various ways of writing on, or in, Osborne, I find that my memory is not less active but it is operating in a different way. Instead of being made to concentrate on very recent memories, of what it is that has to be done and how to do it correctly, I can now forget all that, trusting the process to sort it out later. The forced memorizing of intentional actions, so as to 'behave right', or to get others to do so, is gone. Instead the spontaneous memory, as in laughter or conversation, the joy or terror of living, can return to 'industrial' action. And primary learning, as for kittens, children and all young things, is back . . . Isn't this the end of the need to pre-plan, to control?

What then has become of repetition, uniformity, the accepted mark of 'the machine'? I was surprised when a friend criticized my assumption that exact repetition is mechanical. He said that if you leave a printing machine, or any other, to itself it immediately begins to drift. The products cease to be exact copies and are all different, but in ways we do not want. We, not the machines, impose the uniformity, he said. So we are the fascists, it does not come from things . . . . . . Six dots. A sign of my presence, not that of a machine. Hmm . . .

'No other devices in the world are quite so badly designed from the point of view of ease of human use.'[2] Mackworth was writing about computers and complaining of a big difficulty that is still with us, I think: the way that anyone who has not adapted to the precision of computer logic is made to feel reduced to nearly nothing, to a complete idiot, when he or she tries to use it for the first time. I believe that one mark of good design in software, or anything else, is that of 'zero learning': the machine assumes one's best qualities, brings them out and enhances them. Then one can use it immediately, without special training, and reach 'beyond oneself'. Why not?

A computer is a complete industrial process, but without any people in it. Is that the real joy of miniaturizing, that it squeezes us out, as nothing else could, from being cogs in a machine that could never work properly until we left it alone?

Software

The more I see of software designing the more I notice resemblance not to design in other fields but to craftsmanship. In each the designing, if such it can be called, is done by the maker, and there is much fitting, adjusting, adapting of existing designs, and much collaboration, with little chance of a bird's eye view, such as the drawing board affords, of how the whole thing is organized, though, in craft evolution, if not in software, the results have the appearance of natural organisms or of exceptionally well integrated designs. But there is an important difference: software is increasingly made by modifying the actual material of previous pieces of software, as a building may be altered for a new use, whereas a waggon-maker, for instance, modifies the form, but does not re-use the material, in making each small step in the gradual evolution of his product. As in natural evolution, each alteration is made without conscious intention, or plan, of what kind of artefact may later appear out of the seemingly blind process of making corrections, here and there, as and when lack of adaptation to the working conditions, or to the materials or the making process, become evident. But there is a tremendous respect for the form, as it has evolved so far, embodying, as it does, the otherwise unrecorded history of a thousand ways in which the artefact and its context can be attuned. Of course the context has to be stable, within limits, for centuries, for craft evolution to be possible. Is there any way, I ask myself, in trying to learn from these various modes of evolution, for the makers of software, and the users of it, to attain this almost magical accord with context when context is itself in flux?

Farm-waggons had been adapted, through ages, so very closely to their own environment that, to understanding eyes, they really looked almost like living organisms. They were so exact. Just as a biologist may see, in any limpet, signs of the rocky shore, the smashing breakers, so any provincial wheelwright could hardly help reading, from the waggon-lines, tales of haymaking and upland fields, of hilly roads and noble horses, and so on.[3]

New versions of existing designs

My experience of designing began with industrial design, which, in the fifties, was a new design profession devoted to the re-thinking and re-shaping of existing designs of manufactured products. The typical design process was for a design consultant (who did not work for one industry, but several, and was trained in art, not engineering) to be given a brief to re-design the appearance of a product, and to re-think how it was used, while retaining, to varying degrees, the existing interior mechanisms and the existing manufacturing plant. Although meeting much resistance at first, from engineering designers, salesmen and others, whose experience was limited to making and selling the existing design, the technique prevailed and now many manufactured products are designed in this way by people of wider training and outlook than that of an industry geared to one type of product. Quite a revolution. What, in essence, was the process of this kind of re-designing? At its worst it was cosmetic, restyling, the imposition, via the introduction of an operationally separated cover-component, of a fashionable appearance calculated to increase sales while minimizing costly disruption of the expensive tooling-up of the mechanical parts, which were hidden from view. Top-down designing, aided by a physical separation from the engineering, which had been designed bottom-up. At its best industrial design means the deriving of a fresh concept for the product as a whole from a radical appraisal of the relevance of both inner and outer components and of the operations of using it (now called ergonomics) so as to find a design that is noticeably better from every point of view. In this re-thinking stability is discarded, at the physical scale, and re-created at the scale of functions, costs, sales.

Stretched versions of a passenger jet, successive revised editions of a popular textbook: in many cases these are less deliberate processes than industrial design, often they are completely unplanned-for, but they seem to produce astonishing metamorphoses of existing designs while retaining the original organization of parts, or classification of subject-matter The underlying concept accurately reflects the context in a way that transcends internal conflicts of design.

Cost reduction

We used to say that an engineer is one who can make for sixpence what any fool can make for half-a-crown. The chief instrument of the astonishing cost-reductions of mass-produced goods, as compared to hand-made, is, of course, not ingenuity of design but investment in tooling-up for repetitive operations. But within mass-production there are still largish differences of cost and plenty of examples of big savings made by re-designing the product to reduce its use of materials, labour or special-purpose tools. A formal technique for doing this, Value Analysis, was invented by L.D. Miles in the fifties[4], and has been used with notable success not only to reduce cost but also to rationalize, and to improve, functional performance. The essence of his method, which is a lot more involved than this little outline description suggests, is, as in industrial designing, to focus on function:

> define element
> define function
> consider alternatives
> evaluate alternatives
> select best

The strength of the method is that, given that the functions of each part *can* be predicted and held stable, everything extraneous to their achievement, using the absolute minimum of resources, can be identified and discarded.

But there is a hidden cost, a severe one, which has only recently become evident. It is that of inflexibility, over-specialization, the realization that this 'plastic world' of homogenized, cost-reduced products is increasingly unalterable, un-repairable, and imposes upon us (from its stabilization at the larger scale of functions) a life, an obligatory way of *using* what is made, that is felt as coercive, not satisfying, with decreasing outlets for individuality. The lesson is obvious, though how to apply it is not: do not stabilize functions.

Adaptable designs

There is a principle evident in the type of exceptionally adaptable desk lamp which is mounted on a spring-balanced jointed arm in which arm-pieces and springs are positioned much as they are in the human arm, or leg. The point about this type of lamp is that the effort to adjust it is less, not more, than the effort of adjusting your own posture, or eyes, to continue reading with the light in the wrong place. Many systems of adjustable components, or so-called flexible designs, fail at this point. The adjustments they offer are seldom used because the effort-of-adjusting is greater than that of adapting, personally or socially, to the worse conditions of leaving the thing unadjusted. Does this happen with software too?

My last example, and perhaps the most relevant to software design, is the street, and the street-pattern of a city. It is relevant because, in both cases, street and software, it is the actual thing itself which is re-used, adapted. A beauty so obvious it is invisible.

Now, after a great war, life goes on in our ruined cities, but it is a different life, the life of different or differently composed groups, guided or thwarted by new surroundings, new because so much has been destroyed. The great heaps of rubble are piled on the city's invaluable substructure, the water and drainage pipes, the gas mains and electricity cables.[5]

The services beneath the streets are, of course, only extensions, invented millennia later, some of them, of the ancient excellence of the pattern of streets, and of the so basic idea of arranging for public space to reach, in this so accessible way, to every house, no matter how many. A similar example, which is quite obviously present also in the different ways in which computer storage and access is provided, is the library, and the book. Together they provide equal access times to every book, and to every page, line, word, letter, by the principle of 'pages', of splitting an enormously long string of symbols into units each with access both in series and in parallel.

Designing as process

The difficulty which we all face, as users of all the things, products, or whatever, that are provided by professions other than our own, is that we are tied by our experience as consumers of products to accept them, and not ourselves, as the starting points of our thinking when asked to define our needs. And, as professionals in the provision of software, or of some other product, we are equally tied to thinking of the product as central and the users as existing only in relation to what we provide. 'We are here to help the others: what the others are for I've no idea.' That is product-thinking, the not always laughable weakness of industrial life.

The alternative view, to be found in the recent developments in design, as in all the arts and sciences of this century, is process-thinking. To see process not as a means but as the end, a purpose in itself. To take the product alone as the criterion is to deny that we exist.

At a break in a concert a most un-announcer-like voice, presumably a member of the orchestra, sitting some way from the microphone, says 'We will play the finale – opus one, number two.' That was the first occasion, in years of listening to the output of professionally organized radio, when I felt the existence of the musicians as persons, as one of them improvised that announcement, presumably in a rare failure of the official announcer to keep track. That tiny lapse in the almost totally impervious homogeneity of a planned professional service is, I believe, the clue for getting out of the trap of means-ends thinking that makes us blind to our needs outside those of serving the system. The essential first step is to accept the roughness, the unprofessional character, the reaction 'that's not design, anyone could do it' of improvised initiatives by users themselves, by us as we are as persons, unspecialized. Once this big jump is made, the way is open to becoming able to making this new life that is so rapidly coming into being as a result of our efforts, into something worth while in itself. In computing, more than in other technologies there is the opportunity to drop product thinking, to let the process come alive to us all.

Designing with changing requirements

The instability of requirements is perhaps the biggest difficulty in trying to design, and re-design, computer software as it grows in scale and in length of life. How does it arise? Hard to say, difficult to predict. My strongest impression is that the direction in which requirements are going to change, both during initial design and later, is not predictable from what either the customers or the clients know at the start.

> The sponsor's brief is treated as a starting point for investigation and is expected to be revised, or evolved, during divergent search ... (but not without the sponsor's agreement).

That quotation is from the central chapter of my book *Design Methods*,[6] in which I was describing how the new methods differ from the traditional ones. The main difference is that the new methods begin with formal ways of researching the problem more widely than the client's brief suggests, so that the interdependency of problem and solution can be properly explored and understood. It is far from easy to perceive, in any instance, why and how the initial requirement-statement can be so misleading and that the actual require-ments, if the design is to be good, must reflect what is learned as designing proceeds. But it is easy to see that, in principle, designing is a highly informative process (essentially one of *un*learning what we thought *was* the case, but is *no longer true* when we have changed the situation by making something new which interacts with what was there before) and that it is wise to act always on the latest available information. 'If we'd known at the start what we've learnt while designing it, we'd never have done it like this.' The practical point, in using the newer design methods to make possible collabora-tive divergent search before the requirements are fixed, is to change the basis of the contract between designers and clients. Both parties have to give up the use of the requirements as a semi-legal basis for control and measurement and agree to work together in the continuous meta-process of evolving the brief and sharing in the eventual decision as to how the problem is to be seen and solved.

Contexts

Context (a name I prefer to environment, because it sounds less like a separate thing from ourselves) is the hardest thing to perceive, because it includes us, our ways of thinking. The fish can't see the water. 'It' is the source of change, of unexpectedness, the real generator of newness, design, of evolution. Aims, purposes, requirements, functions: these are words for how we see what is needed. But when we name them we tend to exclude the main part, the least predictable: ourselves, our minds, and how they change once we experience something. It is ourselves, not our words, that are the real purpose of designing. The biggest mistake is to take the product alone as the aim. It is always secondary.

The best kinds of evolution we know, natural, linguistic, hand-crafted, are planless but highly responsive to change of context – with astonishingly coherent results. Functions, statements of requirements, are essential but temporary. Without them we cannot begin, but unless we can change them we cannot finish, cannot discover. The essence of natural and linguistic evolution is to adapt parts, existing parts, to new functions, disregarding the old ones. This almost miraculous process is possible only when the context is mobile, is sensitive to the new functions of existing parts and is not tied to the old functions. This, the largest scale of change there is, supposes fluidity, not fixity, at its most abstract level, at the scale of aims, ends.

So, for continuous designing, do not stabilize functions. To fix the functions inhibits the human adaptiveness, present in everyone, but inhibitable, upon which long-life designing depends. How, in practice, to cope with changes in requirements and specifications? First, recognize that the 'right' requirements are in principle unknowable by users, customers, or designers at the start. Devise the design process, and the formal agreements between designers and customers and users, to be sensitive to what is learned by *any* of these parties as the design evolves. Organize collaboration so that each person concerned has (a) the liberty to experiment and improvise and (b) the means to test his or her improvisations to the operation of the whole. The extent of (a) and (b) may vary greatly from person to person but must always be such as to prevent destructive change, or the making of blocks to other changes.

Collaboration and communication

Creative collaboration is perhaps the main challenge of our time. Before computing it was not possible, in principle, at the scale at which we now operate and organize. The scale of billions and at the scale of everyone's minds. It is bound to be difficult, but it is, I believe, the hidden question behind the quest for long-life designing. The attempt to act together as if all the things we make comprise one thing, a unity. As we do ourselves. But a unity that leaves us incredibly free, to make or mar. What are the blocks to collaborative design? What stops us acting together as a context for our works, adapting freely to what we discover in doing what we do? The blocks are product-thinking, function-fixing, role-fixing, cost-reducing, and our identification of ourselves with these things instead of with our thoughts, feelings, minds, common-sense awareness of what is needed but what we are not paid to do. All this leaves us over-adapted to the status quo (which we identify with self, with security, when in fact it is what destroys the self, the being, the joy of living). That is why, I believe, we seem to lose the adaptiveness, the biological adaptiveness, with which we are born. The first practical step to unblocking, to being free to be inventive, and collaborative, is to widen, and to overlap, our job specifications, our roles. Once that happens the whole context begins to become mobile.

As larger groups begin to work together in design, we need not only looser roles but more public ways of thinking aloud. More visible design processes so that everyone can see what is being decided, and why, *before*, not after, the main decisions are made. Collaboration before concept-fixing is perhaps the main strength of the new design methods. The other strength is to provide means of *un*learning, publicly, with changing, not fixed, self-images.

Attentiveness to context, not to self-expression, is the skill we have to foster, to encourage, to share. In natural evolution inattentiveness is death. So is inability to adapt to what we see happening. The context, not the boss, has to become the manager of what is done, and how. The bosses' role becomes that of designing the meta-process, designing the situation so that designing collaboratively is possible, so that it flows. 'It' being the interaction of what everyone is noticing with what everyone is doing. To find out how to re-structure the design situation so that the blocks are removed, so that initiatives are both encouraged and enabled to be self-correcting, given attentiveness, the right tools and so on. A first step is to change the contractual basis of collaboration between designers, customers, users, all concerned: make it independent of functions, requirements. Find some better level for agreements.

How, in principle, is the context, the design situation, to be organized if all this is to be possible? The general aim is to enable all concerned to take initiatives in the light of accurate knowledge of the effects of what they are doing. In practice this sounds very difficult. I would suggest beginning by loosening specifications so as to allow 'unprofessional' degrees of roughness to be acceptable in improvisations from any quarter and to consciously drop professional standards wherever they seem to have local, not universal importance. Secondly, I would try progressively to do away with the need for 'forced communication', via manuals, meetings, memos, etc., and try more and more for the kind of collaboration-without-communication that is possible in the evolution of language.

John Chris Jones

REFERENCES

1 Young, J.Z., *An Introduction to The Study of Man*, Oxford, 1971.
2 Mackworth, N.H., 'Originality', *American Psychologist*, 20, 1964, pp. 51–66.
3 Sturt, George, *The Wheelwright's Shop*, Cambridge, 1923.
4 Miles, L.D., *Technique of Value Analysis and Engineering*, New York, 1961.
5 Brecht, Bertolt, *Collected Plays*, vol. 5, (ed. Ralph Mannheim and John Willet), New York, 1972.
6 Jones, J. Christopher, *Design Methods*, London, 1970.

ACKNOWLEDGMENTS
·
CONTRIBUTORS
·
INDEX

Acknowledgments

•

The editor and publisher are grateful for permission to include the following works in this anthology:

© Marshall Berman, *All That Is Solid Melts Into Air*: expanded and revised extract based on the edition first published by Verso Editions, 1983

© Kenneth Frampton, *Place-form and Cultural Identity*

© Christopher Alexander, *A City is not a Tree*: this version published in ZONE 1/2, New York, 1986

© Richard Bolton, *Architecture and Cognac*

© Nigel Coates, *Street Signs*

© Peter Fuller, *The Search for a Postmodern Aesthetic*

© Peter Dormer, *The Ideal World of Vermeer's Little Lacemaker*

François Burkhardt, *Avantpostmodernism*, first published in *Cahiers du CCI* (Centre Pompidou): No 2, 'Design actualities fin de siècle', Paris, 1986. Translation © Martin Ryle, 1987

© Claudia Donà, *Invisible Design*

© Peter York, *Culture as Commodity*, based on a paper given to the International Design Conference, Aspen, Colorado, 1986

Jean Baudrillard, *System of Objects*, first published as *Système des Objects*, Editions Gallimard, Paris, 1968. Translation © Penny Sparke

Thierry Chaput, *The Chaos of Microaesthetics*, first published in *Cahiers du CCI* (Centre Pompidou): No 2, 'Design actualities fin de siècle', Paris, 1986. Translation © Martin Ryle, 1987

Philippe Lemoine, *The Demise of Classical Rationality*, first published in *Cahiers du CCI* (Centre Pompidou) No.2,'Design actualities fin de siècle', Paris, 1986. Translation © Martin Ryle, 1987.

Acknowledgments

© Mike Cooley, *Architect or Bee*, Langley Technical Services, Slough, 1980

© Tom Mitchell, *The Product As Illusion*

© John Chris Jones, *Essays in Design*, John Wiley, 1984; this passage originally commissioned by Les Belady of IBM for a conference on long-life software.

The editor also thanks Steve Braidwood, Tony Fry, Julian Gibb and Phil Goodall for their help in developing the project, and in particular Mike Marqusee for his invaluable assistance throughout.

Contributors

•

CHRISTOPHER ALEXANDER   Winner of the first medal for research ever awarded by the American Institute of Architects, Christopher Alexander is a practising architect and builder, Professor of Architecture at the University of California, Berkeley, and head of the Center for Environmental Structure. He is the author of seminal works such as *A Pattern Language* and *A Timeless Way of Building*.

JEAN BAUDRILLARD   Born in 1929, Baudrillard is Professor of Sociology at the University of Paris. His writings have explored the mutations of the contemporary world under the influence of new productive methods, advertising, television and new consumer psychology. He is the author of *The Mirror of Production* (1975), *For a Critique of the Political Economy of the Sign* (1981), *Simulations* (1983) and many other books.

MARSHALL BERMAN   Born in New York City and a veteran of sixties activism. Berman's provocative articles have appeared in *Dissent, American Review* and the *Village Voice*. In his widely-praised *All That Is Solid Melts Into Air* (Verso 1983) Berman mixed literary, architectural, sociological, and political studies in a passionate reconsideration of the modern city. He has taught at Stanford, the University of New Mexico, New York University and is currently a professor at the City University of New York.

RICHARD BOLTON   An artist, teacher and writer, Richard Bolton has taught at the Cranbrook Academy of Art, Wayne State University, Southern Illinois University, and has worked for Harvard University Press. His articles on photography, advertising, and postmodernism have appeared in *Exposure, Photo Communique, Afterimage*, and elsewhere. His work has been exhibited in Detroit and Cincinnati and he is represented in the permanent collections of Cranbrook Academy, Detroit Institute of Fine Arts, Cincinnati Art Museum, and the Erie Arts Centre. Bolton is currently at the Visual Language Workshop of the Massachussets Institute of Technology.

FRANÇOIS BURKHARDT was born in Switzerland and educated in Lausanne and Hamburg. He was director of the Museum of Fine Arts in Hamburg from 1969 to 1971, and of the International Design Centre in Berlin from 1971 to 1984. Since 1984, he has been Director of the Centre de Création Industrielle at the Centre Pompidou in Paris. He has taught at the department of Architecture at Kiel, at the School of Fine Arts in Berlin, and at the Domus Academy in Milan. The author of numerous articles, he has also co-written *Produkt-form Geschichte: 150 Jahre deutsche Design* (Reimer Verlag Berlin, 1973)

THIERRY CHAPUT studied as a designer and ergonomist, and then worked as a designer and journalist for some years. From 1978 to 1986 he was in charge of the Centre de Création Industrielle at the Centre Pompidou; in 1985 he co-curated, with Jean-François Lyotard, the exhibition 'Les Immatériaux' (The Immaterial). He was in charge of exhibitions for two years at the 'City of science and industry' at La Villette, and since 1987 has been Secretary General of ACM Siggraph, France. He also teaches at the University of Paris VII. He has been widely published, in *Parachute, Le Monde, New York Times, Modo, Autrement* and others.

NIGEL COATES After graduating from the Architectural Association, London, in 1974, Nigel Coates embarked on a multi-faceted career involving teaching in Britain and the United States, writing, and architectural and furniture design. He was a founder of the controversial NATO group (Narrative Architects Today) whose influential 'Gamma-City' exhibition was shown at the Air Gallery, London, in 1986. NATO have also exhibited at the ICA Gallery, Boston. Coates has established a world-wide reputation with his innovative shop designs in London, Tokyo and Sapporo. His furniture is manufactured in Japan.

MIKE COOLEY A former development engineer in the aerospace industry, Mike Cooley was national President of TASS, the British engineering union, in 1972, and a leading member of the Lucas Aerospace Combine Shop Stewards Committee which pioneered trade union initiatives in industrial conversion. Author of *Architect or Bee? The Human/Technology Relationship*, Cooley has been a director of the Centre for Alternative Industrial and Technological Systems and is currently a Director of the Greater London Enterprise Board.

CLAUDIA DONÀ, an Italian journalist and design historian, lives and works in Milan. A member since 1977 of the editorial staff of *Modo*, of which she was editor-in-chief 1983-4, she has also written for *Interni, Gap, Zoom and Abitare*. She is a design consultant at the University of Illinois at Chicago, Architecture and Design Department. Donà has curated several exhibitions including 'Home of Juliet' (Verona 1982), 'Unexpected Consequences: Art, Fashion, Design' (Prato 1983), 'New Intentions of Design' (Reggio Emilia 1982), 'Telematic Ulysses' (Chicago 1986). Her current research is directed towards the development of a new language for high-tech, based on ancient mythologies.

PETER DORMER   Author and critic, Peter Dormer has written on design and the applied arts for *Art Monthly*, the *New Statesman*, *Architectural Review*, *The Guardian*. He is the author of *The New Ceramics*, *The New Jewelry* and *The New Furniture* (all Thames and Hudson). He has curated numerous exhibitions, including 'Fast Forward' at the ICA, and 'British Design in Vienna' (1986), and lectured in Europe and North America.

KENNETH FRAMPTON   An architect and architectural historian, Kenneth Frampton studied at the Architectural Association in London and practised professionally before devoting most of his time to teaching. Formerly on the faculty of Princeton University and the Royal College of Art, he is now chairman of the Department of Architecture at Columbia University. Among his many publications is *Modern Architecture: A Critical History* (Thames and Hudson, 1980). Professor Frampton was a fellow of the Wissenschaftskolleg in Berlin during the preparation of this contribution.

PETER FULLER   A regular contributor to *Art Monthly*, *The Burlington Magazine* and *Art and Design*, Peter Fuller is one of Britain's most prominent – and distinctive – cultural critics. He has lectured throughout the USA, Europe and Australia, and his books *Art and Psychoanalysis, Images of God, The Australian Scapegoat* and the autobiographical *Marches Past* have been widely reviewed and discussed. His most recent film for television, a project about art and science called *Naturally Creative*, was first screened on Britain's Channel Four.

JOHN CHRIS JONES   A London-based writer, researcher and artist, John Chris Jones was Professor of Design at the Open University in England, and continues to lecture occasionally at conferences; he is visiting professor at NHIBS, Antwerp. He left full-time teaching in 1974 to concentrate on his own work, and is the author of *Design Methods*, and *Essays in Design* (John Wiley), both of which are published in several languages, and of *Technology Changes* (Princelet Editions). He has contributed to many publications including *Modo*, *Design* and *Futures*.

PHILIPPE LEMOINE is a Professor at the Institute of Political Studies in Paris and since 1985 has been a member of the general board of the Lafayette-Monoprix chain. From 1971 and 1976 he was a research engineer before moving to the Ministry of Industry. In 1982 the French Prime Minister put Mr Lemoine in charge of a study group into information technologies. He is vice-chairman of the national committee on technology, employment and work.

TOM MITCHELL   Born in 1960, Tom Mitchell came to Britain on a Marshall Scholarship and is now completing his Ph.D. in Fine Art Psychology at Reading University. He has written for *Design* magazine on user-behaviour in environments and is developing methods of participatory design – whereby people affected by the end products of design can take part in the design process itself.

Contributors

JOHN THACKARA studied philosophy before spending five years in architectural book publishing. After a two-year break in Australia and South-East Asia, Thackara became editor of *Design* magazine, a post he held for four years. As a freelance journalist and critic he wrote, lectured and broadcast widely in Europe, the United States and Australia, and recently published *New British Design* (Thames and Hudson, 1986). From 1987 the *Guardian*'s design correspondent, he is also a member of the Advisory Board of the Institute of Contemporary Arts in London. Thackara is a director of the London-based research company Design Analysis International, and is Style editor of *Harpers and Queen* magazine.

PETER YORK is the author of *Style Wars* and *Modern Times* and co-author of the best-selling *Sloane Ranger* trilogy. A contributing editor to *Vanity Fair* in New York and *Design* and *Blueprint* magazines in Britain, York is considered Britain's leading 'anthropologist' of urban styles, cults, elites, youth and class sub-cultures. He is a founding partner of SRU Ltd, the business consultancy group.

—234—

Index

•